AF484495

# Pharmaceutical Engineering

Ms. Prerana Sahu, Mr. Divyansh Sahu, Dr. Gyanesh Kumar Sahu, Dr. Harish Sharma

# Contents

## Unit I

• Flow of fluids: Types of manometers, Reynolds number and its significance, Bernoulli's theorem and its applications, Energy losses, Orifice meter, Venturimeter, Pitot tube and Rotometer.

• Size Reduction: Objectives, Mechanisms & Laws governing size reduction, factors affecting size reduction, principles, construction, working, uses, merits and demerits of Hammer mill, ball mill, fluid energy mill, Edge runner mill & end runner mill.

• Size Separation: Objectives, applications & mechanism of size separation, official standards of powders, sieves, size separation Principles, construction, working, uses, merits and demerits of Sieve shaker, cyclone separator, Air separator, Bag filter & elutriation tank.

## Unit II

• Heat Transfer: Objectives, applications & Heat transfer mechanisms. Fourier's law, Heat transfer by conduction, convection & radiation. Heat interchangers & heat exchangers.

• Evaporation: Objectives, applications and factors influencing evaporation, differences between evaporation and other heat process. principles, construction, working, uses, merits and demerits of Steam jacketed kettle, horizontal tube evaporator, climbing film evaporator, forced circulation evaporator, multiple effect evaporator& Economy of multiple effect evaporator.

• Distillation: Basic Principles and methodology of simple distillation,flash distillation, fractional distillation, distillation under reduced pressure, steamdistillation & molecular distillation

## Unit III

• Drying: Objectives, applications & mechanism of drying process, measurements & applications of Equilibrium Moisture content, rate of drying curve. principles, construction, working, uses, merits and demerits of Tray dryer, drum dryer spray dryer, fluidized bed dryer, vacuum dryer, freeze dryer.

• Mixing: Objectives, applications & factors affecting mixing, Difference between solid and liquid mixing, mechanism of solid mixing, liquids mixing and semisolids mixing. Principles, Construction, Working, uses, Merits and Demerits of Double cone blender, twin shell blender, ribbon blender, Sigma blade mixer, planetary mixers, Propellers, Turbines, Paddles & Silverson Emulsifier

## Unit IV

• Filtration: Objectives, applications, Theories & Factors influencing filtration, filter aids, filter medias. Principle, Construction, Working, Uses, Merits and demerits of plate & frame filter, filter leaf, rotary drum filter, Meta filter &Cartridge filter, membrane filters and Seidtz filter.

• Centrifugation: Objectives, principle & applications of Centrifugation, principles, construction, working, uses, merits and demerits of Perforated basket centrifuge, Non-perforated basket centrifuge, semi continuous centrifuge & super centrifuge.

**Unit V**

• Materials of pharmaceutical plant construction, Corrosion and its prevention: Factors affecting during materials selected for Pharmaceutical plant construction, Theories of corrosion, types of corrosion and there prevention. Ferrous and nonferrous metals, inorganic and organic non metals, basic of material handling systems.

# Preface

Pharmaceutical engineering encompasses the study, design, production, and distribution of pharmaceuticals. The first step in the engineering process is to identify a particular disease or condition and investigate the impact of both historical and contemporary medications used to treat it.

Overall, in this main objective of writing the book is to provide readers with a broad spectrum of scientific information in a concise and systemic manner. This would create an interest and include ideas for further ideas for further process of learning and working on the Pharmaceutical Engineering. The content in each chapter is well organized.

This has been our attempt to fulfill the needs of undergraduate students of reputed universities especially for third semester B.Pharm students. This book was developed with the needs of both teachers and students in mind, covering every subject within the acceptable bounds of the suggested curriculum. We hope the book fulfils students' requirements and proves to be beneficial.

We would like to express our profound gratitude to Notion Press for their co-operation and interest taken in publishing this book.

Suggestions for making the book still more valuable to our students will be thankfully considered for the future editions of the book.

Ms. Prerana Sahu

Mr. Divyansh Sahu

Dr. Gyanesh Kumar Sahu

Dr. Harish Sharma

Date:24-07-2024

# UNIT I



*Syllabus*

• Flow of fluids: Types of manometers, Reynolds number and its significance, Bernoulli's theorem and its applications, Energy losses, Orifice meter, Venturimeter, Pitot tube and Rotometer.

• Size Reduction: Objectives, Mechanisms & Laws governing size reduction, factors affecting size reduction, principles, construction, working, uses, merits and demerits of Hammer mill, ball mill, fluid energy mill, Edge runner mill & end runner mill.

• Size Separation: Objectives, applications & mechanism of size separation, official standards of powders, sieves, size separation Principles, construction, working, uses, merits and demerits of Sieve shaker, cyclone separator, Air separator, Bag filter & elutriation tank.

## FLOW OF FLUID: -

Fluid includes both liquids and gases.

 ➤ A material that is not permanently resistant to deformation is known as a fluid. Layers of fluid will slide over one another in an attempt to alter the form of a mass of fluid until a new shape is achieved. There will be shear forces during the form shift, the amount of which is determined by the fluid's viscosity and the sliding rate. However, all shear strains will vanish once a final form is achieved. When a fluid is at equilibrium, shear stresses are absent.

 ➤ A fluid's density varies in response to pressure and temperature. A minor variation in pressure has no discernible impact on the density of a liquid. When it comes to gases, changes in pressure and temperature have a noticeable impact on density.

 ➤ The facts of fluid mechanics include two divisions:

(i) fluid statics and

(ii) fluid dynamics.

Fluids in equilibrium at rest undergo contractions due to fluid statics. The study of fluids in situations where one part is moving in relation to another is known as fluid dynamics.

## MANOMETERS: -

Manometers are instruments that measure pressure differential using the idea of balancing a liquid column by using either the same or a different liquid column.

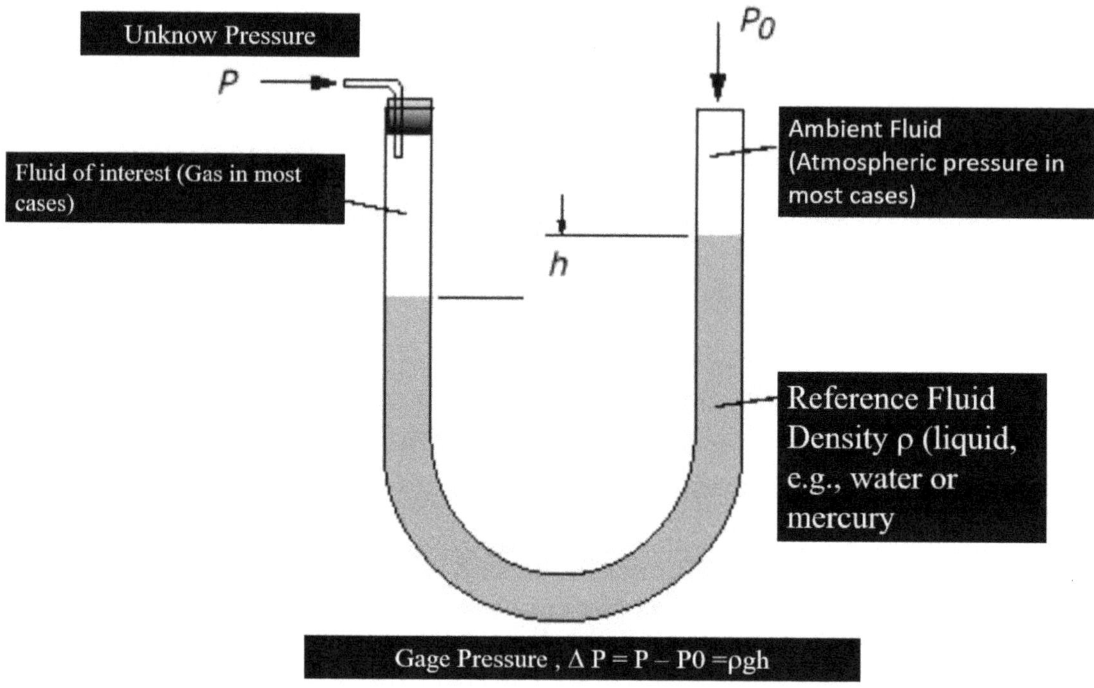


**Simple Manometer**

A simple manometer is a tool used to gauge the pressure of a fluid confined in a pipe or vessel at a specific spot. The most often used manometer is this one. It is composed of a liquid (A) with a density of P0, kilogramme per metre cube, contained in a glass U tube. Liquid B, with a density of P kg/m^ cube, fills the arms above liquid A. Since the liquids A and B are immiscible, it is easy to visualise the interface. One arm will have a greater meniscus of liquid A than the other if two different pressures are applied to it.

Manometers are used to measure the pressure of any fluid.

Liquid A with density A is placed within a U-tube. The fluid B, whose density is B, fills the arms of the U-tube above liquid A. Fluid B and liquid A are not miscible. One U-tube arm experiences pressure P1, whereas the other arm experiences pressure P2. A greater meniscus in one U-tube branch than the other will arise from the pressure differential (P1 P2).

This pair of surfaces is separated vertically by R. The manometer's reading, R, is used to calculate the pressure differential (P1 ∧ P2).

When the two locations on the datum, (2 and 3), are in equilibrium, the forces

plane will be equal. Let the cross-sectional area of the U-tube be S.

All the forces are expressed in gravitational unit.

    Total downward force at point (b)= Forces at point (a) +

        force due to column of fluid B in between points

(a) and (b).

$$= P1S + (m + R) \rho B (g / gc) S$$

    Total downward force at point (c) = Force at point (e) + Force due to column of fluid B in between points

(e) and (d)

+ Force due to column of liquid A in between point

(d) and (c)

$$= P_2S + m \rho_B (g/gc) S + R \rho_A (g/gc) S$$

At equilibrium:

Force at point (b) = Force at point (c)

$$\text{or, } P_1S + (m + R) \rho_B (g/gc) S = P_2S + m \rho_B (g/gc) S + R \rho_A (g/gc) S$$

$$\text{or, } P_1 - P_2 = R \rho_A (g/gc) + m \rho_B (g/gc) - m \rho_B (g/gc) - R \rho_B (g/gc)$$

$$= R (\rho_A - \rho_B) \, g/gc.$$

$$\text{or, } \Delta P = P_1 - P_2 = R (\rho_A - \rho_B) \, g/gc.$$

It should be highlighted that, as long as P1 and P2 are measured from the same horizontal plane, this connection is independent of the U-tube's distance (m) and cross-sectional area (S).


## DIFFERENTIAL MANOMETER: -


A differential manometer is a type of manometer used to measure the pressure differential between any two places in a fluid-filled pipe or vessel. Differential manometers are used sometimes. It is possible to measure tiny pressure variations with this manometer. It is a sensitive instrument that can measure gas pressures as low as a few heads.

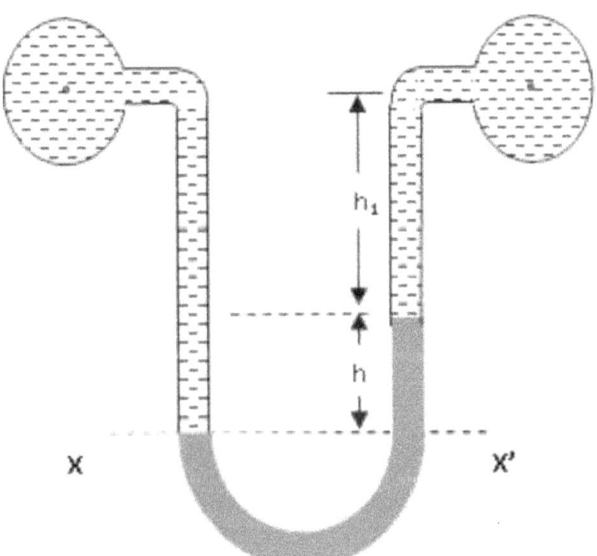


**Differential Manometer**


The differential manometer construction is shown in the diagram. Another name for the differential manometer is two-fluid. U-shaped manometer. It includes two almost identical-density immiscible liquids, A and B. Both arms of the U tube have larger chambers. Therefore, variations in the reading R have no discernible effect on the meniscus of the liquid in these larger chambers.

A differential manometer is used to monitor tiny pressure variations. The two liquids (A and C) in the manometer have to be immiscible. In order to prevent the meniscus 2 and 6 from moving noticeably as the reading changes, larger chambers are added to the manometer.

So, the distance between (1) and (2) = Distance between (6) and (7)

Total downward force on point (3)

Fleft = P1S + a ρA g/gc S + b ρA g/gc S

Total downward force on point (4)

Fright = P2S + a ρB g/gc S + d ρA g/gc S + RρC g/gc S

At equilibrium

$$Fleft = Fright$$

P1S + a ρA g/gc S + b ρA g/gc S = P2S + a ρB g/gc S + d ρA g/gc S + RρC g/gc S

P1 – P2 = (d – b) ρA g/gc + RρC g/gc = – R ρA g/gc + RρC g/gc. = R (ρC – ρA ) g/gc

**Δ P = P1 – P2 = R (ρC – ρA ) g/gc**

From this it reviews that the smaller the differences ρC – ρA, the larger will be the reading R on the manometer for a given value of ΔP.


## INCLINED MANOMETER: -

A manometer that monitors the minuscule pressure variations between any two places in a fluid that is enclosed in a pipe or vessel is called an inclined manometer. Differentia manometers are modified to become inclined manometers. This kind of manometer improves pressure determination accuracy, especially for tiny heads.

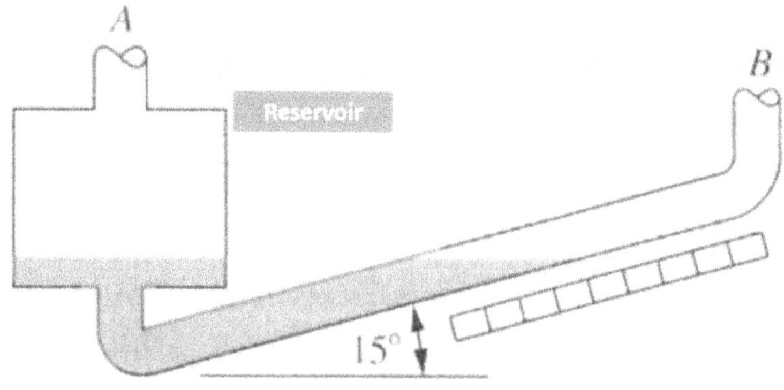


**Inclined Manometer**

This kind of manometer is used to measure minute variations in pressure. The leg with one meniscus in this kind of manometer needs to travel a significant distance along the tube. In this case, R1 magnifies the real reading R by a large number.

Were, **R = R1 sin α**

where α is the angle of leaning of the inclined leg with the horizontal plane. In this case

$\Delta P = P1 - P2 = R (\rho A - \rho B) g/gc.$

To ensure that the meniscus's movement in this expansion is minimal within the gauge's range, an enlargement in the vertical leg is required for this sort of gauge.

The value of R is multiplied into a considerably bigger distance R1 by making α small.

## FLUID DYNAMICS

Study of flow properties of fluid in motion.

### *Nature of Fluid Flow—Reynolds Experiment*

Similar to turbulent or viscous flow, settled fluid in a pipeline may also be turbulent.

These can be practical in the classical Reynolds ex- pertinent.

The Reynolds experiment apparatus assemblage is showed in below figure



**The assembly of the apparatus of the Reynolds experiment**

Osborne Reynolds carried out the experiment in 1883. In the Reynolds experiment, a glass tube was attached to a water reservoir such that the water's flow through the tube could be adjusted in velocity. A nozzle was installed at the tube's intake end to allow for the introduction of a fine stream of colored water.

Following investigation, Reynolds found that the color strand persisted through the tube at low water velocity. It can be shown that there was no mixing in any area of the tube and that the fluid ran in parallel, straight lines by positioning one of these jets at different cross-sectional positions. It was discovered that as the velocity was increased, the strand eventually vanished and the liquid's overall mass became continuously colored. Put differently, the liquid particles were completely mixed since they were no longer traveling in a straight line down the tube's long axis. Instead, they were moving erratically.

Streamline flow or viscous flow is the term used to describe fluid motion that occurred in parallel straight lines.

Turbulent flow is the term used to describe the fluid's erratic motion. The speed at which a fluid flow changes from a streamline or viscous flow to a turbulent flow is known as the critical velocity.

## THE REYNOLDS NUMBER

From Reynolds' experiment it was found that critical velocity depends on

1.  The internal diameter of the tube (D)

2.  The average velocity of the fluid (u)

3.  The density of the fluid ($\rho$) and

4.  The viscosity of the fluid ($\mu$)

Further, Reynolds showed that these four factors must be combined in one and only one way namely ($Du\rho / \mu$). This function ($Du\rho / \mu$) is known as the Reynolds number. It is a dimensionless group.

it has been shown that for straight circular pipe, when the value of the Reynolds number is less than 2000 the flow will always be viscous.

i.e.    $NRe < 2000 \Rightarrow$ viscous flow or streamline flow

$NRe > 4000 \Rightarrow$ turbulent flow

Dimensional analysis of Reynolds number

$[D] = L$ (ft)

$[u] = L/\theta$ (ft / sec)

$[\rho] = M / L3$ (lb/ft3)

$[\mu] = M / (L\theta)$ {lb/ (ft sec)}

$$\left[ \frac{Du\rho}{\mu} \right] = \frac{(L)\,(L/\theta)\,(M/L^3)}{\dfrac{M}{L\theta}} = \frac{L\,L\,M\,L\,\theta}{M\,\theta\,L^3}$$

$$= 1 \Rightarrow \text{dimensionless group}$$

Applications:

(1) Under specific experimental settings, the viscous or turbulent character of the flow may be predicted using the Reynolds number.

(2) The speed at which particles (or globules) settle determines the physical stability of suspensions (or emulsions). Stokes' law is used to the study of particle sedimentation. The speed at which the particles settle in this investigation must not be too quick to induce turbulence. Consequently, the kind of flow—turbulent or laminar—matters. As a result, Reynolds number is added to Stokes' equation.

(3) Whether a liquid flows in a turbulent or viscous manner affects how quickly heat is transferred through it.


## BERNOULLI'S THEOREM

Bernoulli's theorem, named after the Swiss mathematician Daniel Bernoulli, relates to fluid dynamics and is a fundamental principle in fluid mechanics. It states that in a steady, ideal fluid flow (non-viscous and incompressible), the total mechanical energy of the fluid, comprising the sum of its potential energy, kinetic energy, and pressure energy, remains constant along any streamline.

Let us consider the system represented in the figure, and assume that the temperature is uniform throughout the system. This figure represents a channel conveying a liquid from point A to point B The pump supplies the necessary energy to cause the flow. Let us consider a liquid mass m (lb) is entering at point A. Let the pressure at A and b are PA and PB (lb-force/ft2) respectively.

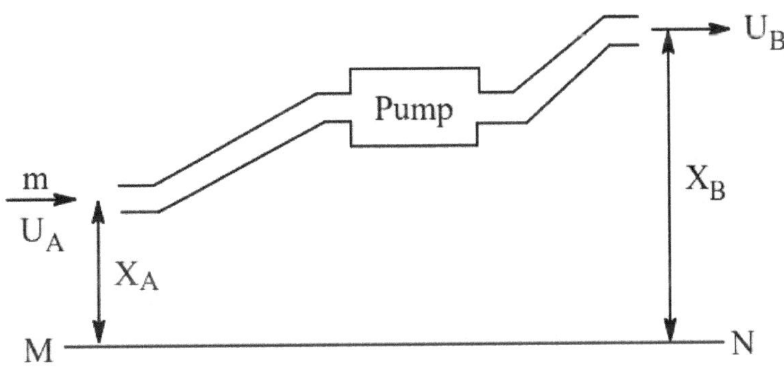


Fig. Bernoullis theorem

The average velocity of the liquid at A and B are uA and uB (ft/sec).

The specific volume of the liquid at A and B are VA and VB (ft3 /lb).

The height of point A and B from an arbitrary datum plane (MN) are XA and XB (ft) respectively.

Potential energy at point A, (W1) = mgXA ft-poundal                    [absolute unit]

          = m (g/gC) XA ft-lb force = mXA ft-lb force          [gravitational unit]

Since the liquid is in motion

∴ Kinetic energy at point A, (W2) = 1 /2. m uA 2 ft-pounda

                    l = (1 /2. m uA 2)/ gC pound-force

As the liquid m enters the pipe it enters against pressure of PA lb-force/ft2 and therefore.

Work against the pressure at point A, (W3) = mPAVA ft-lbf.

N.B. Force at point A = PA S [S = Cross-section area]

Work done against force PA S = PA (S h) = PA V

∴ Total energy of liquid m entering the section at point a will be (E1) = W1 + W2 + W3

E1 = [ mXA + (1 /2. m uA 2)/ gC + mPAVA] ft-lbf.

After the system has reached the steady state whenever m (lb) of liquid enters at Another m (lb) pound of liquid is displaced at B according to the principle of the conservation of mass. This m (lb) leaving at B will have energy content of E2 = [mXB + (1 /2. m uB 2)/ gC + mPBVB] ft-lbf.

Energy is added by the pump. Let the pump is giving w ft-lbf / lb energy to the liquid

E3 = m w ft-lbf.

Some energy will be converted into heat by friction. It has been assumed that the system is at a constant temperature; hence, it must be assumed that the heat is lost by radiation or by other means. Let this loss due to friction be F ft-lbf / lb of liquid.

E4 = − mF ft-lbf [negative sign for loss]

∴ The complete equation representing energy balance across the system between points A and will therefore be E1 + E3 + E4 = E2

or, mXA + (1 /2. m uA 2 )/ gC + mPAVA + m w − mF = mXB + (1 /2. m uB 2 )/ gC + mPBVB

Now, the unit of energy term is ft-lbf / lb

∴ The BERNOULLI'S THEOREM.

$$X_A + \frac{U_A{}^2}{2g_c} + P_A V_A + w - F = X_B + \frac{U_B{}^2}{2g_c} + P_B V_B$$

The density of the liquid ρ be expressed lbm / ft3, then

VA = 1 / ρA and VB = 1 / ρB then Bernoulli's equation can be written in the form also

$$X_A + \frac{U_A{}^2}{2g_c} + \frac{P_A}{\rho_A} + w - F = X_B + \frac{U_B{}^2}{2g_c} + \frac{P_B}{\rho_B}$$

**ENERGY LOSSES**

In the pipe, "loss of energy" is an expression found in Bernoulli's equation. In compliance with the rule of conservation of energy, energy balances must be accurately reported. As a result, the energy losses must be calculated. There are several methods in which fluids lose energy when passing through a pipe. Among them are:

1. Friction losses

2. Losses in fittings

3. Enlargement losses

4. Contraction losses

These are discussed in the following sections.

Friction Losses

Frictional forces result in a pressure loss (AP pascals) during fluid flow. The losses might also be affected by the viscous or turbulent fluid flow. The pressure decrease in a fluid caused by friction is generally:

- ➢ directly proportional to the velocity of the fluid (u), m/s

- ➢ directly proportional to the density of the fluid (p), kg/m$^3$

- ➢ directly proportional to the length of the pipe (L), m

- ➢ inversely proportional to the diameter of the pipe (D), m

These relationships are proposed in Fanning equation for calculating the friction losses, irrespective of the nature of flow (viscous or turbulent).

These relationships are proposed in Fanning equation for calculating the friction losses, irrespective of the nature of flow (viscous or turbulent).

Fanning equation:
$$\Delta P_f = \frac{2 f_u^2 \, L\rho}{D}$$

Where,

$\Delta Pf$ = pressure drop due to friction (lb/ft2)

F / A = resisting force (ft-lbf per ft2 of contact area)

L = length of pipe (ft)

D = inside diameter of the pipe (ft)

$\rho$ = density of fluid (lbm / ft3)

u = average velocity of fluid (ft / s)

$\mu$ = viscosity of fluid (lbm / ft / s)

gc = 32.2 (lbm ft / lbf s2)

For many decades Fanning's equation was used:
$$\Delta P_f = \frac{2 f u^2 \, L \, \rho}{g_c D} \; ----- \; \text{eqn (2)}$$

In Fanning's equation the value of 'f' was taken from tables. This equation however has been widely used for so many years that most engineers still use the Fanning's equation, except that instead of taking values of 'f' from arbitrary tables a plot of the equation f = (Du$\rho$ / $\mu$) is used. The graph (Graph-1) is not that much accurate: Error: $\pm$ 5 to 10 % may be expected for laminar flow.

By combining Hagen Poiseulles equation, a new form of equation can be obtained.

$$f = \frac{16}{\dfrac{Du\rho}{\mu}} = \frac{16}{\text{Reynolds No}}$$

## MEASUREMENT OF FLUID FLOW

*ORIFICE METER*

Objective: To measure the flow of fluids.

i) Velocity of fluid through a pipe (ft/sec)

ii) Volume of liquid passing per unit time (ft3 /sec, ft3 /min, ft3 /hr).

Description

A thin plate with an opening that allows a fluid to pass through is called an orifice meter. The plate can be fitted into a pipe line or positioned at the side or bottom of a container.

A manometer is fitted outside the pipe. One end at point A and the other end at point B (see fig.). The pressure difference between A and B (i.e. before and after the orifice) is read, and the reading is then converted to fluid flow-rate.

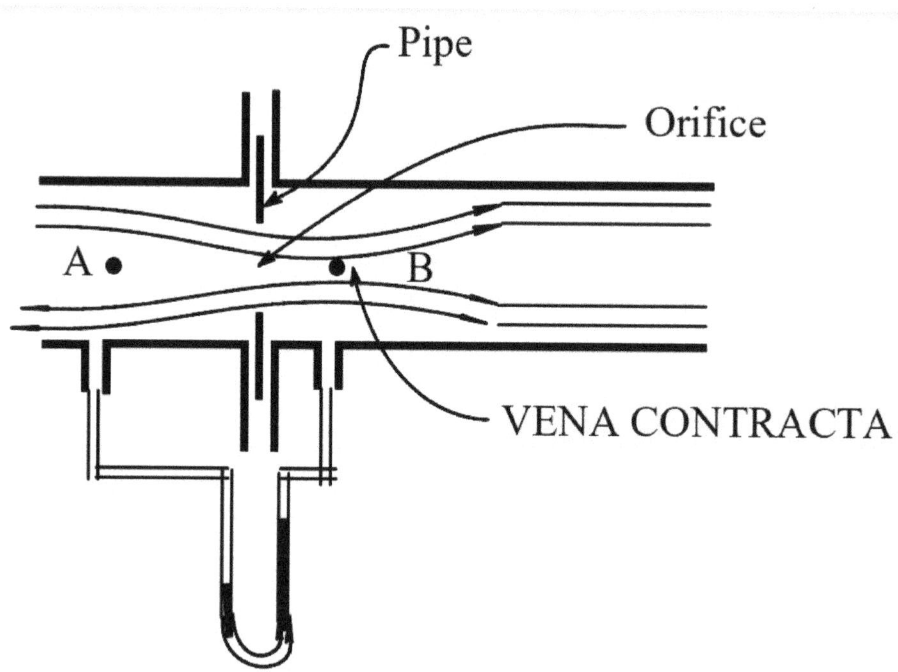


ORIFICE METER

**Derivation**

Bernoulli's equation is written between these two points, the following relationship holds

$$X_A + \frac{U_A^2}{2g_c} + \frac{P_A}{\rho_A} - F + w = X_B + \frac{U_B^2}{2g_c} + \frac{P_B}{\rho_B} \quad \ldots\ldots\ldots\ldots\ldots(1)$$

| Conditions | Equation (1) changes to: |
|---|---|
| i) The pipe is horizontal<br>$\therefore X_A = X_B.$ | $\dfrac{U_A^2}{2g_c} + \dfrac{P_A}{\rho_A} - F + w = \dfrac{U_B^2}{2g_c} + \dfrac{P_B}{\rho_B}$ |
| ii) If frictional losses are assumed to be inappreciable then $F = 0$ | $\dfrac{U_A^2}{2g_c} + \dfrac{P_A}{\rho_A} + w = \dfrac{U_B^2}{2g_c} + \dfrac{P_B}{\rho_B}$ |
| iii) If the fluid is a liquid then<br>$\rho A \approx \rho B = \rho$ (let) | $\dfrac{U_A^2}{2g_c} + \dfrac{P_A}{\rho} + w = \dfrac{U_B^2}{2g_c} + \dfrac{P_B}{\rho}$ |
| iv) Since no work is done on the liquid, or by the liquid between A and B.<br>$\therefore w = 0$ | $\dfrac{U_A^2}{2g_c} + \dfrac{P_A}{\rho_A} = \dfrac{U_B^2}{2g_c} + \dfrac{P_B}{\rho_B} \quad \text{...........................} (2)$ |

Equation (2) may be written as:

$$U_B^2 - U_A^2 = \frac{2g_C}{\rho}(P_A - P_B) \quad \text{........................}(3)$$

Since, $PA - PB = \Delta P$, and since $\Delta P/\rho = \Delta H$

$\therefore$ equation (3) can be written as

$$\sqrt{U_B^2 - U_A^2} = \sqrt{2g_C\,\Delta H} \quad \text{.................................}(4)$$

N.B.    $P_A = H_A\,\rho\,g\,/\,g_c$

       $P_B = H_B\,\rho\,g\,/\,g_c$

       $P_A - P_B = (H_A - H_B)\rho\,g\,/\,g_c$

or,     $\Delta P = \Delta H\,\rho\,g\,/\,g_c.$

Since, $g\,/\,g_c \approx 1.0$ hence, $\Delta H = \Delta P\,/\,\rho$

If the pipe to the right of the orifice plate were removed so that the liquid issued as a jet from the orifice, the minimum diameter of the stream would be less than the diameter of the orifice. This point of minimum cross-section is known a vena-contracta.

The vena contracta yielded Point B. In actuality, the orifice diameter is known, but the stream's diameter at the vena-contracta is unknown. As a result, equation (4) may be expressed in terms of the velocity through the orifice. To account for the discrepancy between this velocity and the velocity at the vena-contracta, a constant (Co) must be added. Friction loss might exist and be factored into the constant as well. Thus, equation (4) becomes:

$$\sqrt{U_0^2 - U_A^2} = C_0\sqrt{2g_C\,\Delta H} \quad \text{...........................}(5)$$

where $U_0$ = velocity through the orifice.

The pressure difference $\Delta P$ between A and B is read directly from the manometer.

In equation (5)

$\Delta H$ is measured from manometer $(\Delta P/\rho)$

gc is constant

C0 is constant and known for a particular orifice meter.

U0 and UA is unknown

So, to solve both U0 and UA another equation is required. We can assume that the volume flow-rate at A and orifice are equal, we can thus deduce the following equation.

$$U_A \frac{\pi d_P^2}{4} = U_O \frac{\pi d_O^2}{4} \qquad \text{or,} \qquad \frac{U_A}{U_O} = \left(\frac{d_O}{d_P}\right)^2 \quad \text{..............................(6)}$$

Were,

dP = diameter of pipe

dO = diameter of orifice

dP and dO are already known

Now we can solve equation (5) and (6) to get the value of both UA and UO.

UA = velocity of fluid in the pipe

$$U_A \times \frac{\pi d_P^2}{4} = \text{volume flow rate of fluid in the pipe.}$$

The constant Co depends on the

- ➢ ratio of the orifice diameter to the pipe diameter
- ➢ position of the orifice taps
- ➢ value of Reynolds number for the fluid flowing in the pipe.

For values of Reynolds number (based on orifice diameter i.e.

$$Re = \frac{d_O u_O \rho}{\mu} \text{ of 30,000 or}$$

above, the value of Co may be taken as 0.61.

**Advantage:**

It is a very easy-to-install gadget that requires little money for installation. Measuring fluids with different viscosities only requires adjusting the aperture diameter.

**Disadvantage:**

The aperture always causes a permanent loss of pressure (head), which reduces as the pipe diameter to orifice diameter ratio grows. This means that operating costs are high, especially over an extended period of time.

**VENTURIMETER**

**Description**

The venturimeter, seen in the picture, is made up of two tapered portions that are put into the pipeline. The taper is sufficiently smooth and progressive to prevent a significant loss of energy. The venturimeter's segment has its minimal diameter at point B. The venturimeter's "throat" refers to this location.

A pipe contains the venturimeter installed in it. A manometer measures the pressure differential between points A and B.

**Derivation**

If the Bernoulli's equation is written between these two points the following relationship holds.

$$X_A + \frac{U_A^2}{2g_c} + \frac{P_A}{\rho_A} - F + w = X_B + \frac{U_B^2}{2g_c} + \frac{P_B}{\rho_B} \quad \dots \dots \dots \dots (1)$$

| Conditions | Equation (1) changes to: |
|---|---|
| i) The pipe is horizontal $\therefore X_A = X_B$ | $\dfrac{U_A^2}{2g_c} + \dfrac{P_A}{\rho_A} - F + w = \dfrac{U_B^2}{2g_c} + \dfrac{P_B}{\rho_B}$ |
| ii) If frictional losses are assumed to be inappreciable then $F = 0$ | $\dfrac{U_A^2}{2g_c} + \dfrac{P_A}{\rho_A} + w = \dfrac{U_B^2}{2g_c} + \dfrac{P_B}{\rho_B}$ |
| iii) If the fluid is a liquid then $\rho A \approx \rho B = \rho$ (let) | $\dfrac{U_A^2}{2g_c} + \dfrac{P_A}{\rho} + w = \dfrac{U_B^2}{2g_c} + \dfrac{P_B}{\rho}$ |
| iv) Since no work is done on the liquid, or by the liquid between A and B. i.e. $w = 0$ | $\dfrac{U_A^2}{2g_c} + \dfrac{P_A}{\rho_A} = \dfrac{U_B^2}{2g_c} + \dfrac{P_B}{\rho_B} \quad \dots \dots \dots \dots (2)$ |

Equation (2) may be written as:

$$U_B^2 - U_A^2 = \frac{2g_C}{\rho}(P_A - P_B) \quad \dots \dots \dots \dots (3)$$

Since, $P_A - P_B = \Delta P$, and since $\dfrac{\Delta P}{\rho} = \Delta H$

$\therefore$ equation (3) can be written as

$$\sqrt{U_B^2 - U_A^2} = \sqrt{2g_c \, \Delta H} \quad \dots \dots \dots \dots (4)$$

> N.B.   $P_A = H_A \, \rho \, g / g_c$
> $P_B = H_B \, \rho \, g / g_c$
> $P_A - P_B = (H_A - H_B)\rho \, g / g_c$
> or,   $\Delta P = \Delta H \, \rho \, g / g_c.$
> Since, $g / g_c \approx 1.0$ hence, $\Delta H = \Delta P / \rho$
> If the pipe to the right of the orifice plate were removed so that the liquid issued as a jet from the orifice, the minimum diameter of the stream would be less than the diameter of the orifice. This point of minimum cross-section is known a vena-contracta.

Since there are practically no losses due to eddies and since the cross-section of the high velocity part of the system is accurately defined hence equation (4) may be written as

$$\sqrt{U_B^2 - U_A^2} = C_V \sqrt{2g_C \, \Delta H} \quad \dots \dots \dots \dots (5)$$

where UB = velocity at the throat of the venturimeter

In case of venturimeter the value of coefficient CV = 0.98.

Comparison between orificemeter and venturimeter:

| Orifice meter | Venturimeter |
|---|---|
| 1. Installation is cheap and easy.<br>2. The power loss is considerable in long run.<br>3. They are best used for testing purposes or other cases where the power loss is not a factor, as in steam lines.<br>4. Installing a new orifice plate with a different opening is a simple matter. | 1. Installation is costly. It is less easier than orifice meter. (*Disadvantage*)<br>2. Power loss is less in long run even negligible (*Advantage*)<br>3. Venturimeters are used for permanent installation.<br>4. Installation of a different opening require replacement of the whole venturimeter. (*Disadvantage*) |

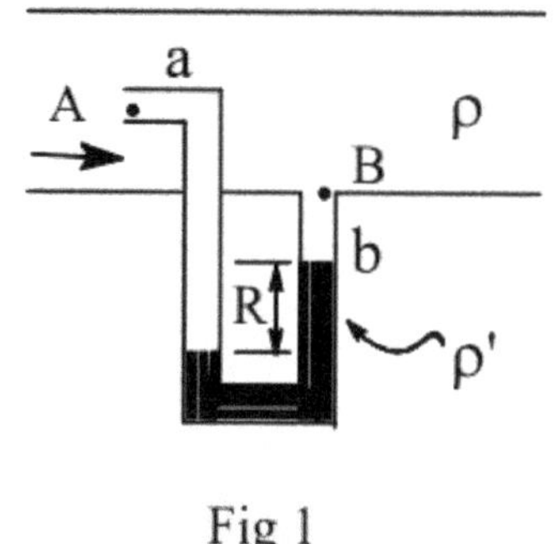

Fig 1

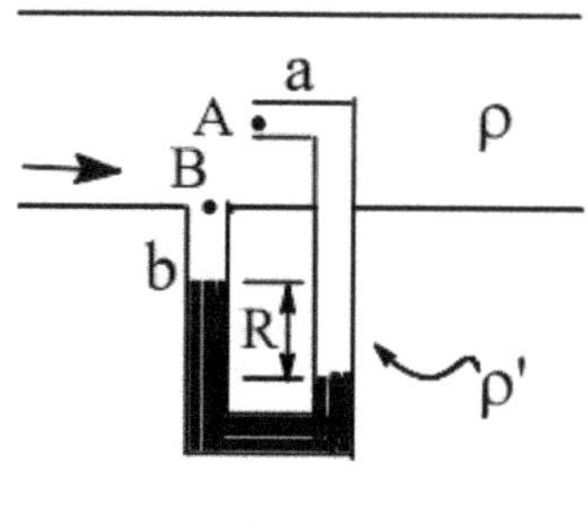

Fig 2

PITOT TUBE

A tool for determining the local velocity along a streamline is the pitot tube. The diagram illustrates the device's configurations. Two arms make up the manometer. The center of the pipe has one arm, "a," positioned in the opposite direction of the fluid's flow. The pipe wall is attached to the second arm, or "b." The reading is the difference in liquid between the manometer's two arms.

The tube in the 'a' hand measures the pressure head ($X_A$) and the velocity head $\left(\dfrac{U_A^2}{2g_c}\right)$. The 'b' hand measures only pressure head ($X_B$).

$$X_A + \frac{U_A^2}{2g_c} = X_B \qquad \text{or, } X_A - X_B = \frac{U_A^2}{2g_c} \qquad \text{or, } \Delta X = \frac{U_A^2}{2g_c} \quad \text{.........(i)}$$

Here $\Delta X_B$ is the pressure head of the fluid whose flow is to be measured that corresponds to R.

Therefore the following equation is how the manometer calculates pressure.

$$\Delta X = (\rho' - \rho)\, R\, g/g_c$$

or, $\qquad = (\rho' - \rho)\, R \qquad\qquad\qquad$ [Since $g/g_c \approx 1$]

where, $\rho' =$ density of the liquid in the manometer

$\qquad \rho \ =$ density of the fluid in the pipe.

Replacing $\Delta X$ in the equation (i) gives,

$$(\rho' - \rho)\, R = \frac{U_A^2}{2g_c} \qquad\qquad [U = U_A \text{ (let)}]$$

$$\therefore\ U = \sqrt{2\,(\rho' - \rho)\, g_c\, R} \qquad\qquad\qquad\dots\dots\dots(ii)$$

The velocity measured is the maximum velocity inside the pipe.

$$U_{max} = \sqrt{2\, g_c\, (\rho' - \rho)\, R}$$

The velocity measured is the maximum velocity inside the pipe.

$$U_{max} = \sqrt{2\, g_c\, (\rho' - \rho)\, R}$$

By orifice meter or venturimeter average velocity of fluid is measured. With pitot tube velocity of only one point (i.e. at the centre of the pipe) is measured. To convert Umax to average velocity (U) the following relationship is taken into concern.

where, $D =$ diameter of the pipe

$\qquad U_{max} =$ maximum velocity of fluid

$\qquad \rho =$ density of the fluid flowing

$\qquad \mu =$ viscosity of the fluid flowing

$\qquad \overline{U} =$ average velocity in the pipe

**Disadvantage of pitot tube**
1. It does not give the average velocity directly.
2. When velocity of gases are measured the reading are extremely small. In these cases some form of multiplying gauge like differential manometer and inclined manometers are used.

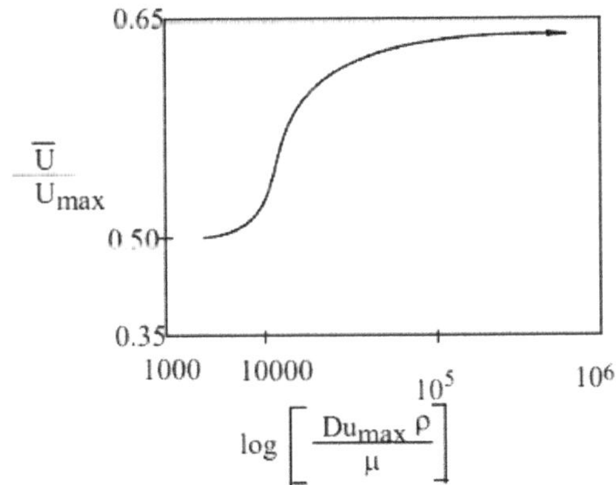


where D= diameter of the pipe
$U_{max} =$ maximum velocity of fluid
$\rho =$ density of the fluid flowing
$\mu =$ viscosity of the fluid flowing
U – average velocity in the pipe

## _ROTAMETER_

Construction of rotameter:

It is basically a vertically mounted, gradually tapering glass tube with the big end facing up in a frame. The tapering tube allows the fluids to flow higher. A solid float or plummet with a diameter less than the glass tube is inserted within the tapered tube. The fluid's velocity determines whether the plummet rises or falls.

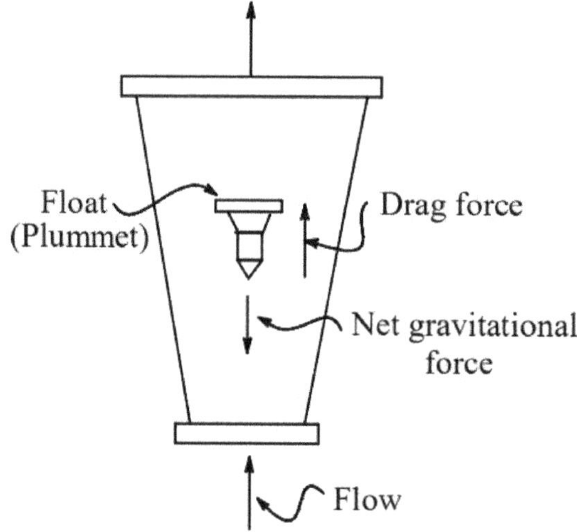


Principles of rotameter:

Three forces are balanced to determine the equilibrium section of the float in the rotameter for a given flow rate.

1.  The weight of the float (w)

2.  The buoyant force of the liquid on the float (B)

3.  The drag force on the float (D)

'w' acts downward and B and D acts upward. At equilibrium:

W = B + D

or, D = W − B

or, FD gC = Vfρfg − Vfρg .

where, FD = drag force

Vf = volume of float

ρf = density of float

ρ = density of fluid

The quantity of $V_f$ can be replaced by $\dfrac{m_f}{\rho_f}$, where $m_f$ is the mass of the float, and equation (i)

becomes: $\qquad F_D\, g_C \;=\; V_f\,(\rho_f - \rho)\, g \qquad\qquad = \dfrac{m_f}{\rho_f}\,(\rho_f - \rho)\,g \;=\; m_f\left(1 - \dfrac{\rho}{\rho_f}\right)g$

For a given meter operating on a certain fluid, the right-hand side of equation- (ii) is constant and independent of the flow rate. Therefore $F_D$ is also constant, when the *flow increases the position of the float must change to keep the drag force constant.*

$$F_D \;=\; K_1\,\dfrac{U_{max}^2}{2g_c} \qquad \text{where, } K_1 = \text{constant}$$

It can be demonstrated that the height at which the plummet is floating is related to the flow rate if the tube is tapered and the difference between the float and tube diameters is minimal.

Advantages:

1. The flow rates can be measured directly.

2. Measured in linear scale and

3. Constant and small head loss.

## SIZE REDUCTION

The process of reducing large solid unit masses (such as chemical or vegetable components) into smaller unit masses—coarse or fine—is known as size reduction.

The process of reducing size is also known as pulverization, diminution, or comminution. Size reduction may often be accomplished by one of two processes: mechanical processing or precipitation.

**Objectives**

Objectives of size reduction

1. Reducing size results in an increase in surface area.

Example-I: After size reduction, the rate at which solid medication particles dissolve multiplies many times. When griseofulvin, an antifungal medication, is delivered in its micronized form, absorption is approximately five times better.

Example-II: After size reduction, the absorptive ability of kaolin and charcoal rises because of their increased surface area.

2. Reduced size results in particles with a limited range of sizes. It is simpler to mix powders with a restricted size range.

3. Finer particle size is necessary for pharmaceutical suspensions. It lowers the sedimentation rate.

4. Particles smaller than 60 μm are needed for pharmaceutical capsules, ointments, suppositories, and insufflations (powders breathed directly into the lungs).

Objectives of size separation

1.  All solid materials include particles of different sizes following size reduction; they never produce particles of the same size. After the particles have been reduced in size, sieves are used to extract fractions with a restricted size range.

2.  If the granules are not within a specific size range during tablet granulation, weight variance will occur during tablet punching.

**Factors affecting size-reduction**

The pharmaceutical business employs a wide range of resources, such as chemicals, plant-based medications, and animal tissues.

**A. Factors related to the nature of raw materials**

Hard materials: The hardest materials to comminute are hard materials like pumice and iodine. These kinds of materials will cause abrasive wear on milling surfaces during size reduction, which will contaminate the material.

Fibrous materials: Crude drugs obtained from plants such as rauwolfia, ginger, glycyrrhiza, etc. are fibrous by nature and cannot be crushed under pressure. Therefore, a cutter mill might minimize their size.

Friable materials: Sucrose and dried filter cakes are easily ground up due to their friability and brittleness in a hammer mill or fluid energy mill.

Plastic materials: During milling, synthetic gums, waxes, and resins become pliable and soft. It is best to cool (make cold) these low melting materials before grinding. These materials are ground in a fluid energy mill and hammer mill.

Hygroscopic materials: Hygroscopic materials absorb moisture quickly, they must be processed inside a closed apparatus, such as a ball mill.

Thermolabile materials: Thermolabile compounds, such as medicines and vitamins, are processed in refrigerated equipment.

Inflammable materials: Certain combinations of fine particles, such as dextrin, starch, and sulfur, have the potential to explode. The mill should be securely earthed, and all electrical switches should be resistant to explosions.

Particle size of the feed: The feed needs to be the right size for a mill to function properly.

Moisture Content: More over 5% moisture content creates a sticky mass and impedes the grinding process.

**B. Factors related to the nature of the finished product**

Particle size: Different impact mills can produce powders that are rather coarse. A fluid energy mill is able to produce extremely tiny particles, such as griseofulvin micronized particles.

Ease of sterilization: Size reduction has to be done in a sterile setting when preparations are used for ophthalmic and parenteral (injection) purposes. Before being used, mills should be steam sterilized.

Contamination of milling materials: It is important to prevent product contamination while dealing with potent drugs and low dosage products. In this situation, wear-free equipment (such as a fluid energy mill) may be utilized.

Laws controlling the amount of energy and power used by mills Energy is given to the equipment (mill) during size reduction. Less than 2% of the energy used actually results in size reduction. Rest of the energy is dissipated (wasted) in:

I.      Elastic deformation of particles

II.     Transport of material within the milling chamber

III.    Friction between the particles

IV.    Friction between the particles and mill

V.     Generation of heat

VI.    Vibration and noise.

**VII.**    Inefficiency of transmission and motor.

Theories of milling

A number of theories have been proposed to establish a relationship between energy input and the degree of size reduction produced.

**Rittinger's theory**

Rittinger's theory suggests that energy required in a size reduction process is proportional to the new surface area produced.

$$E = K_R (S_n - S_i)$$

where, E = energy required for size reduction

KR = Rittinger's constant

Si = initial specific surface area

Sn = final specific surface area

Application: It is most applicable in size reducing brittle materials undergoing fine milling.

**Bond's theory**

Bond's theory states that the energy used in crack propagation is proportional to the new crack length produced

$$E = 2K_B \left( \frac{1}{\sqrt{d_n}} - \frac{1}{\sqrt{d_i}} \right)$$

where, E = energy required for size reduction

$K_B$ = Bond's work index

$d_i$ = initial diameter of particles

$d_n$ = final diameter of particles

*Application*: This law is useful in rough mill sizing. The work index is useful in comparing the efficiency of milling operations.

**Kick's theory**

Kick's theory states that the energy used in deforming (or fracturing) a set of particles of equivalent shape is proportional to the ratio of change of size, or:

$$E = K_K \, \log \frac{d_i}{d_n}$$

where, E = energy required for size reduction

KK = Kick's constant

di = initial diameter of particles

dn = final diameter of particles

Application: For crushing of large particles Kick's theory most useful.

**Walker's theory**

Walker proposed a generalized differential form of the energy-size relationship:

$$dE = -K \frac{dD}{D^n}$$

where E = amount of energy (work done) required to produce a change

D = size of unit mass

K = Constant        n = constant

For n =1.0 Walker equation becomes Kick's theory used for coarse particles > 1 $\mu$m.

For n =1.5 Walker equation becomes Bond's theory. This theory is used when neither Kick's nor Rittinger's law is applicable.

For n =2.0 Walker equation becomes Rittinger's theory used for fine particles < 1 $\mu$m size.

## Methods of size reduction

Depending on the material, there may be variations in the size reduction mechanism. Therefore, a unique treatment plan might be essential for each medications.

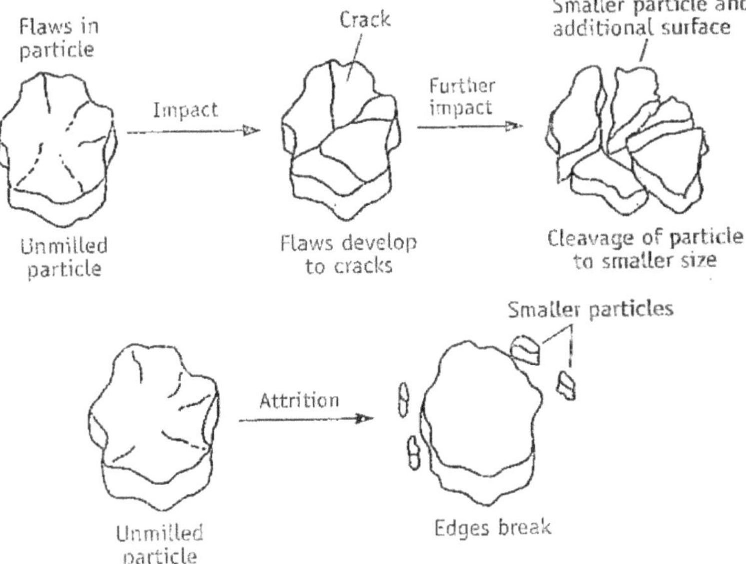



Drugs are generally uncomplicated to grind. The process is divided into two categories: superfine grinding (particles smaller than a micrometer) and fine grinding (#200). These classes comprise the majority of pharmaceutical processes, however before extraction, vegetable drugs are coarsely ground.

## MODES OF STRESS APPLIED IN SIZE REDUCTION

Different types of stresses are applied in order to reduce size. The following are common size reduction techniques.

1. Cutting: The material is sliced using one or more sharp blades. It works well for grinding up fibrous or waxy materials. For instance, a cutter mill.

2. Compression: In this mode, pressure is applied to smash the material between rollers. When a particle is compressed, the applied stress creates deformation (a crack tip) in an area that is distant from the main stress application point rather than directly causing the particle to fail. E.g. roller mill.

3. Impact: This involves the operation of hammers or bars at high speeds. A lump of material splits apart when it comes into contact with the rotating hammers. This process keeps going until the necessary number of particles are obtained. E.g. hammer mill. When moving particles collide with a stationary surface, impact also happens. Similar to this, fast-moving particles clash with one another to create smaller particles. E.g. fluid energy mill.

4. Attrition: In this procedure, the substance is broken down by rubbing it across two surfaces, i.e. surface phenomenon. It is generally necessary for fine grinding. E.g. fluid energy mill.

## CLASSIFICATION OF SIZE REDUCTION EQUIPMENT

A. Crushers, e.g. edge runner mill, end runner mill.

B. Grinders:

    I.    Impact mills, e.g. hammer mill.

II.     Rolling-compression mills, e.g. roller mill.

III.    Attrition mills, e.g. fluid energy mill.

IV.     Tumbling mills, e.g. ball mill.

C. Ultrafine grinders, e.g. fluid energy mill.

D. Cutting machines, e.g. cutter mill. Some of them are discussed individually in the following sections.

## SIZE REDUCTION – EQUIPMENT

The equipment described in this chapter are also used in small-scale plants. The basic principles and working remain the same even in largescale operations. Other variants are also included, in brief.

| Degree of size reduction | Typical methods | Examples |
|---|---|---|
| Large pieces | Cutter or compression mills | Rhubarb |
| Coarse powders | Impact mills | Liquorice, cascara |
| Fine powders | Combined impact and attrition mills | Rhubarb , belladonna |
| Very fine powders | Fluid energy mills | Vitamins and antibiotics |

## HAMMER MILL

Method of size reduction: Impact

Construction and working principle:

A sturdy metal shell encircling a central shaft to which four or more hammers are mounted makes up a hammer mill. When the shaft is rotated, the swivel joints on these mount the hammers to a radial position. When materials are cut down to a suitable size, a screen in the lower portion of the case allows them to escape. The materials are gathered in a container that is positioned beneath the screen.

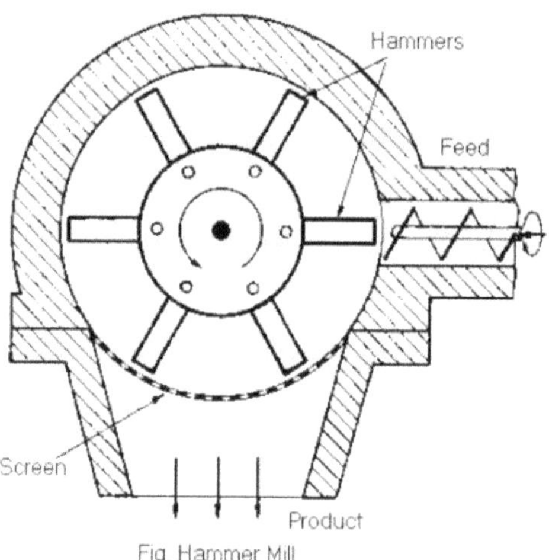

Fig. Hammer Mill

- The screen can be adjusted to the necessary particle size.

- According to the purpose of operation the hammers may be square-faced, tapered to a cutting form or have a stepped-form.

- For greater effect, the interior of the casing can have an angular shape rather than a smooth, circular one.
- The rotor spins at 80 revolutions per second.

Advantages:

I. It is rapid in action, and is capable of grinding many different types of materials.

II. The product can be controlled by variation of rotor speed, hammer type and size and shape of mesh.

III. Operation is continuous.

IV. Since no surface touches another, there is extremely minimal chance of mill material contamination.

Disadvantages:

I. Excessive operating speed produces heat, which could harm thermolabile materials or medications that contain resin, fat, or gum.

II. The feed rate needs to be managed to prevent choking of the mill.

III. Foreign elements, such as metal fragments or stones, may cause harm to the hammer mill due to its high speed of operation.

Applications: Powdering of crystals and filter cakes.

## BALL MILL

Construction

A hollow cylinder that is rotated on its horizontal axis makes up the ball mill. There are balls or pebbles inside the cylinder.

Cylinder:

- The cylinder's composition could be rubber, porcelain, or metal.
- Rubber minimizes abrasion. In pharmaceutical practice, the cylinder's diameter varies from 1 to 3 meters.

..Balls:

- Balls occupy about 30 to 50% of the volume of the cylinder.
- The cylinder's diameter and the feed size determine the balls' diameters. Balls range in diameter from 2 to 15 cm.
- Balls could be made of porcelain, metal, or stones.

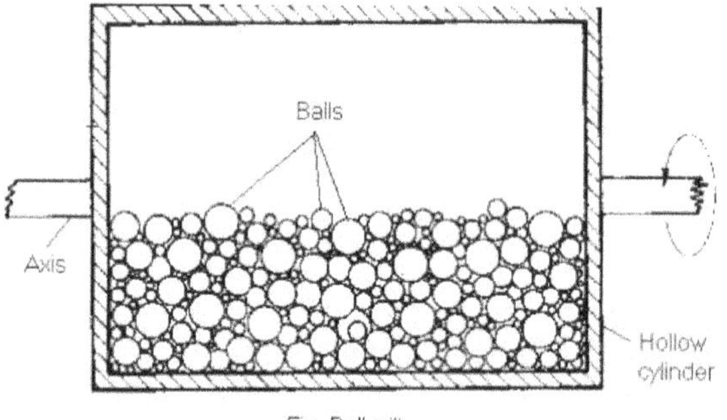



Fig. Ball mill

Working Principle

The cylinder has an aperture through which larger particles are fed. The opportunity has ended. At the ball mill's critical speed, the cylinder rotates.

The following variables determine a ball mill's ideal size reduction:

Feed quantity: Too much feed can cause a cushioning effect, while insufficient feed will cause the mill to become less efficient.

Speed of rotation of the cylinder:

• Only a small amount of size decrease will occur when the bulk of the balls slides or rolls over one another at low speeds.
• Centrifugal force will cause balls to be hurled against the cylinder wall at high speeds, preventing grinding. It is known as the ball mill's crucial speed when centrifugation only starts at the second-third of its speed. The balls are propelled nearly to the top of the mill at this speed, whereupon they cascade across the mill's diameter. This means that attrition between the balls and particle collision between the balls result in the greatest size decrease. It is often measured in cycles per second (cps).

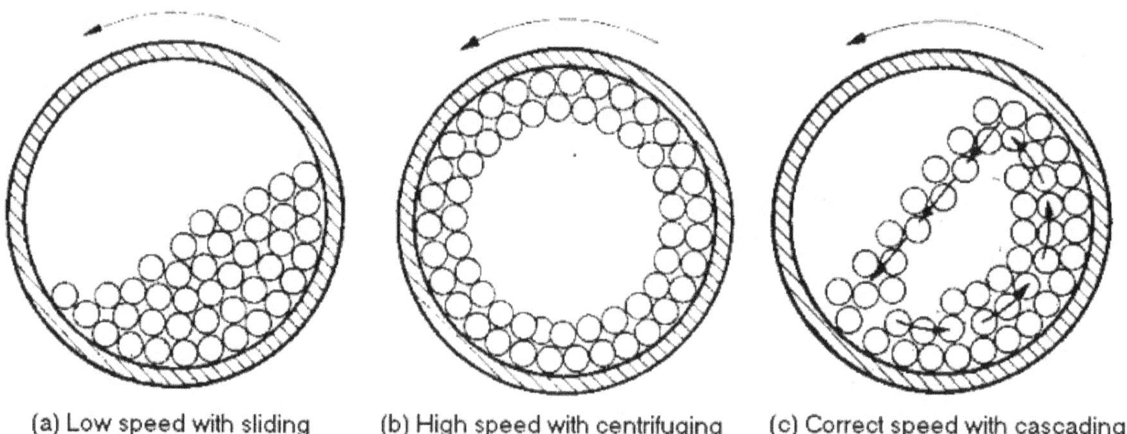



Advantages

I.    It can grind a broad range of materials with varying degrees of hardness.

II. It can be used with hazardous substances because it may be used in an enclosed form.

III. It can produce very fine powders.

IV. It works well for both wet and dry milling. In order to prepare medicinal suspensions, wet grinding is necessary.

Disadvantages

I. Wear occurs from the balls and the inside surface of the cylinder hence there is possibility of contamination of product with mill material. Abrasive materials increase wear.

II. Soft or sticky materials that hold the balls in aggregates or induce caking on the mill's sidewalls may be problematic.

III. The ball mill is a very noisy machine, particularly if the cylinder is made of metal.

Applications:

Before pharmaceutical compounds are manufactured, ores are ground in large ball mills. Smaller ball mills are employed for the grinding of suspensions, medicines, and excipients.

Various types of ball mills:

**Hardinge mill:** The cylinder in these ball mills has a conical end that faces the discharge point. The smaller balls in this mill are gathered in the conical section, while the larger balls stay inside the cylinder. Consequently, the cylinder portion is used for coarser grinding, and the conical portion's apex is used for finer grinding. When compared to a standard cylindrical ball mill, the result is more homogeneous and finer.

**Tube mill:** Compared to a traditional ball mill, they can grind to a finer product because of their lengthy cylinder design.

**Rod mill:** They have rods inside instead of balls, and the rods run the entire length of the mill. Since rods don't aggregate like balls do, these rods are helpful when working with sticky materials.

**Vibration mill:** Instead of rotation, vibratory vibrations are used in these kinds of mills. The vibration is created by the springs supporting the cylinder. With a vibration amplitude of up to 20 mm and a rotational frequency of 15 to 50 per second, the cylinder rotates in a circular motion.

## FLUID ENERGY MILL

Construction:

It consists of a loop of pipe, which has a diameter of 2 to 20cm. The height of the loop may be up to 2m. Several nozzles are fitted at the bottom of the pipe. A classifier is fitted at the product collection point.

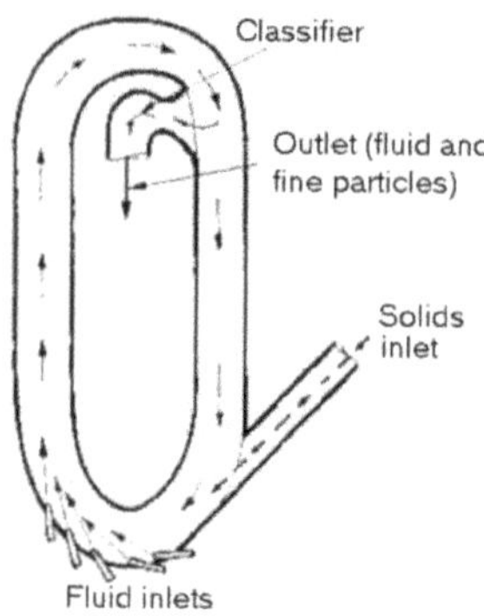


Working principle

A high-pressure fluid, often air, is injected through nozzles located at the bottom of the loop. This results in a high circulation velocity that causes turbulence. The feed inlet allows solids to enter the stream. High levels of turbulence cause the particles to collide and attrition to ensue. The device is equipped with a classifier to separate the larger particles from the finer ones and send them back into the air stream for additional size reduction. A 100 mesh screen is used to filter and size-reduce the feed before it is sent to the mill. The result may be as small as 5 μm or smaller.

Advantages:

I.    The particle size of the product is smaller than that produced by any other method of size reduction.

II.    Expansion of gases at the nozzles lead to cooling, counteracting the usual frictional heat that can affect heat-sensitive (thermolabile) materials.

III.    Since the size reduction is by inter-particulate attrition there is little or no abrasion of the mill and no contamination of the product.

IV.    For oxygen or moisture sensitive materials inert gases like nitrogen can be used instead of normal air.

V.    This method is used where fine powders are required like micritization of griseofulvin (an antifungal drug), antibiotics etc.

## EDGE RUNNER MILL

The materials are crushed into fine powders by the slow rotation of two huge grinding wheels or stones in a big bowl inside an edge runner mill or roller stone mill.

Principle: The shearing forces created by the revolving stones are the basis for how an edge runner mill operates. Because of their high weight, the stones quickly crush the materials, minimizing their size.

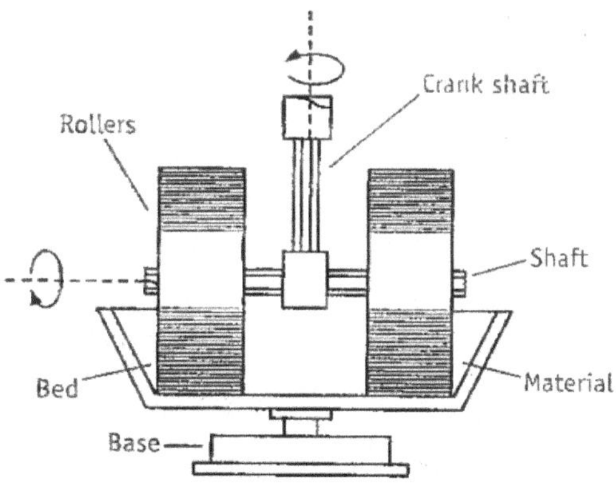



Construction:

The existence of two heavy rollers composed of stone or metal that roll on a second bed of stones or granite accounts for the edge runner mill's weight of several tons. Each roller has its own axis of rotation and is driven by a central shaft. They travel around the bed on a horizontal shaft farther.

Working: It utilizes a batch processing system. The shallow stone bed is where the material to be crushed is kept. It remains in the path of the stone wheel, which rotates around both its axis and the stone bed. This is maintained by a scrapper. By shearing and crushing, the outer portion of the wheel travels a longer distance than the inner half in order to reduce size. Following a predetermined amount of time spent crushing the material, the resultant materials are gathered and sieved to produce the required size.

Uses:

1) It is used for crushing hard materials into fine powders.

2) It is used for plant-based product.

Advantages: -

    I.      It can produce very fine particles of drugs.

    II.     It does not required much more attention while operating.

    III.    Simple and easy to install.

Disadvantages: -

    I.      It cannot be used for sticky materials.

    II.     The milling process is time taking.

    III.    Produce noise.

**END RUNNER MILL**

A form of mortar and pestle known as an end runner mill has a flat-bottomed pestle and shallow mortar. It functions similarly to the wet grinding that households use.

Construction:

The end-runner mill is powered by a motor and has a weighted pestle positioned eccentrically inside a metal, granite, or ceramic mortar. The material is crushed and rubbed between the spinning mortar and the rotating pestle, which rotates due to friction and is free to rise and fall within the mortar. This creates a dual impact and shear grinding action.

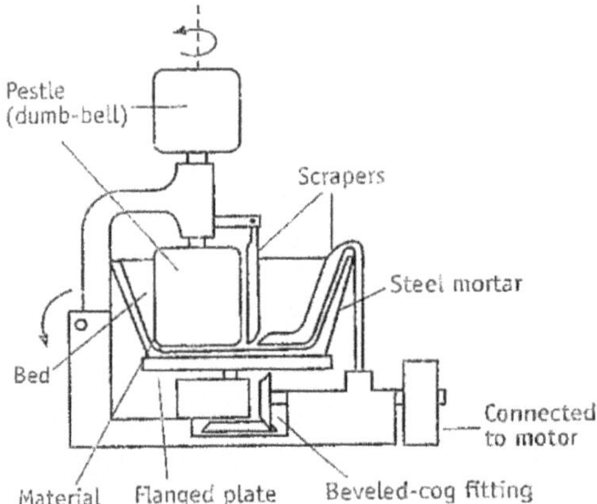


The material is continuously returned to the grinding area by spring-loaded scrapers, and emptying and cleaning are made easier by the pestle's ability to swing out of the mortar at the conclusion of the operation.

Uses: When working with fibrous materials such as bark, wood, fruits, leaves, etc., the end runner mill produces a powder that is fairly fine.

Advantages:

I.      It produces fine particles.

II.     Requires less attention during the milling operation.

Disadvantages:

I.      It is not suitable for milling sticky materials.

II.     Machine noise leading to noise pollution

## SIZE SEPARATION

**Definition:** Size separation is a unit process in which a mixture of different sized particles is divided into two or more parts using screening surfaces. Sieving, sifting, and screening are other names for size separation. This method is predicated on the physical distinctions between the particles, including their density, size, and form.

**Application/uses of size separation:** Determination of particle size & size distribution used for production of tablet and capsule. It is a quality control tool for analysis of raw material. To optimize the process condition such as method of agitation, time of screening, feed rate etc. To measure the efficiency of size reduction equipment's.

**SIEVES**

Pharmacopeial testing sieves are made of wire cloth with square meshes that are woven from wires made of stainless steel, brass, and other metals.

Number of sieves: No of meshes in a length of 2.54 cm in each transfer direction parallel to the wires.

Nominal size of aperture: Distance between the wires. Length of the side of the square aperture. (in mm or μm).

Nominal diameter of the wire: Made of suitable diameter in order to give a suitable aperture and sufficient length.

Approximate % sieving area: The area of the meshes as a percentage of the total area of the sieve. Generally, the sieving area is kept within the range of 35-40% in order to give suitable strength to the sieve.

Tolerance average aperture size: Fine sieves cannot be woven with same accuracy.

Sieve Analysis Equivalent diameter Sieve diameter, ds , is the particle dimension that passes through a square aperture (length = x).

Range of analysis: The International Standards Organization (ISO) sets lowest sieve diameter of 45 μm. Powders are usually defined as particles having a maximum diameter of 1000 μm, so this is the upper limit. In practice sieve analysis can be done over a range of 5 to 125000 μm.

ISO Range: - 45 to 1000 μm

Range available in practice: 5 to 125000 μm

Sample preparation

- Powders in dry state is usually used.

- Powders in liquid suspension can also be analysed by sieve.

Principle of measurement with sieve:

A set of sieves is used in sieve analysis. Every sieve is made of woven, punched, or electroformed mesh that is physically barriers to particles. These meshes are frequently made of brass or stainless steel and have known aperture diameters. A stack or "nest" of sieves is a series of sieves organized so that the largest aperture is at the top and the smallest aperture is at the bottom in sieve analysis.

1. A sieve-nest usually comprises 6 to 8 sieves with an aperture progression based on √2 or 2√2 change in diameter between adjacent sieves.

2. Initial weight ($W_0$) of powder sample was taken on the first sieve (i.e. topmost sieve). The sieve-set was closed and shaking was started. After shaking for a stipulated time, the sieve-set was taken out. All the sieves were disassembled.

3. The powder retained on each sieve was collected on a paper (bearing the mesh number) and weighed.

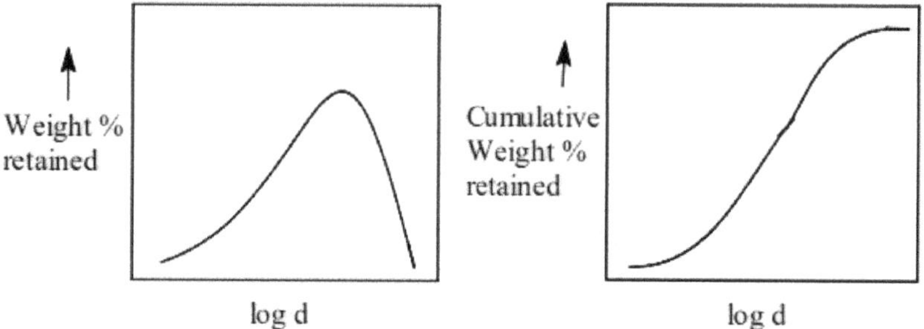


## STANDARDS OF SIEVES

It is required that wire-mesh sieves will be made from wire of uniform, circular cross-section and for each sieve the following particulars are stated:

Number of sieves

This is the number of meshes in a length of 25.4mm (i.e. 1 inch), in each direction. Nominal size aperture This is the distance between the wires, so that it represents the length of the side of the square aperture.

N.B. While it is the diameter of the largest sphere that would pass the mesh, it is not necessarily the maximum dimension of the particle, plate like particles will pass through diagonally and long fibrous particles require only suitable orientation.

## OFFICIAL STANDARDS FOR POWDERS

in general, powders are vaguely described as coarse and fine powders. However, it is essential to identify with some guiding specifications. Indian Pharmacopoeia has prescribed standards for powders for pharmaceutical purposes. Accordingly, degree of coarseness or fineness is ex pressed with reference to the nominal aperture size of sieve through which powder is able to pass. The relevant grades of powders and sieve number along with nominal aperture size. The IP 1996 specifies five grades of powder.

**Grades of Powders and Sieve Number alongwith Nominal Aperture Size as per IP**

| Sl. No. | Grade of powder | Sieve through which all particles must pass | Nominal mesh aperture size | Sieve through which 40 % particles pass | Nominal mesh aperture size |
|---|---|---|---|---|---|
| 1 | Coarse powder | 10 | 1.7 mm | 44 | 355 µm |
| 2 | Moderately coarse powder | 22 | 710 µm | 60 | 250 µm |
| 3 | Moderately fine powder | 44 | 355 µm | 85 | 180 µm |
| 4 | Fine powder | 85 | 180 µm | — | — |
| 5 | Very fine powder | 120 | 125 µm | — | — |

## Construction

Pharmaceutical testing sieves are made of wire cloth with square meshes that are woven from brass, bronze, stainless steel, or any other acceptable maximum metals. It is not appropriate to coat or plate sieves. The material of the sieve and the substance to be sieved cannot react with one another.

**Types of Sieves**

The primary considerations for sieves are given to the size and shape of aperture opening. Square meshes are arranged as per the specifications. Sieves commonly used in pharmaceutical processing include:

- Woven wire sieves

- Bolting cloth sieves

- Bar screens (closely spaced bars)

- Punched plates

## SIZE SEPARATION EQUIPMENTS

## SIEVE SHAKER

An equipment used in particle analysis is the sieve shaker. In order to sort materials according to particle sizes, it is used to shake a stack of test sieves that are arranged in ascending order (biggest aperture at the top and smallest aperture at the bottom). In order to perform material separation, reduce sample size, and support particle analysis, sieve shakers can be used in place of human hand sifting.

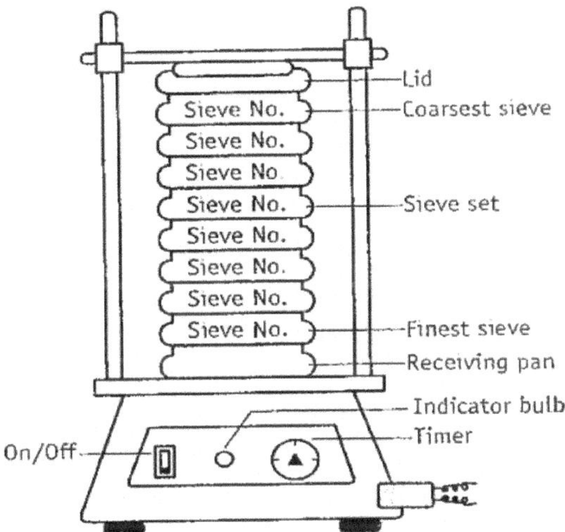


Working: -Sieves are arranged in a nest with the course at the top. A powder sample (50 g) is placed on the coarsest sieve. This sieve set is fixed to the mechanical shaker apparatus and shaken for a certain period of time (20 min). The powder retained on each sieve is weighed.

Practical considerations: - Taking precautions is necessary to obtain repeatable outcomes. Sieving is influenced by the type of motion; vibratory motion is the most effective, followed by side-tap, bottom-pat, rotary motion with tap, and rotating motion. The shaker's motion type and intensity are set and consistent. Shakers can be purchased commercially.

The sample's weight and shaking time are additional variables. With a lower limit of estimation of particle diameter 50 pm, sieves generated by photo-etching and electro-forming processes are employed to obtain a better estimate of the size distribution study.

Advantages: -It is inexpensive, simple and rapid with reproducible results.

Disadvantages: -

(1) Lower limit of particle size is 50 pm.

(2) If powder is not dry, apertures get clogged with particles, leading to improper sieving.

(3) During shaking, attrition (particles colliding with each other) occurs causing size reduction of particles. This leads to error in estimation.

Variants: -

Electromagnetic sieve shaker—It is useful for analysing powders under controlled conditions. Sonic sifter—This apparatus utilises sonic oscillations. A mechanical pulse action is used to reduce blinding and agglomeration in the sub-sieve sizes.

SHAKING SCREEN

Principle: Particles of different sizes are separated by passing them through a sieve, which oscillates to-and-fro continuously.

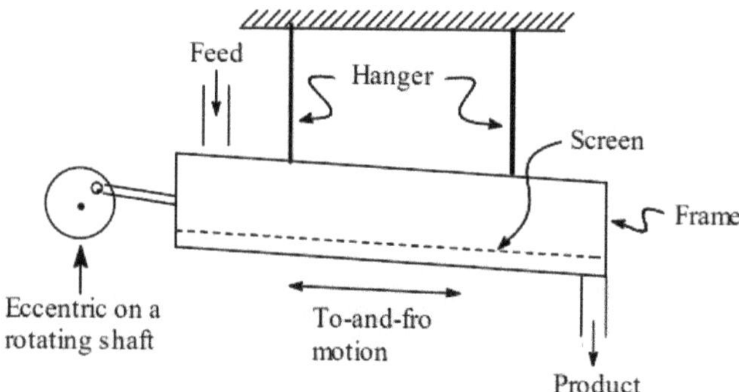


Construction: A metal frame with a screen fastened at the bottom makes up a shaking screen. Either a detachable bolted frame or direct riveting can be used to fit the screen cloth. To provide for freedom of movement, hanger rods are used to suspend the metal frame. The metal frame can be suspended in an inclined or horizontal orientation. An ordinary eccentric is used to join one side of the frame to a spinning shaft. There is a reciprocating (to-and-fro) action across the entire frame.

Working: Reciprocating shakes of the screen are permitted. The feed, or item to be screened, is fed in from one side of the screen. First, fine particles are filtered out. The over-sized particles are gathered at one end while the remaining materials continue ahead.

Advantages: It requires low-head room and low power requirement.

Disadvantages: High cost of maintenance of screens and supporting structures. Its capacity is low.

SHAKING AND VIBRATING SCREENS (ROTEX SCREEN)

Principle: Rotex screens use an eccentric mechanism to provide oscillating agitation, or to-and-fro motion. Rubber balls create additional vibrations.

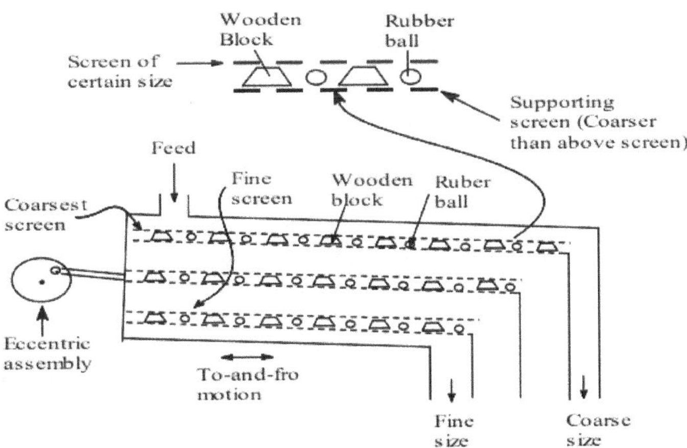



Construction: This apparatus consists of a series of screens with a horizontal axis that is slightly angled at a 5 degree angle. Every screen set has two layers. The lower screen is a coarser screen that serves as a supporting sieve, while the upper screen has a set size. Wooden blocks arranged at various intervals are situated between these two screens. Rubber balls are positioned in between the wooden pieces. There is only one unit in this two-sieve system. A number of these units are set up descendingly, with a sieve or bigger hole at the top and a finer opening at the bottom. The overall assembly of screens is supported on sliding contacts at the lower end. The upper end of the screen system is connected to an eccentric pin on a flywheel.

Working: The screen system is allowed to agitate with the use of eccentric. The screens shake, causing the balls to fly between them. As the balls strike the slanted surface of the wooden blocks, they deflect upward and impact the screen fabric, preventing the mesh from being blocked. The feed is introduced at the top of the screen. The substance moves through the upper screen and onto the next screen. This process continues until all of the materials have been sorted into fractions. The fractions are gathered individually at the outflow point.

Uses: Rotec screen is used for handling a variety of dry powders, granules and dry foods.

## CYCLONE SEPARATOR

Principle

Cyclone separators employ centrifugal force to separate solids from fluids. The separation process is dependent on particle size and density. It is also feasible to transport tiny particles with the fluid.

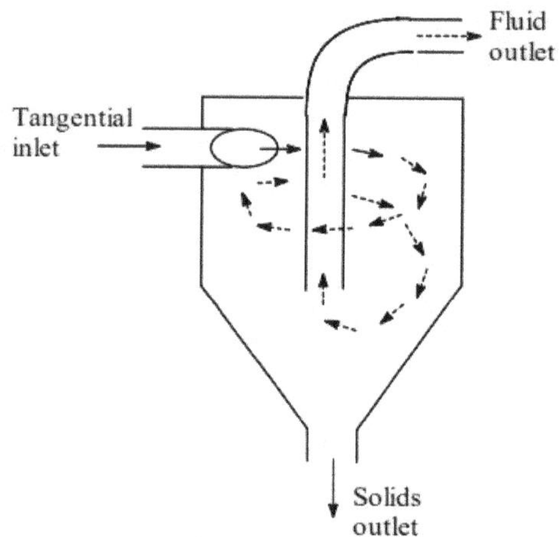


## Construction

It consists of a short vertical cylindrical jar with a conical base. The upper half of the vessel has a tangential inlet. The solid outlet is located at the base. The fluid exit is located in the center of the top section and continues inwardly into the separator. This structure prevents air from short-circuiting directly from the fluid's input to its output.

## Working

Solids to be separated are suspended in a stream of fluid (typically air or water). Such feed is supplied tangentially at a high velocity, resulting in rotating movement within the tank. The particles are thrown against the vessel's wall due to centrifugal force. As the fluid's (air) speed decreases, the particles fall to the base and accumulate at the solid exit. The fluid (air) can exit through the center outlet at the top.

## Uses

1. Cyclone separators are used to separate solid particles from gases.

2. It is also used for size separation of solids in liquids.

3. It is used to separate the heavy and coarse fraction from fine dust.

## AIR SEPARATOR

### Principle

The cyclone separator cannot separate fine materials based on their size. For such separations, an air current mixed with centrifugal force is used. The finer particles are swept away by air, while the coarser particles are hurled by centrifugal force and sink to the bottom.

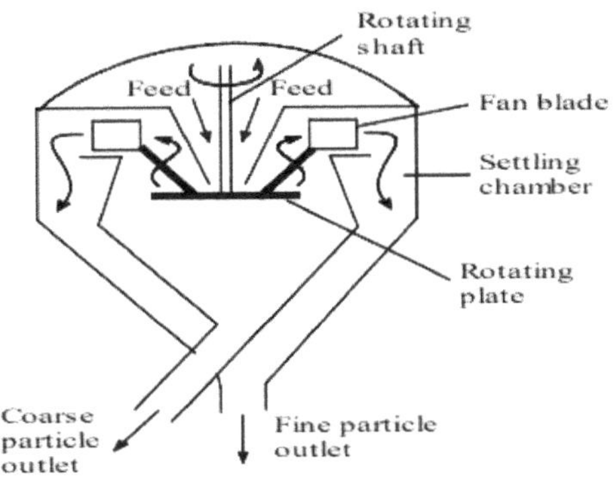



## Construction

It is composed of a cylindrical vessel with a conical base. A spinning plate is mounted on a shaft located in the center of the vessel. The same shaft is also used to connect a set of fan blades. At the vessel's base, there are two outlets: one for finer particles and one for coarse particles.

## Working

A motor powers the rotation of the disc and fan. The feed (powder) enters the vessel from the centre and falls off the spinning plate. The whirling fan blades create a draft (flow) of air in the direction indicated in the diagram. The draft of air picks up the fine particles and transports them into the settling chamber, where the air velocity is sufficiently slowed so that the fine particles are dropped and removed through the fine particle exit. The coarse particle outlet removes particles that are too heavy to be taken up by the air stream.

## Uses

Air separators are frequently coupled to ball mills or hammer mills to separate and return larger particles for further size reduction.

## BAG FILTER

### Principle

A bag filter separates fines (or dust) from milled powder in two phases. The milled powder is initially pushed through a bag (made of cloth) with suction applied to the opposite side of the feed entry. This helps the separation. In the next phase, pressure is used to shake the bags, causing powder adhered to the bag to fall off and be collected from the conical base.

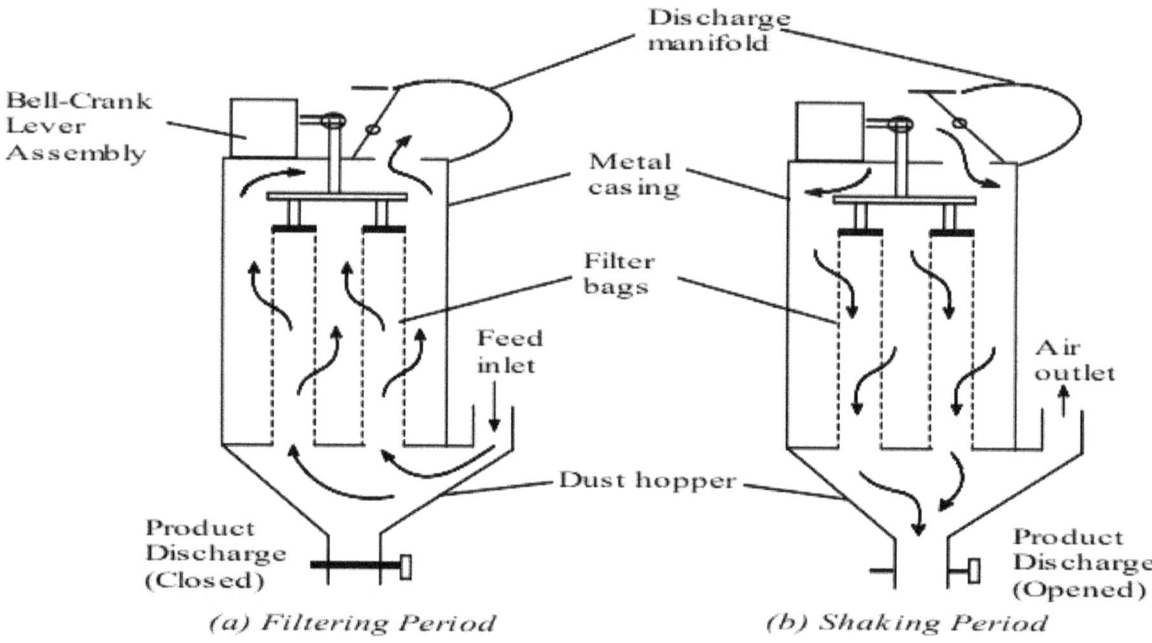



Construction

It is made up of several cotton or wool fabric bags. These are suspended in a metallic container. A hopper is placed at the bottom of the filter to receive the feed. A vacuum fan and exhaust through the discharge manifold are installed on top of the metal container. A bell-crank lever mechanism at the vessel's top is used to switch from filtration to shaking.

Working

(a) Filtering period: During this time, the vacuum fan generates a pressure lower than the air pressure inside the vessel. The gas to be filtered enters the hopper, travels through the bags, and exits the top of the apparatus. The particles remain within the bags.

(b) Shaking period: During this time, the bell-crank lever closes the discharge manifold and allows air to enter via the top, breaking the vacuum. At the same time, it violently jerks the bags to release them from dust. Fine particles are gathered at the conical base.

Uses

1. Bag filters are used along with other size separation equipment, e.g. a cyclone separator.

2. They are use on the top of fluidized bed dryer for drying to separate the dusts.

3. They are used to clean the air of a room.

4. Household vacuum cleaner is a simple version of bag filter.

COTTRELL PRECIPITATOR

Principle

If a gas is exposed to a strong unidirectional electrostatic field, it becomes ionized and drifts towards one electrode. If a finely divided solid particle (or liquid droplet) is suspended in the gas, it will become charged and migrate to the same electrode as the ionized gas.

Construction

There will be two electrodes:

(i) Discharge electrode and

(ii) Collecting electrode.

• The discharge electrode is usually a wire, chain, wire screen or other arrangement with a large surface.

• The collecting (or smooth) electrode may be parallel plate or pipe.

• In case of parallel plate design the gas flows parallel to plates. Plate dimensions: Length = 10 to 18 ft Width = 3 to 6 ft.

• In case of pipe design the pipes are placed vertically and a wire (discharge electrode) is fitted at the centre of the pipe. Gas flows from the bottom to the top of the pipe. At the bottom of the pipe a hopper is given to collect the particles. Pipe dimensions: Height 6 to 15 ft.

Working

AC current is first stepped up with a step-up transformer to raise the potential difference to 50,000 to 60,000 volts. Then the voltage is made unidirectional by a motor-disc assembly where the motor is rotating at a speed similar to the frequency (i.e. cycles per second or Hz) of the AC current. This results in a pulsating but unidirectional electrostatic field. The particles will be charged and precipitated on the smooth plate or pipe, which is then collected through the hopper.

Use The Cottrell process is successfully used for the removal of fine dusts from all kind of waste gases.

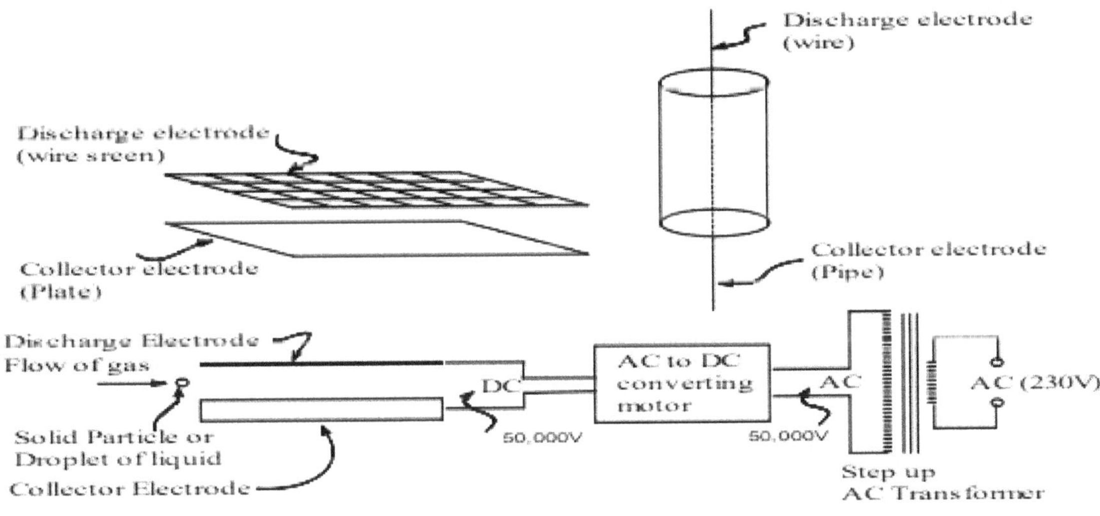


SIZE SEPARATORS BASING ON SEDIMENTATION THEORY (ELUTRIATION TANK)

Principle: Size separation by sedimentation utilizes the differences in settling velocities of the particles with different diameter (d) and these can be related to Stoke's law.

Stoke's law

When a solid particle is suspended in a liquid the particle settles downward at a velocity, V. This velocity is called sedimentation rate. It is found that this rate of sedimentation depends on the diameter of the particle, density of the liquid and particle, viscosity of the liquid and the acceleration due to gravity. All these parameters can be combined in the form of Stoke's equation:

$$V = \frac{d^2(\rho_1 - \rho_2)g}{18\eta}$$

## CONTINUOUS SEDIMENTATION TANK

A shallow tank is arranged with inlet and outlet pipes as shown in the figure. Particles entering the tank will be acted upon by a force that can be divided into two components:

(i) a horizontal component due to the flow of liquid carrying the particles forward and

(ii) a vertical component due to gravity, which causes the particles to fall towards the bottom of the tank. This component is governed by Stoke's law so that the velocity of sedimentation is proportional to the square of the diameter of the particles. Thus, the particles will settle at the bottom of the tank in such a way that the course (largest) particles will settle near to the inlet of liquid and the finest particles near to the outlet of the liquid. Partitions are arranged at the floor of the tank to enable collection of different size fraction particles.

Where, d = diameter of the particle

$\rho1$ = density of the particle

$\rho2$ = density of the liquid

g = acceleration due to gravity

$\eta$ = viscosity of the liquid.

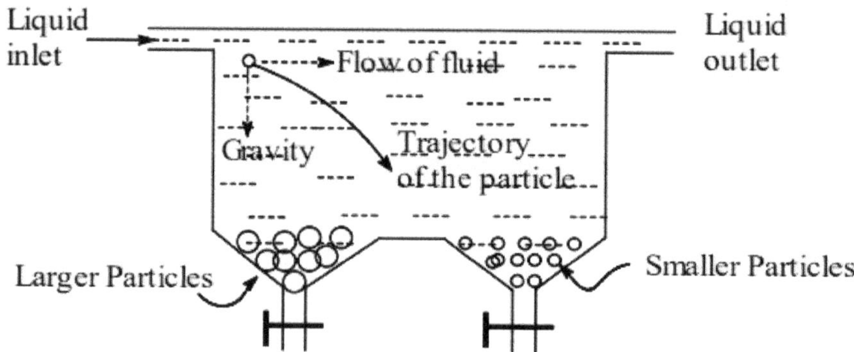


**QUESTION BANK**

Multiple choice questions: -

Each question carries one mark

1. Which one of these instruments is suitable for measuring minute pressure differences in a fluid?

   a) Diaphragm pressure gauge

   b) Inclined manometer

   c) Simple manometer

   d) U-tube differential manometer

2. The velocity distribution of a fluid in a pipe is parabolic for one of the following types of flow.

   a) non-uniform laminar flow

   b) non-uniform turbulent flow

   c) Uniform laminar flow

   d) Uniform turbulent flow

3. In a pipe, laminar flow has a centre line velocity of 0.1 m/s. What is the average velocity?

   a) 5 cm/s

   b) 10 cm/s

   c) 15 cm/s

   d) 20 cm/s

4. What is the unit for pressure energy in hydraulics?

   a) Joules

   b) $Kg^x m/s2$

   c) Metre

   d) Pascal

5. Two pipe systems are said to be equivalent in their lengths, in one of the following conditions.

   a) Both the systems are connected in series

   b) Discharge and diameter are same.

   c) Friction factor and discharge are same

   d) Same head loss is produced by the same discharge

6. In which portion of a pipe, the flow of liquid is high?

   a) At the actual surface of pipe wall,

b) Central portion

c) Near the pipe wall

d) Transition region

7. In the flow of fluids, the inertial forces depend on one of the following.

a) Mass

b) Mass and velocity

c) Mass, velocity and density

d) Mass, velocity, density and viscosity

8. Measurement of time of flow is important for the determination of flow of fluids in one of the following.

a) Displacement meter

b) Orifice meter

c) Rotameter

d) Venturi meter

9. Which of the following gives direct reading of flow of fluids?

a) Orifice meter

b) Pitot tube

c) Rotameter

d) Venturi meter

10. Which one of the following does NOT require manometer in the construction of flow meters.

a) Orifice meter

b) Pitot tube

c) Rotameter

d) Venturi meter

11. The fluid particles flowing in a fluid follow one of the following.

a) Constant velocity

b) Variable velocities

c) Velocity as high as possible

d) Zero velocity

12. Which of the following can be considered as an ideal fluid?

a) Compressible fluid

b) non-viscous fluid

c) Plastic fluid

d) Viscous fluid

13. Fluid is a substance which does NOT offer resistance to change one of the following. Identify.

a) Flow

b) Pressure

c) Shape

d) Volume

14. Which one of the following instruments is used for measuring the speed of a submarine moving in a deep sea?

a) Orifice meter

b) Pitot tube

c) Rotameter

d) Venturi meter

15. Alcohol is used in manometers because of one of the following proper¬ties?

a) Clear visibility

b) Low density

c) Low surface tension

d) Low vapour pressure

<u>Short Answer Question: -</u>

Each question carries 5 marks

1. Describe the types of flow patterns exhibited by liquids in motion.

2. Differentiate fluid statics and fluid dynamics. Name the fluid flowmeter, which gives point velocity.

3. Write Bernoulli's equation and explain the symbols used therein with a labelled diagram.

4. Describe Reynolds classic experiment elucidating different types of flow patterns, when a liquid flows through a closed channel.

5. Explain the characteristics of different types of flow. Add a note on Reynolds number.

<u>Long Answer Question: -</u>

Each question carries 10 marks

1. Give a neat sketch of two fluid manometers and explain its working principle.

2. Explain the working, principle and construction of venturi meter. Write the expression for the volumetric flow rate of fluid through it.

3. Explain the energy losses that occur when a fluid flows through a pipe with relevant equations.

## Size reduction:

1. Which one of the following is NOT a mode of stress in size reduction?

    A. Classification B. Collision C. Compression D. Cutting

2. Which one of the following parameters of finished product does NOT influence the selection of size reduction equipment?

    A. Porosity B. Shape C. Surface roughness D. True density

3. Which -are the modes observed in a ball mill for size reduction?

    A. Attrition and cutting B. Compression and impact C. Cutting and compression D. Impact and attrition

4. Which mill includes a screen as an integral part of the size reduction?

    A. Ball mill B. Colloid mill C. Edge runner mill D. Hammer mill

5. Which one of the following is NOT TRUE in case of construction of hammer mill?

    A. Hammers are flat or sharp edges B. Hammers are rigid or swing type C. Metal sheet with holes or slots D. Woven type of screen

6. Clearance between the stator and rotor is critical factor in one of the following size reduction mills.

    A. Colloid mill B. Fluid energy mill C. Hammer mill D. Rotary cutter mill

7. Which one of these is NOT a facility in colloid mill?

    A. Clearance between stator and rotor B. Dry grinding of feed C. Recirculation of milled product D. Water jacket for reducing the heat

8. If a given material is fibrous in nature, which mill is preferred?

    A. Ball mill B. Colloid mill C. Fluid energy mill D. Rotary cutter mill

9. The sterile product CANNOT be obtained by one of the following mills.

    A. Colloid mill B. Cutter mill. C. Fluid energy mill D Roller mill

10. Which principle operates in the hammer mill?

    A. Attrition B. Crushing C. Cutting D. Impact

SHORT ANSWER QUESTION

1. List special precautions to be taken while thermolabile substances are subjected to size reduction process.

2. The powder must contain fewer amounts of fines when it is meant for percolation process of extraction. Why?

3. What are the advantages of swinging type of hammer compared to rigid hammers?

4. Powders of same particle size that are obtained by different equipment have same physicochemical characteristics. Justify.

5. List the areas in which size reduction equipment is used in tablet production.

LONG ANSWER QUESTION

1. Describe the milling equipment with the help of a neat diagram that uses the principle of shear and impact.

2. Explain the theories related to the size reduction of a powder.

3. Explain the advantages and disadvantages of size reduction process.

## Size separation:

1. Size classification is also known in one of the following terms.

    A. Size analysis B. Size distribution C. Size reduction D. Size separation

2. Size separation is NOT based on one of the following properties.

    A. Particle density B. Particle shape C. Particle size D. Particle texture

3. Which one of the screens is used for size separation of big and heavy particles?

    A. Bar screens B. Bolting cloth sieves C. Punched plate screens D. Woven wire screens

4. Which one of the screens is attached to the hum-Mur screens?

    A. Bar screens B. Cloth sieves C. Punched screens D. Woven wire screens

5. Which one of the following indicates the nominal size of aperture?

    A. Area of mesh as percentage B. Distance between two adjacent wires C. Number of meshes per linear length D. Wire having specified diameter that gives suitable aperture

6. During size separation, movement of particles can be enhanced by one of the following modes.

    A. Agitation B. Attrition C. Gravitation D. Mixing

7. Brushing method hastens the movement of one of the following materials.

    A. Coarse materials B. Dry materials C. Light materials D. Sticky materials

8. Flywheel is used to enhance the motion of particles by one of the following modes.

    A. Brushing mode B. Centrifugal mode C. Gyration mode D. Oscillation mode

9. Which equipment is used for sieve analysis?

    A. Alpine air jet sieve B. Cyclone separator C. Rotex screen D. Shaking screen

10. Fluidised state is NOT used in one of the following

g equipment.

    A. Air separator B. Alpine sieve C. Cyclone separator D. Rotex screen

## SHORT ANSWER QUESTION

1. Explain the working of a cyclone separator and its usefulness.

2.  Describe the method of size separation using the Rotex shaker screen.

3.  Explain various grades of powders official in pharmacopeia.

4.  Give details about the various standards fixed by the pharmacopoeia for sieves.

5.  Describe the specifications of standard sieves as per IP.

# UNIT II

*Syllabus:*

1. Heat Transfer: Objectives, applications & Heat transfer mechanisms. Fourier's law, Heat transfer by conduction, convection & radiation. Heat interchangers & heat exchangers.

2. Evaporation: Objectives, applications and factors influencing evaporation, differences between evaporation and other heat process. principles, construction, working, uses, merits and demerits of Steam jacketed kettle, horizontal tube evaporator, climbing film evaporator, forced circulation evaporator, multiple effect evaporator& Economy of multiple effect evaporator.

3. Distillation: Basic Principles and methodology of simple distillation, flash distillation, fractional distillation, distillation under reduced pressure, steam distillation & molecular distillation.

## 1. HEAT TRANSFER

Heat transfer is the process of transferring heat from a high-temperature system to a lower-temperature system. Heat transfer in thermodynamic systems refers to the transport of heat over the system's boundary caused by a temperature differential between the system and its surroundings.

## Classification of heat flow process

When two objects at different temperatures are brought into thermal contact, heat flows from the object at higher temperature to the object at lower temperature. The mechanisms by which the heat may flow are (i) conduction, (ii) convection and (iii) radiation.

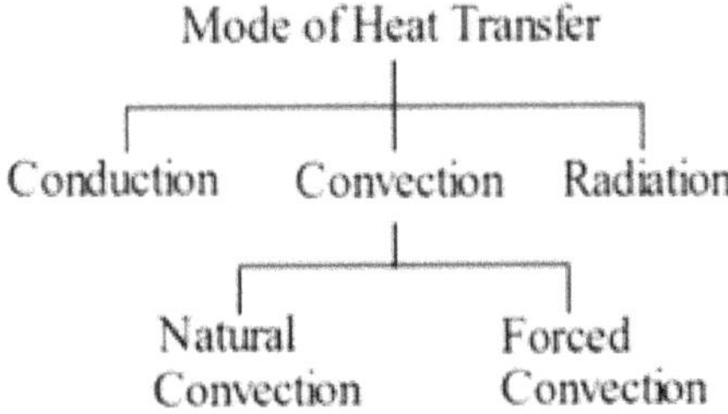


## Conduction

Conduction occurs when heat flows through a body without any apparent motion of materials.

Mechanism: Thermal conduction in metallic materials occurs due to unbound electrons (similar to electrical conductivity). Solids are poor heat conductors, whereas liquids conduct heat via the passage of momentum over the temperature gradient. In gases, conduction occurs through the random motion of molecules, causing heat to be "diffused" from hotter to colder locations. Examples include heat flowing through the brick wall of a furnace or the metal wall of a tube.

## Convection

Convection is the term used to describe heat movement that occurs through the transfer of materials. In this situation, heat flows through the actual mixing of warmer and cooler regions of the same substance. Convection is limited to the transfer of heat in fluids. Heat moves through fluids via both conduction and convection, and it is difficult to distinguish between the two routes due to the eddies created by the change in density with temperature. Examples Heat transfer occurs through turbulent flow bodies and a current of warm air from a room heater moving across the room.

Natural and forced convection:

The forces used to create convection currents in fluids are two types.

Natural convection: When a fluid is heated the warmer part becomes lighter than the cooler part. Due to this difference in density the cooler (higher density) fluid moves down wards and the warmer (lighter density) move upwards and thus forming convection current. Thus heat is transferred with mass. This method of heat transfer is called natural convection.

Forced convection: If the current (or movement of fluid) is caused not by the density difference but by some agitator or by some mechanical devices then the type of heat flow associated with it is called forced convection.

## Radiation

Radiation heat flow refers to the transmission of heat through space via electromagnetic waves. When radiation passes through empty space, it is neither turned into heat nor diverted from its intended route. If radiation strikes a material, the energy is transmitted (passes through the material), reflected, or absorbed. Only the energy absorbed is transformed to heat energy.

CONDUCTION The basic law of heat transfer by conduction can be written in the form of the rate equation:

$$\text{Rate} = \frac{\text{Driving force}}{\text{Resistance}}$$

The driving force is the temperature gradient.

## Fourier's law

Fourier's law states that the rate of heat flow through a uniform material is proportional to the area perpendicular to the heat flow (A), the temperature drop (dt) and inversely proportional to the length of the path of flow.

Consider an area A of a wall of thickness L. Let the temperature be uniform over the area A on one face of the wall. Both sides of the wall has a temperature gradient. If a thin thickness dL, parallel to the area A, be taken at some intermediate point in the wall, with a temperature difference of dt across such a layer, then Fourier's law may be represented by he equation:

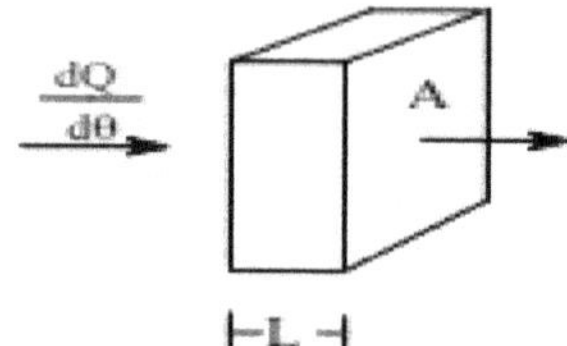

$$\frac{dQ}{d\theta} = -\frac{kAdt}{dL} \qquad\qquad \text{eqn 1}$$

Where k = proportionality constant If the temperature gradient dt/dL does not vary with time (this case is observed at steady state of heat flow) then the rate of heat flow is constant with time and

$$\frac{dQ}{d\theta} = \text{constant} = q = -\frac{KAdt}{dL} \qquad \text{eqn. 2}$$

Since normally we know only the temperature at the two faces of the wall hence integrating the Fourier's equation:

the Fourier's equation: $$\frac{q\,dL}{A} = -k\,dt \qquad\qquad \text{eqn. 3}$$

On integration, if $t_1$ is the higher temperature than $t_2$.

$$q\int_0^L \frac{dL}{A} = -\int_{t_1}^{t_2} k\,dt = \int_{t_2}^{t_1} k\,dt \qquad\qquad \text{eqn. 4}$$

If A does not vary with L (i.e. the case of a flat wall) then equation 4 integrates to

$$\frac{qL}{A} = k(t_1 - t_2) = k\,\Delta t$$

or, by rearranging we get

$$q = \frac{k\,A\,\Delta t}{L} \qquad\qquad \text{or, } q = \frac{\Delta t}{L/kA} \quad \text{eqn. 5}$$

In equation 5 $\Delta t$ is the driving force and the resistance is L / k A.

Thermal conductivity

The proportionality in constant k in equation $q = kA\Delta t/L$ is called the thermal conductivity (also called the coefficient of thermal conductivity) of the material of which the wall is made.

If q is expressed in Btu

$\theta$ in hr

A in ft2

t in $^0$F and

L in ft

The unit of k will be :

$$\frac{(Btu)\ (ft)}{(hr)\ (ft^2)\ (^0F)}$$

The numerical value of the thermal conductivity depends upon (i) The material of which the body is made of The thermal conductivities of liquids and gases are smaller compared to solids. For example at $212^0F$ the thermal conductivity of

silver is 240 $(Btu)(ft) / (hr)(ft^2)(^0F)$

water is 0.35 $(Btu)(ft) / (hr)(ft^2)(^0F)$ and

air is 0.017 $(Btu)(ft) / (hr)(ft^2)(^0F)$

(ii) and upon its temperature. The variation of thermal conductivity with temperature is meager (very small) but it is assumed that the variation is linear; that is:

$k = a + b\,t$

where a and b are constants and t is the temperature.

**Compound resistances in series**

Consider a flat wall constructed of a series of layers.

- L1, L2, L3 are the thickness of the layers.

- K1, K2, K3 are the thermal conductivities of the layers

- Let the area of the compound wall, at right angles to the heat flow be A.

Let $t_0$, $t_1$, $t_2$ and $t_3$ be the temperatures at the surfaces of the wall and at each junction according to the figure where $t_0 > t_1 > t_2 > t_3$. Therefore, $\Delta t = \Delta t_1 + \Delta t_2 + \Delta t_3$

where, $\Delta t_1 = t_3 - t_0$.

$\Delta t_1 = t_1 - t_0$.

$\Delta t_1 = t_2 - t_1$.

$\Delta t_1 = t_3 - t_2$.

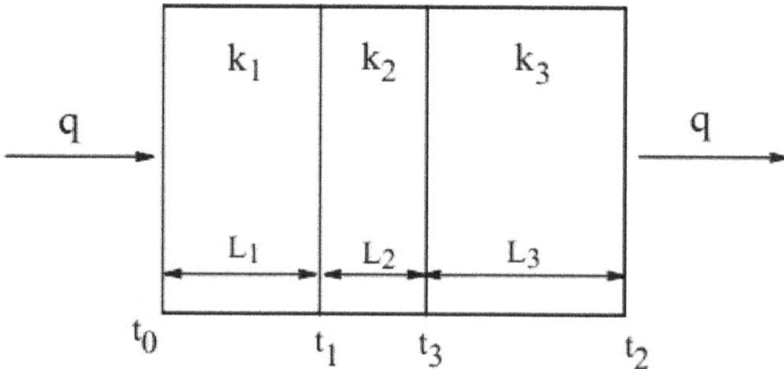


Again from Fourier's law

$$q_1 + \frac{k_1 \, A \, \Delta t_1}{L_1} \quad \text{or,} \quad \Delta t_1 = q_1 \frac{L_1}{k_1 \, A} = q_1 \, R_1$$

$$q_2 + \frac{k_2 \, A \, \Delta t_2}{L_2} \quad \text{or,} \quad \Delta t_2 = q_2 \frac{L_2}{k_2 \, A} = q_2 \, R_2$$

$$q_3 + \frac{k_3 \, A \, \Delta t_3}{L_3} \quad \text{or,} \quad \Delta t_3 = q_3 \frac{L_3}{k_3 \, A} = q_3 \, R_3$$

Since all the heat passing through the first resistance must pass through the second and in turn, pass through the third, so $q_1$, $q_2$ and $q_3$ must be equal and all of them can be represented by q. From equation (1–4):

$$\Delta t = \Delta t_1 + \Delta t_2 + \Delta t_3$$
$$= q \, R_1 + q R_2 + q R_3.$$
$$= q \, (R_1 + R_2 + R_3)$$
$$\therefore \quad q = \frac{\Delta t}{R_1 + R_2 + R_3}$$

If the equivalent resistance of the compound wall is R then

$$q = \frac{\Delta t}{R} = \frac{t_3 - t_0}{R_1 + R_2 + R_3}$$

$$\therefore \quad R = R1 + R_2 + R_3.$$

HEAT FLOW THROUGH A CYLINDER

Let us consider the hollow cylinder represented by the figure.

$r_1$ = inside radius

$r_2$ = outside radius

$t_1$ = inside temperature

$t_2$ = outside temperature

N = length of the cylinder

km = mean thermal conductivity of the material of the cylinder

It is desired to calculate the rate of heat flow through the wall.

Let us consider a very thin cylinder, concentric with the main cylinder with a radius r where $r_1 < r < r_2$.

The thickness of the wall of that cylinder is dr temperature difference across dr is dt.

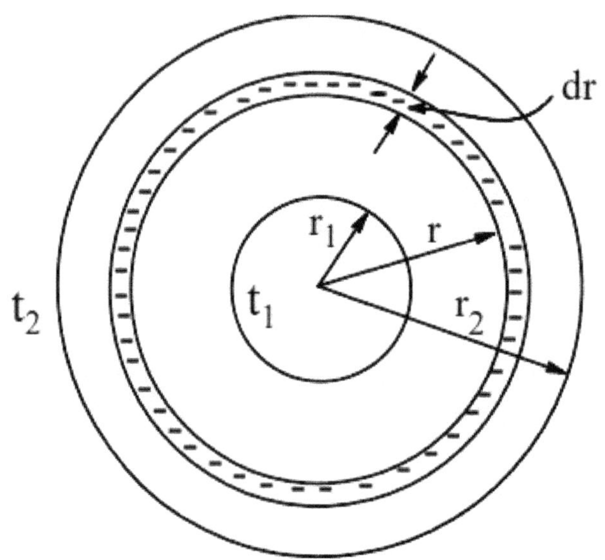


Then applying Fourier's law over the thin wall will give:

$$q = - \frac{k_m \, A \, dt}{dr}$$

where A = total area of the thin wall

$$= -(2\pi r N) \, k \, \frac{dt}{dr}$$

$$\therefore \quad \frac{dr}{r} = - \frac{2\pi N k_m}{q} \, dt$$

$$\text{or,} \quad \int_{r_2}^{r_1} \frac{dr}{r} = - \frac{2\pi N k_m}{q} \int_{t_1}^{t_2} dt$$

$$\text{or,} \quad \left[\ln r\right]_{r_1}^{r_2} = -\left(\frac{2\pi N k_m}{q}\right)(t_2 - t_1)$$

$$\text{or,} \quad \ln \frac{r_1}{r_2} = \frac{2\pi N k_m}{q}(t_1 - t_2)$$

$$\text{or,} \quad \boxed{q = \frac{k_m (2\pi N)(t_1 - t_2)}{\ln \frac{r_2}{r_1}}}$$

PRINCIPLES OF HEAT FLOW IN FLUIDS

Heat transfer from a warmer liquid to a colder liquid, usually through a solid wall separating the two liquids, is found in various heat transfer equipment, which include heat exchangers and evaporators. The heat transferred may be in the following forms:

(i) latent heat accompanying a phase change such as condensation , vaporization

(ii) sensible heat without any phase change. Mechanisms of heat transfer through a fluid: Both by conduction and convection.

Heat flow from one fluid to another fluid separated by a solid wall

For example, a liquid flows through a pipe and is heated by steam from the outside. In this situation, heat will be transferred from steam to liquid. Both the steam and the liquid have Reynolds numbers greater than 4000, indicating that they are flowing in turbulent motion. In this situation, steam will build a thin film on the outside surface of the pipe, while liquid will form another film on the interior surface of the pipe wall [because the flow is very slow near the solid wall hence in the film viscous flow will prevail]. For example:Beyond these films, the steam and liquid stay in tumultuous motion, indicating that complete mixing is taking place. Conduction transports heat through this stationary layer, and forced convection mixes it with the rest of the fluid. Because the bulk of the fluids are in constant motion, heat transfer within them is extremely quick. Because the fluids' thermal conductivities are low, even though the films are very thin, they provide a significant obstacle to heat flow.

Temperature gradients in forced convection

Let us consider that heat is flowing from a hot fluid through a metal wall to a cold fluid.

• The dotted lines $F_1F_1$ and $F_2F_2$ on each side of the solid wall are representing the boundaries of the films in viscous flow; all parts of the fluids to the right of $F_1F_1$ and to the left of $F_2F_2$ are in turbulent flow.

• The temperature gradient from the bulk of the hot fluid to the metal wall is represented by the curved line $t_a t_b t_c$. The temperature $t_a$ is the maximum temperature in the hot fluid (i.e. in the bulk of the fluid). The temperature $t_b$ is the temperature at the boundary between the viscous and turbulent flow. The temperature $t_c$ is the temperature at the actual interface between the fluid and the solid wall.

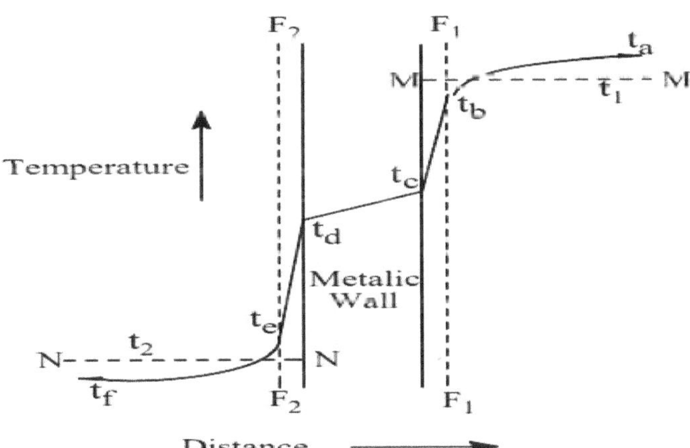


Fig. Temperature gradients in forced convection

The temperature $t_c$ is the temperature at the actual interface between the fluid and the solid wall. Similarly for fluid 2 the curved line is $t_d t_e t_f$. • When a thermometer (or any heat sensing instrument) is inserted into the bulk of the fluid it will show a temperature $t_1$ and $t_2$ respectively for the two fluids. This $t_1$ is neither $t_a$ nor $t_b$ but this will be an average temperature and $t_a < t_1 < t_b$. $t_1$ is shown as a straight line MM. The same remarks will apply for fluid 2 also whose average temperature $t_2$ is represented by the line NN. • The temperature gradient $t_d t_c$ is caused by the flow of heat in pure conduction through the solid wall and this $(t_c - t_d)$ smaller than $(t_1 - t_2)$.

Surface coefficients

Since the thickness of the film is not known, the simple equation of conduction cannot be applied in this case. The difficulty is circumvented by the use of surface coefficient. The surface coefficient on the hot side is defined by the relation.

$$h_1 = \frac{q}{A_1(t_1 - t_c)}$$

where, $h_1$ = surface coefficient of the fluid on the hot side [Btu/(ft$^2$ $^0$F s)]

$q$ = amount of heat flowing from hot to cold fluid. [Btu / s]

$A_1$ = area of the metal wall on the hot side in a plane at right angle to the heat flow.[ft2 ]

$(t_1 - t^C)$ = temperature gradient. [$^0$F]

If we compare $q = h_1 A_1 (t_1 - t_C)$ equation with $\quad q = \dfrac{k\,A\,\Delta t}{L} \quad$ then it is evident that

$h_1$ is analogous to $(k / L)$ and $(1/h_1A_1)$ is the resistance term same as that of $(L / kA)$ and $h_1$ contains the effect of both the viscous film and of the thermal resistance of the turbulent core that causes the temperature difference $(t_1 - t_C)$.

In the same way h2 may be defined as $\quad h_2 = \dfrac{q}{A_2(t_d - t_2)}$

So the resistance imparted by the hot side = $1 / h_1 A_1$.

Resistance imparted by the metallic wall = $L / kA_m$.

Resistance imparted by the cold side = $1 / h_2 A_2$.

**Overall heat transfer coefficient**

If this resistances are substituted in the equation for compound resistance in series.

$$q = \frac{t_1 - t_2}{R_1 + R_2 + R_3}$$

Then,

$$q = \frac{t_1 - t_2}{\dfrac{1}{h_1 A_1} + \dfrac{L}{k A_m} + \dfrac{1}{h_2 A_2}}$$

If the numerator and denominator are multiplied with $A_1$ then

$$q = \frac{A_1 \Delta t}{1/h_1 + A_1 L / kA_m + A_1 / h_2 A_2}$$

So the overall heat transfer coefficient U1 is defined by the equation

$$U_1 = \frac{1}{1/h_1 + A_1 L / kA_m + A_1 / h_2 A_2}$$

Therefore $q = U_1 A_1 \Delta t$ states that the rate of heat transfer is the product of three factors: overall heat transfer coefficient ($U_1$), temperature drop ($\Delta t$), and area of heating surface ($A_1$).

For a tubular pipe $A_1 = \pi D_1 l$ where $D_1$ and $l$ are the inner diameter and length of the pipe respectively. Similarly $A_2 = \pi D_2 l$ and $Am = \pi D_m l$. So another form of overall heat transfer coefficient:

$$U_1 = \frac{1}{1/h_1 + D_1 L / kD_m + D_1 / h_2 D_2}$$

Analogous equation can be written for $U_m$ and $U_2$.

**Fluids in natural convection**

For example, if a fluid comes into contact with a heated surface, the fluid immediately near to the tube tends to rise due to its lower density and is replaced by a cooler fluid. Natural convection is the circulation of fluids produced by temperature changes in density. The fluid's velocity of circulation is determined by density variations in the system's geometry, which includes the size, shape, and arrangement of the heating surface as well as the shape of the heating vessel in which the fluid is confined. For the simple case of a fluid outside a single horizontal cylinder with a large extent of fluid surrounding the cylinder, the heat-transfer coefficient for natural convection has been correlated by an equation containing three dimensionless groups the Nusselt number (Nu), the Prandtl number (Pr) and the Grashof number (Gr):

$$Nu = \psi \,(Gr, Pr)$$

where $\quad Nu = \dfrac{hD_o}{k_f}, \qquad Gr = \dfrac{D_o^3 \rho_f^2 \beta g \Delta T_o}{\mu_f^2}, \qquad Pr = \dfrac{c_p \mu_f}{k_f}$

where

$h$ = average heat transfer coefficient, based on the entire pipe surface

$k_f$ = thermal conductivity of fluid

$c_p$ = specific heat of fluid at constant pressure

$\rho_f$ = density of fluid

$\beta$ = coefficient of thermal expansion of fluid

g = acceleration of gravity

$\Delta T_o$ = average difference in temperature between outside of pipe and fluid distant from wall

$\mu_f$ = viscosity of fluid

When hot bodies lose heat to their surroundings they do so both by radiation and convection. In the lower temperature range convection is more important, in higher temperature range radiation is more important.

**Heat transfer through boiling liquids**

Consider a horizontal tube or a group of horizontal tube immersed in a pool of pure liquid with steam or other source of heat inside the tubes. $\Delta T$ is the difference in temperature between the tube wall temperature and the temperature of the liquid (under the pressure of the vapour space above the liquid).

• When the $\Delta T$ is very small the rate of heat transfer is nearly similar to that of a non-boiling liquid.

• As the $\Delta T$ is increased, the coefficient of heat transfer is increased rapidly because the stirring effect of the increasing number of bubbles released produces currents in the liquid that accelerates the heat transfer. This increasing coefficient multiplied with the increasing $\Delta T$, results in an even more rapid increase in the total heat transferred per unit area.

• However, if the temperature of the surface is continually increased, a point is found where the heat-transfer coefficient reaches a maximum.

• At higher $\Delta T$ beyond the maximum value the heat transfer rate is sharply lowered. Actually the bubbles of vapour formed on the heating surface are discharged rapidly to rise through the liquid. This type of boiling is called nucleate boiling. At critical $\Delta T$, these bubbles coalesce into a continuous film of vapour that insulates the tube, and this reduces the heat transfer rate with increasing $\Delta T$.

With polished horizontal tube in reasonably pure water, this critical point is reached at relatively modest value of $\Delta T$, possibly 45 to 500F. With rougher commercial steel tubes the critical $\Delta T$ is much higher.

In case of nucleate boiling how easily the bubbles will leave the surface depends on the following factors:

• roughness of the tube and the type of roughness: For instance a rough surface with small sharp projections makes it possible to detach bubbles from points more easily than from a smooth surface.

• the tendency of the liquid to wet the tube: A liquid that wets the tube strongly tends to pinch off the bubbles of gas and liberate them more quickly than a liquid that does not wet the surface easily.

• the difference in density between the bubble and the liquid

• the physical arrangement of the surface: For instance, a vertical tube with bubbles rising inside it, will always show a much higher critical $\Delta T$ than a horizontal tube, with bubbles formed on the outside.

**Heat flow through condensing vapours**

For example: When a saturated vapour, such as steam, conducts heat to a metal surface and condenses, it can take one of two completely different forms. One is film condensation, whereas the other is drop-type condensation.

Film-type condensation: In this case the condensed liquid wets the surface on which it is condensing and forms a continuous film of condensate. If the condensate is occurring on the outside of the tube then this film of condensate drops off the underside of the tube. If the tube is vertical then the condensate runs down the whole length of the tube. For the case of a horizontal tube in true-film type condensation on which there is condensing a saturated vapour, free from any non-condensed gas and moving at low velocities, Nusselt has derived the following equation:

$$h = 0.725 \sqrt[4]{\frac{k^3 \rho^2 g \lambda}{D \mu \Delta T}}$$

where

$\lambda$ = latent heat of vaporisation of vapor,

Btu/lb $\rho$ = density of condensate, lb/ft$^3$.

k = thermal conductivity of condensed vapour $\dfrac{(Btu)(ft)}{(ft^2)(h)(^0F)}$

g = acceleration due to gravity (ft/hr$^2$)

$\mu$ = viscosity of condensate film, (ft-lb-hr) units

D = outside pipe diameter, ft

$\Delta T$ =temperature difference between vapor and metal, $^0$F.

For the case of a vertical tube with all other conditions same as above Nusselt has given the equation:

$$h = 0.943 \sqrt[4]{\frac{k^3 \rho^2 g \lambda}{L \mu \Delta T}}$$

where L = the length of the tube.

• The film coefficient between condensing vapours and metal walls increases with increasing temperature of the vapour, because of decreased viscosity of the film condensate.

• Coefficient (h) decreases with increasing temperature drop, because increasing temperature drops cause faster condensation and hence thicker liquid films.

• The presence of non-condensable gas accumulates near the heating surface and adds to their resistance to that of the liquid film.

Drop-wise condensation

In this situation, the condensed liquid does not soak the surface but rather gathers in droplets ranging in size from microscopic to visible to the human eye. These drops grow for a while before falling to the surface, leaving an apparently naked space in which more drops can form. These two modes of condensation produce quite different film coefficients of heat transfer. Coefficients obtained from drop-wise condensation are significantly higher than those produced from film type condensation, given that all other surface parameters remain constant.

RADIATION

Any solid body at any temperature above absolute zero radiates energy. This radiation is an electromagnetic phenomenon and takes place without the necessity of any medium. The approximate range of wavelengths for infra-red radiation (or heat rays) is 0.8 to 400 μm. In industries, most of the cases, the thermal radiation corresponds to wavelengths from 0.8 to 25 μm.

**The Black Body**

Not all substances radiate heat at same rate at a given temperature. So a theoretical hot body is defined, which is called 'black body'.

Definition: A 'black body is defined as that body which radiates maximum possible amount of energy at a given temperature.

Example: It has been shown that the inside of an enclosed space, at a constant temperature throughout, viewed through an opening so small that the amount of energy escaping through the opening is negligible, corresponds to a black body.

Practical e.g. In practice, a convenient black body is made from a tube of carbon plugged at both ends with a small observation hole in the center of one end.

Industrial e.g. The inside of furnace at completely uniform temperatures, viewed through a small opening, is a black body. The interior of the furnace and all the objects within the furnace can also be considered black bodies.

**Rates of radiation**

If the radiation energy emitted by a hot body is plotted against the wave lengths emitted then graphs of the nature shown in the fig will be obtained. The total amount of radiation emitted by a black body would be given by integrating the curves of the figure (Effect of temperature on amount and distribution of black-body radiation)

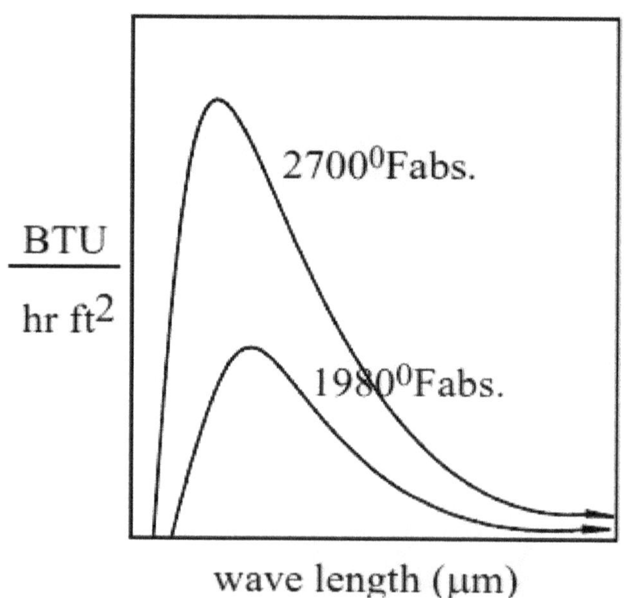


the result is the Stefan-Boltzmann law

$$q = b \, A \, T^4$$

where

$q$ = energy radiated per hour (BTU/hr)

$A$ = area of radiating surface (sqft)

$T$ = absolute temperature of the radiating surface $^0R$ (Rankine) = $t^0F + 460$

For black bodies the value of $b = 0.174 \times 10^{-8}$ Btu / (hr sqft $^0F^4$)

No actual body radiates quite as much as the black body. The radiation by any actual body can be expressed as

$$q = \varepsilon \, b \, A \, T^4$$

where $\varepsilon$ is the emissivity of the body.

• The emissivity is a fraction less than 1 and is the ratio of the energy emitted by the body in question to that emitted by a black body at the same temperature.

• When a radiant energy falls on a cooler body either the energy is reflected or transmitted or absorbed. The fraction of the radiation energy falling on a body that is absorbed is represented by $\alpha$, the absorptivity, which is always less than 1. If the reflected energy can be neglected then the energy absorbed by anybody is equal to the radiation falling on it.

• It can be shown that the absorptivity of a given substance at a given temperature and its emissivity at the same temperature must be equal.

That is, $\varepsilon = \alpha$

Since the $\varepsilon$ of a black body is 1 hence the $\alpha$ of the black body will also be equal to 1. Therefore the black body absorbs all the radiation falling on it – an important property of black body.

• The value of $\alpha$ for a given surface at a given temperature varies somewhat with the wavelength of the radiation involved. To avoid complication due to this the concept of gray body has been introduced. The absorptivity of a gray body at a given temperature is constant for all wavelengths of radiation.

• When a small black body of area A and temperature $T_2$ is completely surrounded by a hotter black body of temperature $T_1$, the net amount of heat transferred from the hotter body to the colder body is, therefore the algebraic sum of the radiation from the two bodies, so that Stefan's law may be written for this case as…

$$q = b \, A \, (T_1^{\,4} - T_2^{\,4})$$

## HEAT EXCHANGERS

Some of the processes that involve heat transfer in pharmaceutical industries are:

• Preparation of starch paste (in steam jacketed kettle)

• Crystallization

• Evaporation

• Distillation: The equipment's used for heat transferring are known as heat exchangers.

Classification of heat exchangers

On the basis of transfer of heat, heat exchangers are classified as:

1. Direct transfer type: The hot and cold fluids are separated by a metal wall through which the heat is transferred from hot fluid to cold fluid. E.g. shell and tube heater,

2. Storage type: First a hot fluid is flown through a porous solid medium to heat the medium, then the cold fluid is flown through the hot solid porous medium to extract the heat from it. This type of heat exchangers is not used in pharmaceutical industries.

3. Direct contact type: Hot fluid is passed through the cold fluid and in this case the hot and cold fluids are not separated physically. For example steam is bubbled through a cold liquid.

Tubular heater

Tubular heaters consists of circular tubes, one fluid flows through the inner tube, while the other flows through the outside space. The heat transfer takes place across the wall of the tube.

1. Single Pass Tubular heater:

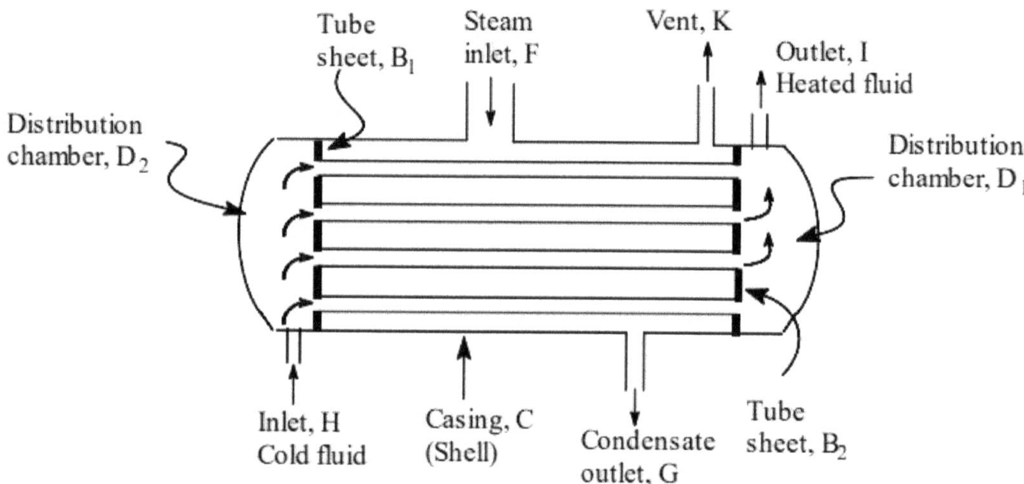


Construction:

It consists of a bundle of parallel tubes, which are relatively thin-walled. The ends of these tubes are fitted to two tube-sheets B1 and B2. The bundles of parallel tubes are enclosed in a cylindrical shell or casing (C, made of cast iron) to which the tube-sheets (B1 and B2) are fitted. Two distribution chambers D1 and D2 are provided at each end of the casing (C). Cold fluid inlet (H) is fitted with distribution chamber D2 and hot fluid outlet (I) is fitted with the distribution chamber D1. Steam inlet F, steam outlet K (called vent) and condensate outlet G are fitted to the shell.

Working:

Steam is introduced through the steam inlet F into the space surrounding the parallel tubes. Heat is transferred to the cold liquid inside the tubes and steam is condensed. The condensate is removed through condensate outlet G placed at the bottom of the casing. Non-condensable gases, if any, escapes through the vent K provided at the top of the shell. The fluid to be heated is pumped through the cold fluid inlet (H) in to distribution chamber D1, flows through the tubes and collects in the distribution chamber D2. Heat is transferred from the steam to the cold fluid through the metal wall. The hot fluid leaves the heater through outlet (I).

Advantages: Large heating surface is packed into a small volume.

Disadvantages:

(a) The velocities of the fluid flowing through these tubes are low because of large crosssectional area or surface area.

(b) The expansion of the tubes and shell takes place due to difference in temperatures. This may lead to loosening of the tube sheets form the casing.

(c) Initial cost and maintenance costs are very high.

2. Floating-head two-pass heater

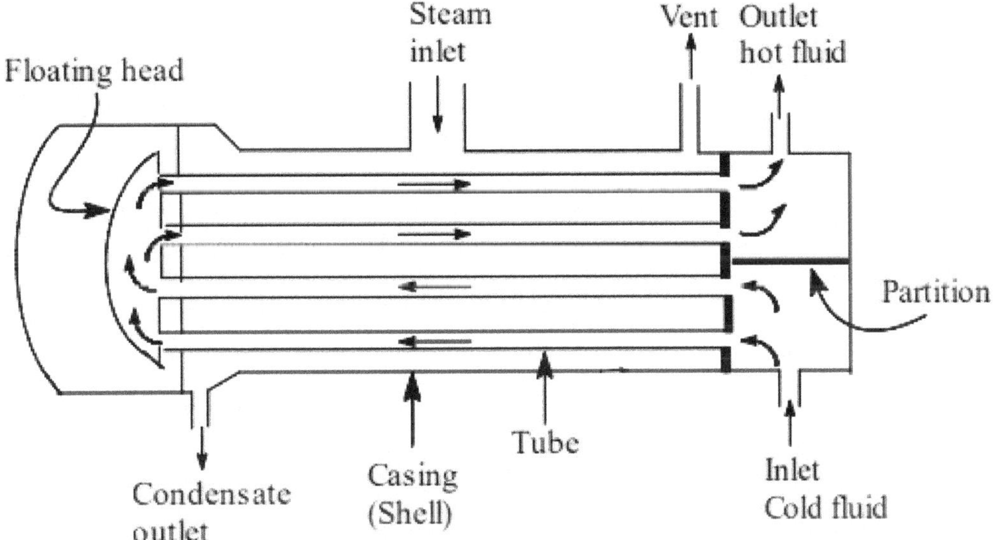


Construction:

It consists of a bundle of parallel tubes. They are enclosed in a shell (casing). The right side of the distribution chamber is partitioned and fluid inlet and outlet are connected to the same chamber. The partition is such that both have equal number of tubes. On left side the distribution chamber is not connected to the casing. It is structurally independent, hence known as floating head. The ends of the tubes are fitted with the floating head. Casing is provided with steam inlet, vent, and condensate outlet.

Working:

Steam is introduced through the steam inlet of the casing (shell). Steam heats the tubes. The condensate escapes through the condensate outlet fitted at the bottom of the casing. Non-condensable gas, if any, escapes through the vent of the casing provided at the top. The cold fluid is introduced through the cold fluid inlet into the right-hand distribution chamber. The fluid flows through few tubes present in the lower part of the distribution chamber. The fluid reaches the floating head and changes direction and flows through the upper tubes again to the right-hand distribution chamber. The hot fluid is taken out through the outlet. During this process the fluid in the tubes get heated due to heat transfer through the metallic wall.

Advantages: Due to differences in temperature the tubes and shells may expand and the joints may get loose. Since, the floating head part is independent of shell (or casing) hence the problem of loosening is prevented in this type of heater.

3. Liquid-to-liquid heat interchanger

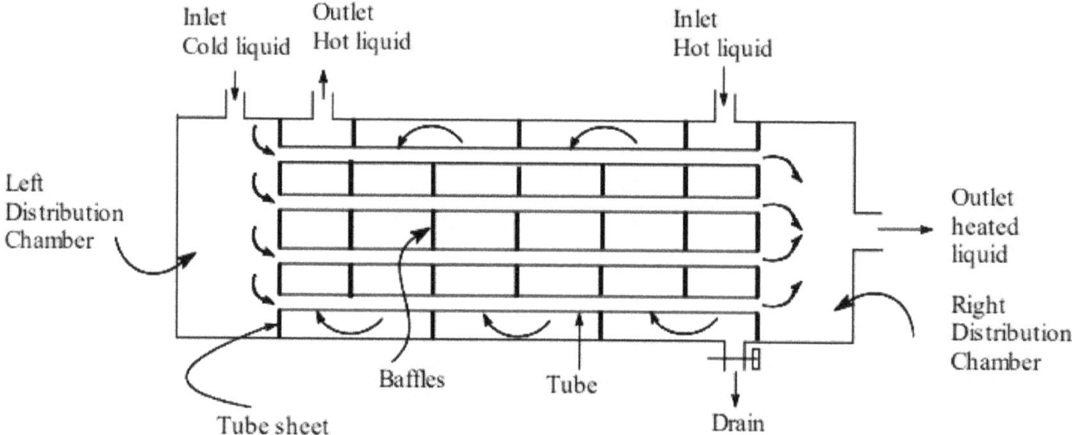



Construction:

The construction is identical to that of a single-pass tubular heater; the only difference is that it includes baffles to extend the direction of flow of the outer liquid. A pair of parallel tubes is attached to two tube-sheets at either end. The tubes and tube sheets are put within the shell. The distribution chamber's left-hand side has a cold liquid intake, while the right-hand side has an outlet. Hot liquid enters the shell from the right-hand top side and exits through the outlet located on the top, left-hand side. Baffles are placed inside the shell at appropriate places. Baffles have perforation on it through which the tubes pass.

Working:

The hot liquid is pumped from the left-top of the shell. The fluid flows through the shell (i.e. outside of the tubes) and moves down directly to the bottom (due to baffle), again moves up – like this it flows from the left to right-hand side of the shell. Baffles increases the velocity of the hot fluid outside the tubes, which creates more turbulence. This reduces the film thickness at the outside of the tube and thus increases the film coefficient and thus heat transfer increases. The baffles also get heated and add to the heat transfer to cold liquid. The cold liquid is pumped through the inlet at the left-hand side distribution chamber. The liquid passes through the tubes and gets heated. The heated liquid is collected from the righthand side distribution chamber.

4. Double-pipe heat interchanger

N.B. In a liquid-to-liquid heat interchanger, the fluid to be heated is passed only once through the tubes before it is discharged, i.e. single pass. The heat transfer in this case is not efficient.

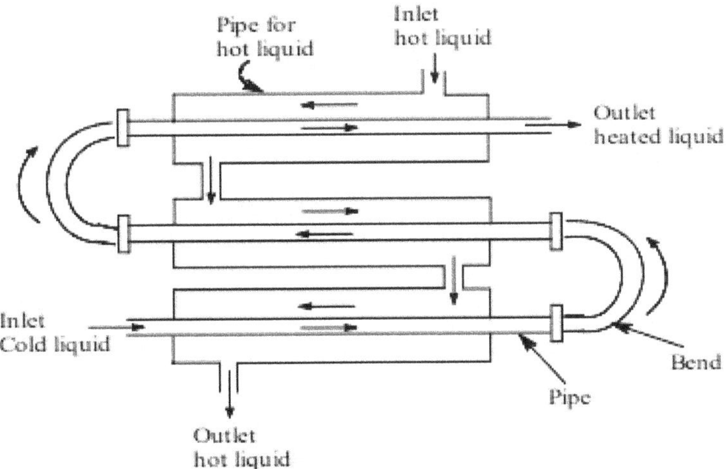


In double-pipe heat interchanger number of pass can be increased as desired.

Construction:

In this instance, two pipes are used, with one placed into the other. Cold fluid is passed through the inner tube. The outer pipe serves as a jacket for the flow of hot fluid. All jacketed portions are joined. Normally, there are few pipe portions. The length of the pipe is likewise shorter. The inner tubes might be constructed of glass or conventional iron. The pipes are linked using typical return bends and stacked vertically. Pipes may have longitudinal fins on their outside surface to improve heat transfer.

Working:

The hot liquid is pumped into the jacketed section. It is circulated through the annular spaces between them and carried from one section to the next section. Finally it leaves the jacket. In this process the pipes get heated. The liquid to be heated is pumped through the inlet of the inner tube. The liquid gets heat up and flows through the bend tube into the next tube-section and finally leaves the exchanger.

Limitation:

Double-pipe heat interchanger is economical when the heating surface area is less than 9 $m^2$.

## SOURCES OF HEAT

1. Steam

2. Electricity: Heating coil made with nichrome wire. Used in heating oven, tray dryer. Air can be heated by passing through heating coil. Water can be heated by using heating element. Heating element is a coil of nichrome wire covered with a non-conductor and enclosed within a steel pipe.

3. Infra-red source: Infra-Red heating source with carbon filament. Used for drying films, coatings etc. as the materials are conveyed under the IR heat source.

### Steam as heating media

Steam has wide-spread application in pharmaceutical industries.

The applications are as follows:

1. Steam has very high heat content. – Under 1 atm pressure saturated steam has 540cal/gm of latent heat.

2. The heat of steam is given up at constant temperature. – When steam condenses no temperature change takes place only the latent heat is given up.

3. The raw material of steam is water. It is cheap and easily available.

4. Steam is clean, odourless and tasteless, so that any accidental contamination of a product is not likely to be serious.

5. Steam is easy to generate, distribute and control.

**Properties of steam**

One kg of water is taken in a closed vessel one side of which is closed by a moving frictionless piston. By changing the weight of the piston the pressure inside the vessel can be changed. Let us imagine that the piston is giving a constant pressure, P and the temperature inside is $0\ ^0C$.

1. State-1: Heat (h) is added until water starts to boil. This h amount of heat is required to raise the temperature of water from $0^0C$ to $t_s$.

So $h = ms\Delta t$

where m = 1 kg, s = specific heat of water = 1000 J/kg/$^0$C

$= 1 \times 1000 \times (t_s - 0)$

$= t_s$ kJ

2. State-2: If more heat is added, q fraction of water will be vaporized. If the latent heat of vaporization of water is L kJ/kg then the steam contains qL kJ amount of heat and the total heat of water and steam = (h + qL) kJ. When steam remains in contact with water that steam is called wet steam and q is known as dryness fraction.

3. State-3: If further heat is added, a point will be reached when all the water will be converted to steam i.e. q = 1. The total heat of the steam is now Hs = (h + L) kJ. The temperature is still ts. Since no water is there in contact with steam hence this type of steam is called dry saturated steam.

4. State-4: If more heat is provided to dry saturated steam then the temperature of the steam will be increase above $t_s$ (say $t_{sup}$). This type of steam is called super-heated steam. The total heat content = $H_s + Hs_{up} = h + L + H_{sup}$.

**Generation of steam**

The steam is generated in central boiler house at high pressure. High-pressure steam may be used to generate electricity by driving a turbine and the low-pressure steam that is exhausted can be used to heat various processes. Under high pressure steam can carried through pipes to different equipments.

**Distribution of steam**

To reduce heat loss, steam is transferred from the boiler via pipework of appropriate size and length. To prevent heat loss, pipes should be lagged, which means they should be covered with a porous, low-conducting material like asbestos, kieselguhr, or glass wool. The porous substance traps a stagnant layer of air surrounding the pipe. An additional approach of limiting heat loss is to cover the pipes with numerous layers of aluminium sheets. The aluminium surface lowers radiation heat loss, while the air trapped within the layer of aluminium sheets reduces heat loss caused by convection and conduction.

**Boiler capacity**

The output of a boiler is often expressed in pounds of steam delivered per hour. Since this value may vary in temperature and pressure over time, a more accurate and complete expression is that of heat transferred over time, expressed as British thermal units per hour. Boiler capacity is usually expressed as kBtu/hour (1000 Btu/hour).

**Steam Pressure**

If pressure increases the temperature of the steam will increase, thus making it super-heated steam. Super-heated steam contains less amount of latent heat compared to dry saturatedsteam. Since the latent heat is the useful heat, steam should be used at the lowest pressure that will give a suitable temperature gradient.

## 2. EVAPORATION

Definition

In theory, evaporation is just the vaporization of a liquid from its surface. Evaporation is a unit operation that removes a solvent from a solution by boiling it in an appropriate vessel and extracting the vapor, leaving a concentrated liquid residue.

Objective of evaporation: To make a solution more concentrated. Generally extracts are concentrated in this way.

Factors affecting evaporation:

(i) Temperature:

Heat is necessary to provide the latent heat of vaporization, and in general, the rate of evaporation is controlled by the rate of heat transfer. Rate of heat transfer depends on the temperature gradient. Many pharmaceutical agents are thermolabile. So the temperature that will cause the least possible decomposition should be used. e.g. Many glycosides and alkaloids are decomposed at temperature below $100^0$C. e.g. Hormones, enzymes and antibiotics are extremely heat sensitive substances. e.g. Malt extract (containing enzyme) is prepared by evaporation under reduced pressure to avoid loss of enzymes. Some antibiotics are concentrated by freeze-drying.

(ii) Temperature and time of evaporation

Exposure to a relatively high temperature for a short period of time may be less destructive of active principles than a lower temperature with exposure for a longer period. Film evaporators used a fairly high temperature but the time of exposure is very short. An evaporating pan involve prolonged heating.

(iii) Temperature and moisture content

Some drug constituents decompose more rapidly in the presence of moisture, especially at a raised temperature (by hydrolysis). Hence, evaporation should be carried out at a low controlled temperature, although the final drying can be performed at higher temperature when little moisture remains. e.g. Belladonna Dry Extract is an example of this type.

(iv) Type of product required

Evaporating pans or stills can generate both liquid and dry goods, but film evaporators exclusively produce liquid products. So, a dilute extract can be concentrated in a film evaporator before dying in an evaporating pan.

## (v) Effect of concentration

As the liquor becomes more concentrated, the quantity of solids increases, raising the solution's boiling point. This increases the danger of damage to thermolabile constituents and reduces the temperature gradient. In general, concentrated solutions have higher viscosity, resulting in thicker boundary layers, and they may deposit particulates on the heating surface, reducing heat transfer. All of these difficulties can be mitigated by turbulent flow conditions.

## EVAPORATORS

Evaporators are classified according to the form of the movement:

(i) Natural circulation evaporators.

(ii) Forced circulation evaporation

(iii) Film evaporators

(i)Natural Circulation Evaporator

## EVAPORATING PAN

*Construction:*

The apparatus comprises of a hemispherical, or shallow pan, made of a suitable material such as copper or stainless steel, and enclosed by a steam jacket. The hemispherical shape provides the optimum surface-to-volume ratio for heating and the biggest area for vapour separation. The pan may include a mounting that allows it to be tilted to remove the product, although the shallow shape makes this arrangement unsteady, and an outlet at the bottom is typical.

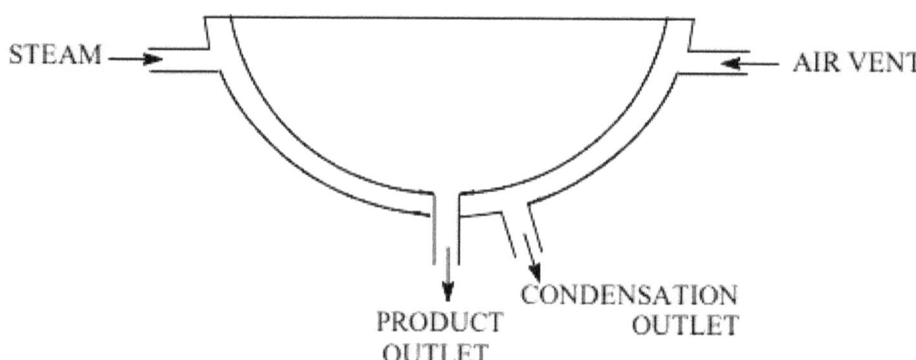


*Working:*

The dilute solution is placed in a pan. Steam is supplied into the jacket via the steam intake to heat the pan. In these evaporators, the liquid moves due to convection currents created by the heating process. The concentrated liquid is collected through the outlet at the bottom of the pan.

*Advantages:*

(a) It is easy and inexpensive to construct.

(b) It is simple to operate, clean, and maintain.


*Disadvantages:*

(a) With only natural circulation, the total coefficient of heat transmission will be low, and particles will most likely deposit on the surface, resulting in product degradation and more degradation in heat transfer.

(b) Also, several products cause foaming..

(c) The entire fluid is heated all the time, which may be unsuitable for thermolabile materials.

(d) The heating surface is constrained and reduces correspondingly as the pan's size expands.

(e) As the pan is open, the vapor escapes into the atmosphere, potentially causing saturation.

(f) These pans can only be used to evaporate aqueous liquids.

(g) Pan evaporation cannot be performed at low pressure.

(h) Can only be used with thermolabile things.


## EVAPORATING STILLS

*Construction:*

It comprises of a jacketed evaporating pan with a cylindrical cover which is attached to a condensing unit. The entire assembly is called still. The cover is secured to the evaporating pan.

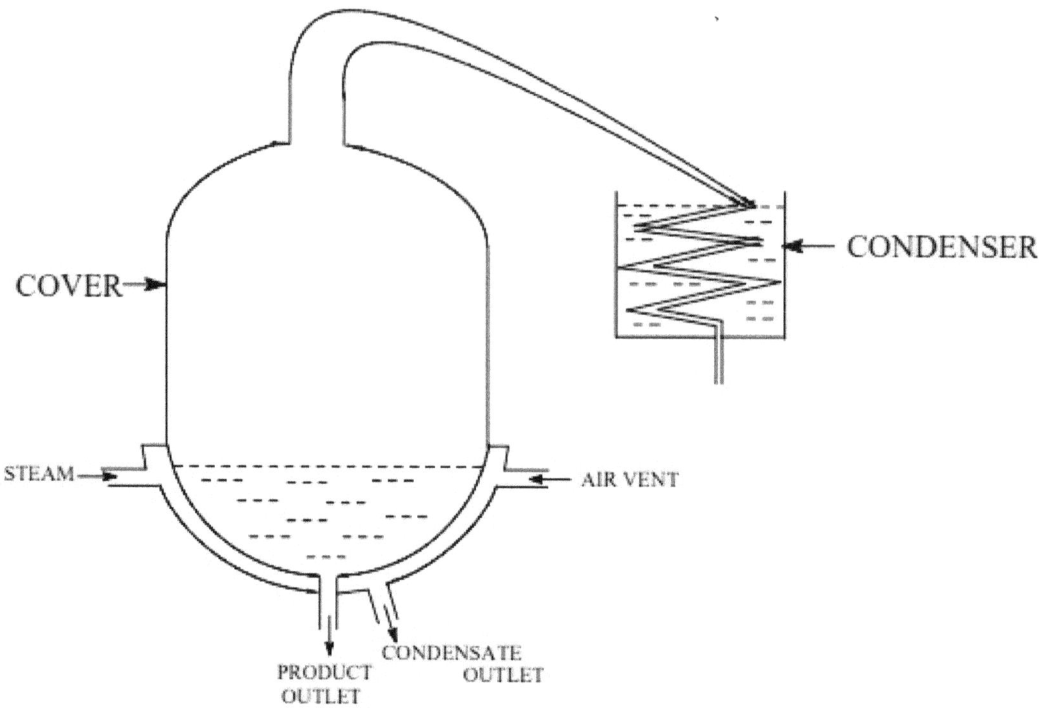


*Working:*

The diluted liquid is fed into the still, and the cap is fastened. Steam is introduced into the jacket. The liquid evaporates, condenses in the condenser, and is then collected. The product (concentrated liquid) is collected via the product outlet.

*Advantages:*

(a) Simple construction and easy to clean and maintain.

(b) The vapor is removed by condensation which (i) speeds evaporation (ii) reduces inconvenience and (iii)allows the equipment to be used for solvents other than water e.g. ethanol.

(c) A receiver and vacuum pump can be fitted to the condenser, permitting operation under reduced pressure and, hence, at lower temperature.

*Disadvantages:*

(a) Natural convection only

(b) All the liquor is heated all the time

(c) The heating surface is limited.

*Uses:*

(i) Aqueous and other solvents may be evaporated

(ii) Thermolabile materials can be evaporated under reduced pressure.

(iii)Removing the still head it is convenient for evaporating extracts to dryness.

## SHORT TUBE EVAPORATOR (Basket type vertical short tube evaporator)

*Construction:*

The evaporator is a cylindrical vessel. The lower portion of the vessel consists of a nest of tubes with the liquor inside and steam outside– this assembly is called calendria. The specifications of calendria are as follows:

Tube length: 1 – 2 m

Tube diameter: 40 – 80 mm

Diameter of evaporator: 2.5 m

Number of tubes: 1000

The feed inlet is at the top of the calendria. The product outlet is placed at the bottom of the evaporator. Steam inlet and outlet is placed from the side of the calendria.

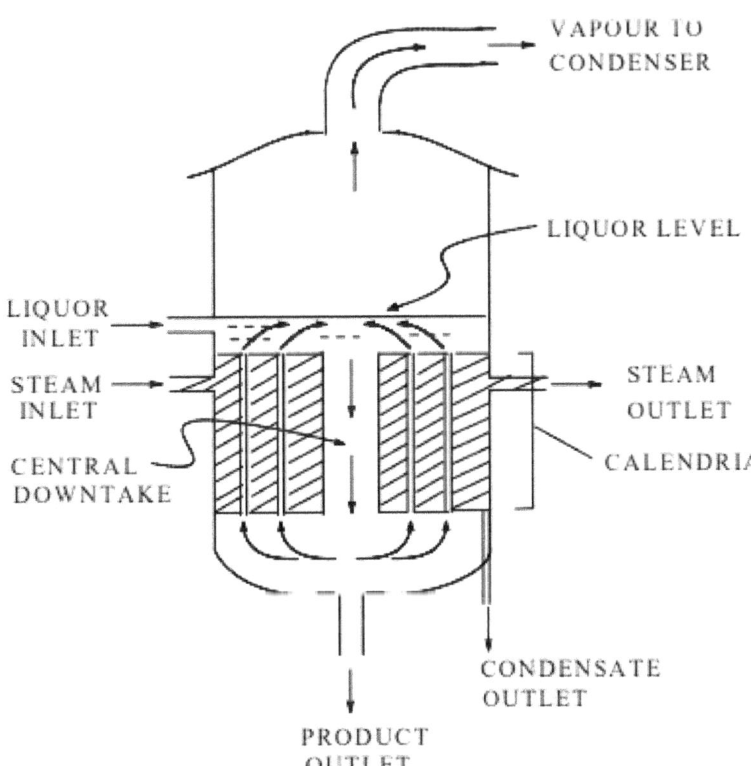


*Working:*

• The feed is introduced through the feed inlet and the liquor is maintained at a level slightly above the top of the tubes (of calendra), the space above this is left for the disengagement of vapor from the boiling liquor.

• The liquor in the tubes is heated by the steam and begins to boil, when the mixture of liquid and vapor will shoot up the tubes (in a similar manner to that of a liquid that is allowed to boil to vigorously in a test-tube).

• This initiates circulation, with boiling fluid climbing up the calendria's smaller tubes before returning down the bigger central downtake.

• The product is collected via the product outlet.

*Advantages*

1. Use of tubular calendria increases the heating area, possibly by a factor of 10 to 15 compared to that of an external jacket.

2. The vigorous circulation reduces boundary layers and keeps solids in suspension, so increasing the rate of heat transfer.

3. Condenser and receiver can be attached to run the evaporation under vacuum with nonaqueous solvents.

*Disadvantages*

1. Since the evaporator is filled to a point above the level of the calendria, a considerable amount of liquid is heated for a long time. The effect of this continual heating can be reduced to some extent by removing concentrated liquor slowly from the outlet at the bottom of the vessel.

2. Complicated design, difficult for cleaning and maintenance.

3. The head (pressure) of the liquor increases pressure at the bottom of the vessel and, in large evaporators where the liquor depth may be of the order of 2 m; this may give rise to a pressure of about 0.25 bar, leading to elevation of the boiling point by 5 to $6^0$C.

## FORCED CIRCULATION EVAPORATORS

Forced circulation evaporators are natural circulation evaporators with some added form of mechanical agitation. Different forms of forced circulation evaporators can be designed.

• An evaporating pan, in which the contents are agitated by a stirring rod or pole could be described as a forced circulation evaporator.

• A mechanically operated propeller or paddle agitator can be introduced into an evaporating pan or still.

• Propeller or paddle agitator can be introduced into the downtake of a short-tube evaporator.

• A typical forced circulation evaporator can be shown as follows:

*Construction:*

The evaporator consists of a short tube calendria and a large cylindrical vessel (body of the evaporator) for separation of vapor and liquid takes place. The liquor inlet is provided at the side of the cylindrical vessel. A pump is fitted in between the calendria and the body of the evaporator. A tangential inlet for liquid under high pressure is placed at neck of the body of the evaporator. The vapor outlet is placed at the top of the body and it may be passed through a condenser to collect the condensed liquid.

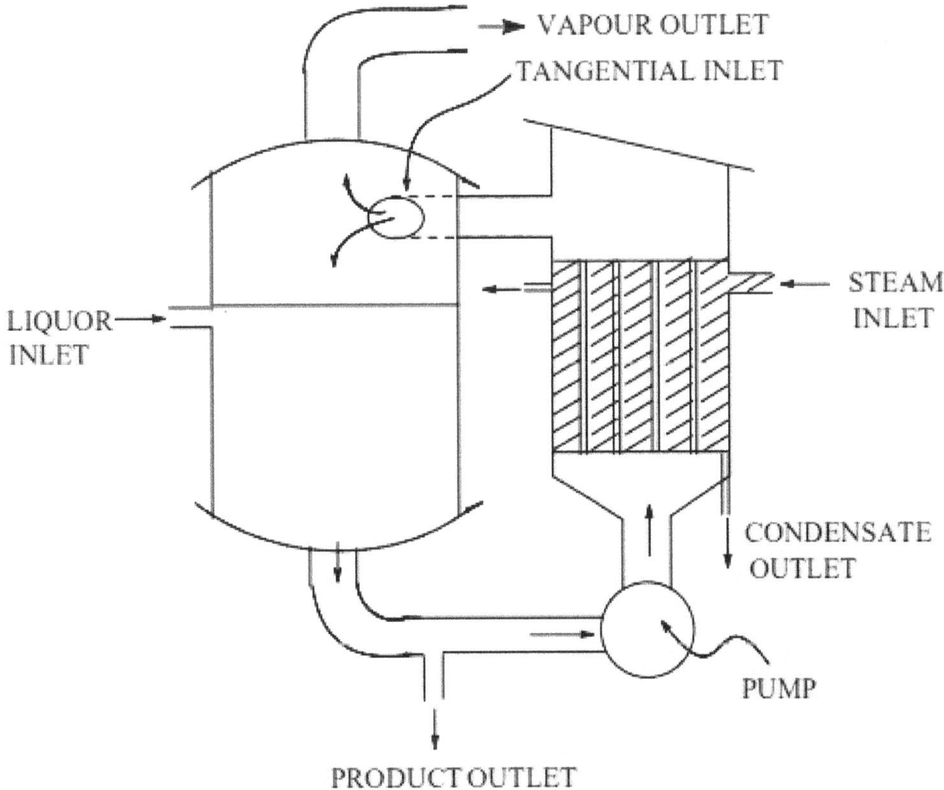



*Working Principle*

Feed is introduced through the liquor inlet. Pump will force the liquid through the calendria. Steam heats the liquid inside the calendria. As it is under pressure in the tubes the boiling point is elevated and no boiling takes place. As the liquor leaves the tubes and enters the body of the evaporator through the tangential inlet there is a drop in pressure and vapor flashes off from the superheated liquor. The concentrated liquid is pumped out through the product outlet and the vapor is collected through the vapor outlet.

*Advantages*

• Rapid liquid movement improves heat transfer, especially with viscous liquids or materials that deposit solids or foam readily.

• The forced circulation overcomes the effect of greater viscosity of liquids when evaporated under reduced pressure.

• Rapid evaporation rate makes this method suitable for thermolabile materials, e.g. it is used in practice for the concentration of insulin and liver extracts.

## FILM EVAPORATORS

Film evaporators spread the material as a film over the heated surface, and the vapor escapes the film.

### Long tube evaporators (Climbing film evaporators)

*Construction and working principle*

The heating unit consists of steamjacketed tubes, having a length to diameter ratio of about 140 to 1, so that a large evaporator may have tubes 50 mm in diameter and about 7 m in length. The liquor to be evaporated is introduced into the bottom of the tube, a film of liquid forms on the walls and rises up the tubes, hence it is called climbing film evaporator. At the upper end, the mixture of vapor and concentrated liquor enters a separator, the vapor passes to a condenser, and the concentrated liquid to a receiver.

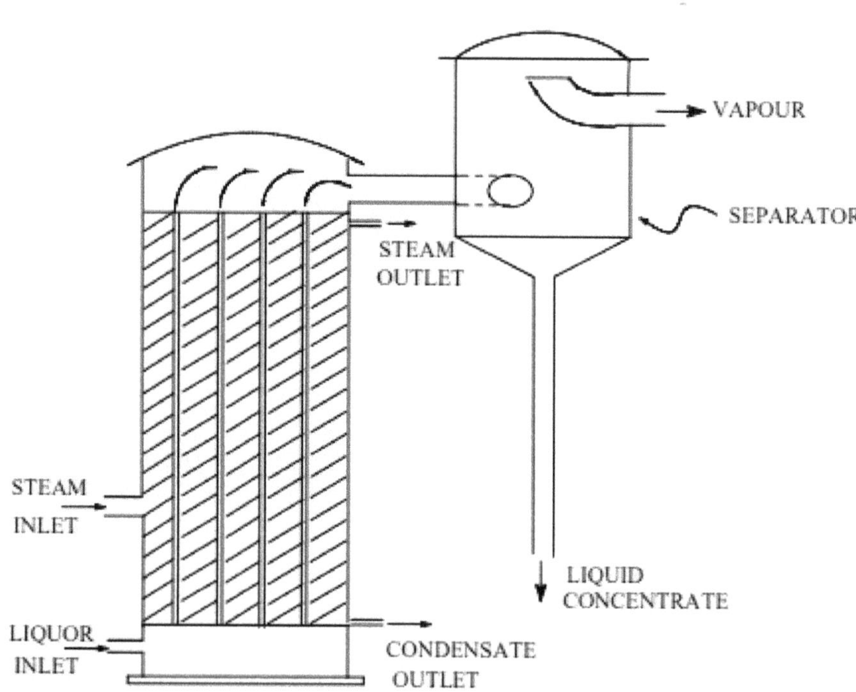


Cold or pre heated liquor is introduced into the tube (fig.-i). Heat is transferred to the liquor from the walls and boiling begins, increasing in vigor (fig.-ii). Ultimately sufficient vapor has been formed for the smaller bubbles to unite to a large bubble, filling the width of the tube and trapping a 'slug' of liquid above the bubble (fig.-iii). As more vapor is formed, the slug of liquid is blown up the tube (fig.-iv), the tube is filled with vapor, while the liquid continues to vaporize rapidly, the vapor escaping up the tube and, because of friction between the vapor and liquid, the film also is dragged up the tube upto a distance of 5 to 6 metres.

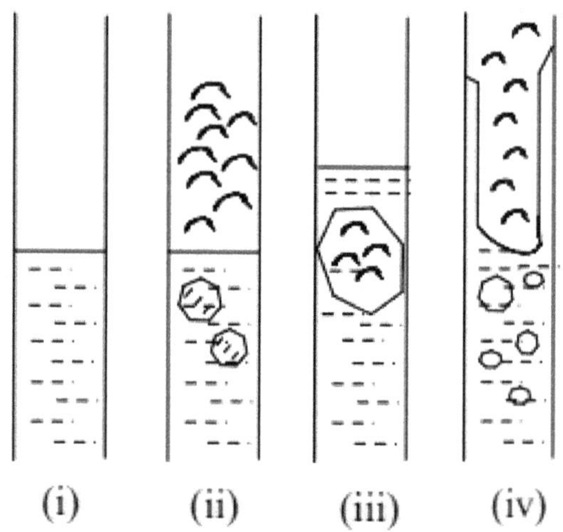


**Long tube evaporators (Falling film evaporators)**

*Construction and working principle*

The heating unit consists of steam-jacketed tubes, having a length to diameter ratio of about 140 to 1, so that a large evaporator may have tubes 50 mm in diameter and about 7 m in length. The liquor to be evaporated is introduced at the top of the evaporator tubes and the liquor comes down due to gravity.

The concentrate and vapor leaves the bottom. They are separated in a chamber where the concentrate is taken out through product outlet and vapor from vapor outlet.

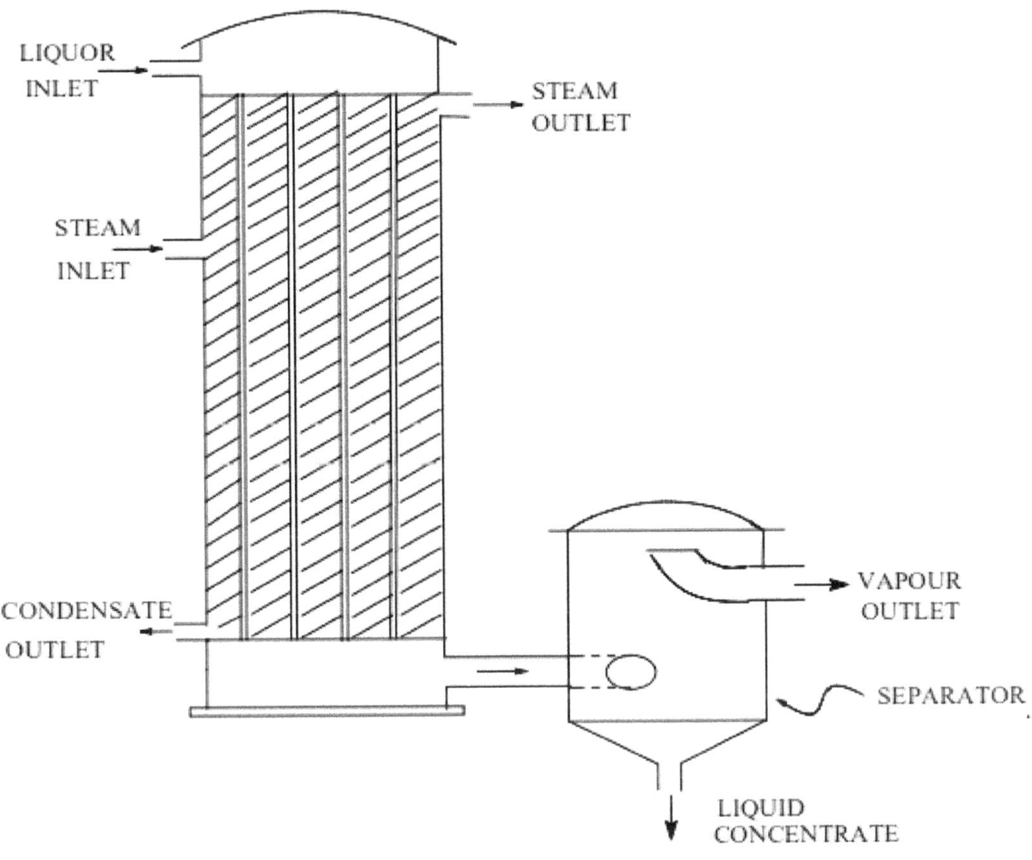


*Advantages of long tube evaporator(s)*

Since the movement of the film is assisted by gravity, more viscous liquid can be handled by falling film evaporator.

(i) Very high film velocity reduces boundary layers to a minimum giving improved heat transfer.

(ii) The use of long narrow tubes provides large surface area for heat transfer.

(iii)Because of increased heat transfer efficiency, a small temperature gradient is necessary with less risk of damage to thermolabile materials.

(iv)Although the tubes are long, they are not submerged, as in the short-tube evaporator; so that there is no elevation of boiling point due to hydrostatic head.

*Disadvantages*

(i) Expense to manufacture and install the instrument is high.

(ii) Difficult to clean and maintain.

(iii)From the operational point of view the feed rate is critical. If too high, the liquor may be concentrated insufficiently, whereas, if the feed rate is to low, the film cannot be maintained and dry patches may form on the tube wall.

**Multiple effect evaporator**

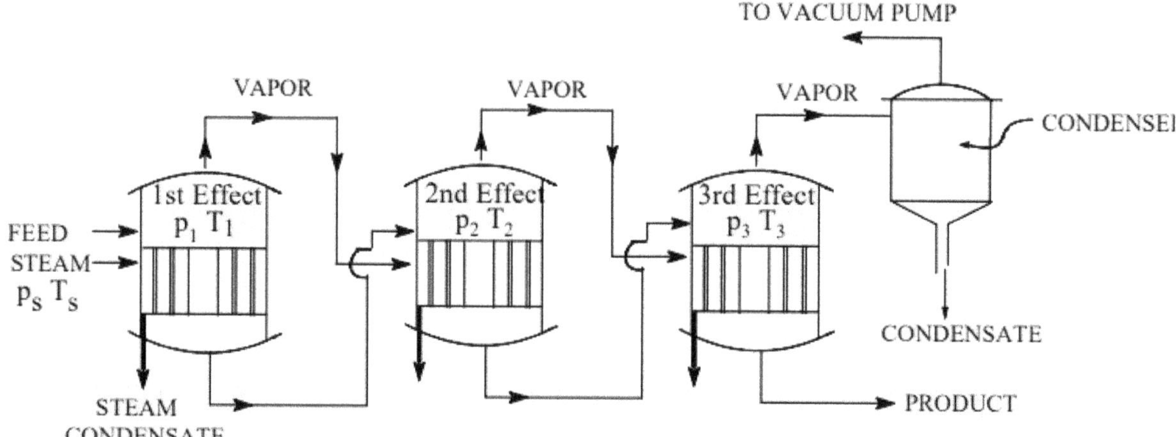



*Triple-effect evaporator: $p_s$, $p_1$, $p_2$, $p_3$ vapor pressures, Ts, T1, T2, T3 temperatures where $p_s > p_1 > p_2 > p_3$.*

In a single effect evaporator steam is supplied for heating the liquor. The total heat is not transferred form the steam. So the rest of the heat is wasted. To use that heat efficiently, connections are made so that the vapor from one effect serves as the heating medium for the next effect.

(i) The dilute feed (liquor) enters the first effect, where it is partly concentrated; it flows to the second effect for additional concentration and then to the third effect for final concentration. This liquor is pumped out of the third effect.

(ii) In the first effect raw steam is fed in which the vapor pressure in the evaporator is the highest, $p_1$. the second effect has the intermediate vapor pressure; i.e. $p_1 > p_2 > p_3$. This pressure gradient is maintained by drawing the vapor through a vacuum pump and condensing after the final effect.

(iii)Depending on the lowering of vapor pressure boiling point of the liquids of 2nd and 3rd effect will also be lowered; i.e. $T_1 > T_2 > T_3$.

(iv)In the 2nd effect vapor from the 1st effect ($T_1$) is heating the liquor (having temperature $T_2$). So there is a temperature gradient ($T_1 - T_2$); consequently the liquor will be heated. Similar heating will be there in the 3rd effect also.

**Methods of feeding**

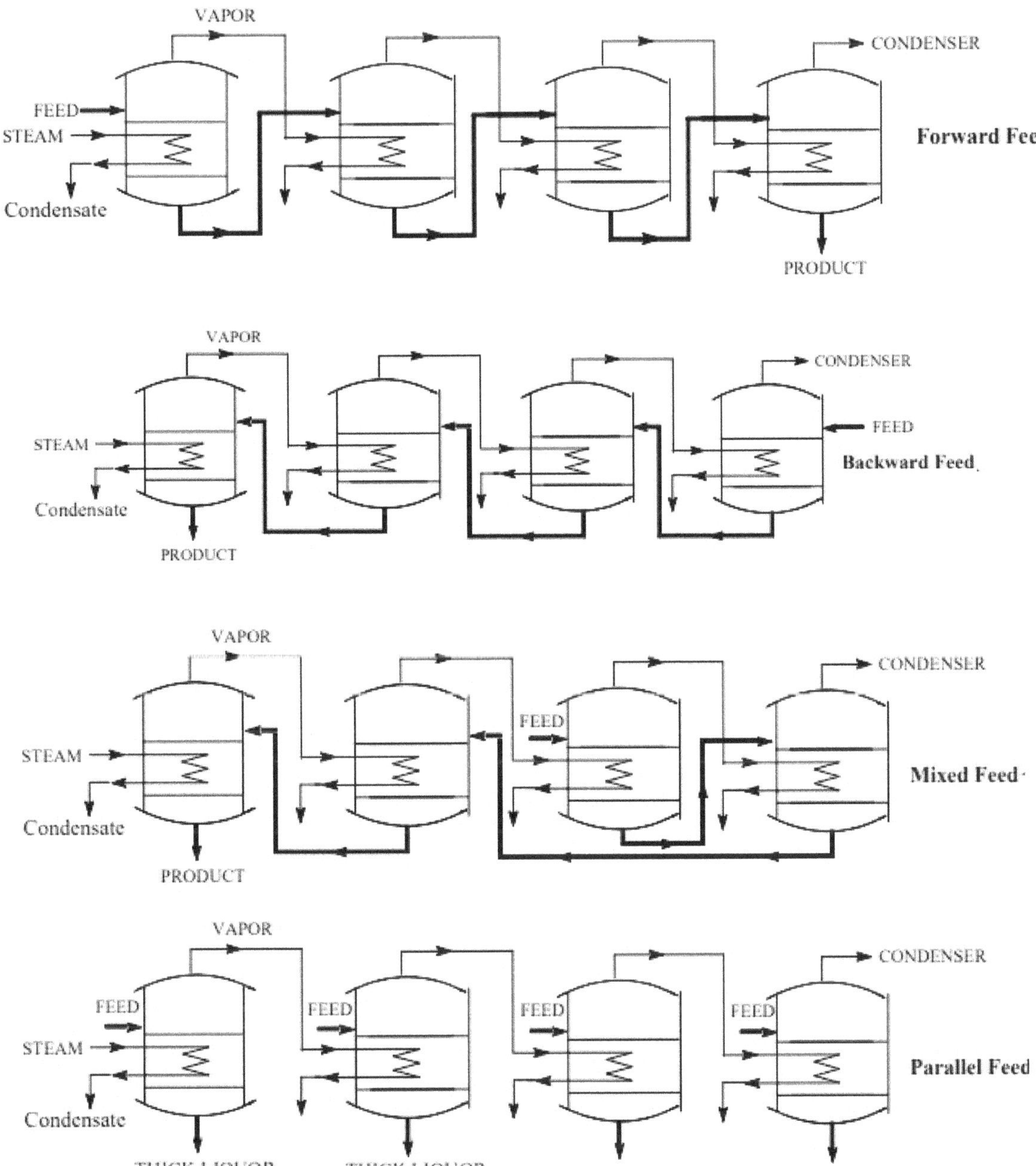


## Forward feed

*Advantages:*

1. Feed moves from high pressure (in effect-2) to low pressure (in effect – 4) chambers, so pumping of liquor is not required.

2. Product is obtained at lowest temperature.

3. This method is suitable for scale-forming liquids because concentrated product is subjected to lowest temperature.

*Disadvantages:*

It is not suitable for cold feed because, the steam input in effect-1 raises the temperature of the feed, and a small amount of heat is supplied as latent heat of vaporization. Therefore, amount of vapor produced will be less than the amount of steam supplied. Lower amount of vapor in effect-1 produces lower amount of vapor in the subsequent effects. Therefore, the overall economy is lower.

**Backward feed**

In backward-feed the feed enters in the last effect and moves towards first effect (i.e IV→III→II→I).

*Advantages:*

It is suitable for cold feed, because the heat used for increasing the temperature in IV effect is already used for heating 3 times. This will give more economy.

**Mixed feed method**

The feed enters in the intermediate effect, moves forward and then backward to effect-I (III→IV→II→I).

Advantages

• Liquid moves from high pressure (III) to low pressure (IV), hence no pump is required. Liquid moves from IV→II→I requires pump.

• Product is obtained from highest temperature (I) hence lowest viscosity.

**Parallel feed**

It is suitable where the feed has to be concentrated slightly.

**ECONOMY OF MULTIPLE EFFECT EVAPORATORS**

Assumptions:

(a) Feed is at boiling point and (b) Loss of heat is negligible

In effect-1

1 Kg of steam transfers its heat to feed. Since feed is at boiling point so the total amount of heat is used as latent heat of vaporization. Therefore, 1 kg steam will produce 1 kg vapor.

In effect – 2

1 Kg vapor from effect-1 will transfer heat to the liquor of effect -2. Here also 1 kg vapor produce 1 kg vapor from the liquor.

In effect – 3

1 Kg vapor from effect-II will produce 1 kg vapor in effect-3.

Therefore, 1 kg steam will produce 3 kg vapor.

Now, economy of a single effect evaporator $= \dfrac{vapor\ produced}{steam\ used} = \dfrac{1\,kg}{1\,kg} = 1$

And economy of a triple effect evaporator $= \dfrac{vapor\ produced}{steam\ used} = \dfrac{3\,kg}{1\,kg} = 3$

So for N number of effects economy will be N times that of a single effect evaporator.

## CAPACITY OF MULTIPLE EFFECT EVAPORATORS

Capacity = total evaporation per hour

= vapor production rate

Capacity is also expressed in terms of total heat transferred because latent heats are nearly constant all over the ranges of pressure ordinarily involved. The heat transferred in the three effects can be represented by the following equations:

$q_1 = U_1 A_1 \Delta t_1$.

$q_2 = U_2 A_2 \Delta t_2$.

$q_3 = U_3 A_3 \Delta t_3$.

Total capacity will be found by adding these equations, giving:

$q = q_1 + q_2 + q_3. = U_1 A_1 \Delta t_1 + U_2 A_2 \Delta t_2 + U_3 A_3 \Delta t_3$.

Assuming that all effects have equal areas $A_1 \approx A_2 \approx A_3 = A$(let) and that average coefficient $U_{avg}$ can be applied to the system. The eqn (i) can be written as:

$q = U_{avg} A (\Delta t_1 + \Delta t_2 + \Delta t_3)$

However the sum of individual temperatures drops equals the total over-all temperature drop between the temperature of the steam and the temperature in the condenser;

therefore

$q = U_{avg} A \Delta t$

This is exactly the same as that of single effect.

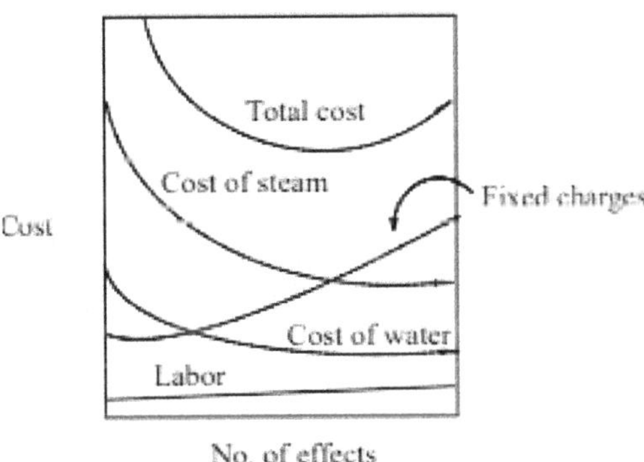


*Conclusion*

It follows from this that if the number of effects of an evaporation system is varied and if the total temperature difference is kept constant, the total capacity of the system remains substantially unchanged.

## 3. DISTILATION

Distillation may be defined as the separation of the constituents of a mixture including a liquid by partial vaporization of the mixture and separate and collect the vapour. Such separation may include

(i) one liquid from non-volatile impurities.

(ii) One liquid from one or more other liquids, with which it may be miscible, partially-miscible or immiscible

N.B. In practice it is difficult to distinguish between evaporation, distillation and drying.

Based on the intention:

(i) When condensation vapour is required the operation is called distillation

(ii) When the concentrated liquid residue is required the operation is called evaporation.

(iii) When the dried solid residue is required as product the process is called drying

BOILING POINT DIAGRAM OF A BINARY MIXTURE

The figure represents the boiling point and equilibrium-composition relationship, at constant pressure. Two liquids A (b.p. $t_A$) and B (b.p. $t_B$) are taken in a chamber of constant pressure. Now at any temperature the vapour composition and liquid composition will give two lines when plotted vs. temperature. In boiling point diagram, temperatures are plotted as ordinates and compositions as abscissas.

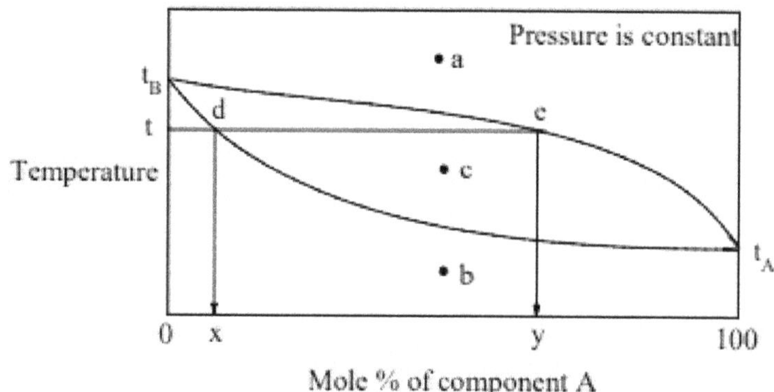


• The diagram consists of two curves, the ends of which coincide with the b.p. of two components ($t_A$ and $t_B$).

• The upper-curve describes vapour composition and lower-curve liquid composition.

• At any temperature t the horizontal line cuts the vapour composition curve at 'e' which corresponds to vapour composition of y (mole%A) and cuts the liquid composition curve at 'd' which corresponds to liquid composition of x (mole% of A). So any two points on the same horizontal line (such as d and e) represent compositions of liquid and vapour in equilibrium at temperature 't'.

• For all points above the top line (such as point 'a') the mixture is entirely vapour.

• For all points below the bottom line (such as point 'b') the mixture is completely liquefied.

• For all points between the two curves (such as point 'c') the system consists partly of liquid and partly of vapour.

RAOULT'S LAW

Raoult's law states that, any particular temperature, the partial pressure of one component of a binary mixture is equal to the mole fraction of that component multiplied by its vapor pressure in the pure state at this temperature.

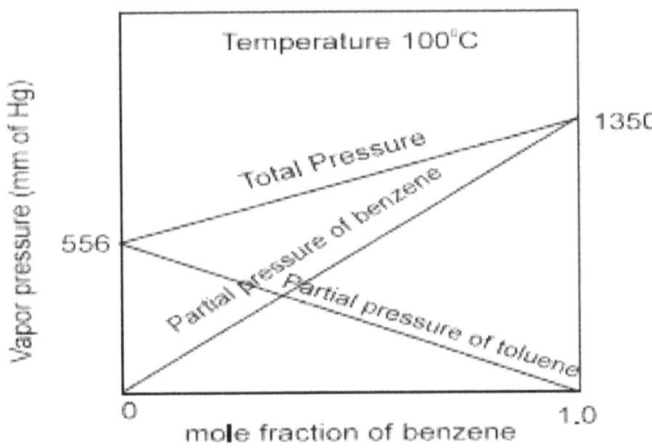


e.g. to illustrate Raoult's law, let us consider the case of benzene and toluene mixture. At a temperature of $100^0C$ toluene has a vapor pressure of 556 mm. Consequently, if partial pressure is plotted against composition, the partial pressures of toluene at various compositions will fall along a straight line from 556 mm for pure toluene to zero for pure benzene. At this same temperature benzene has vapor pressure of 1350 mm, and its vapor pressure will change linearly from zero for 0% benzene to 1350 mm for pure benzene. The total pressure for any composition will be the sum of the two partial pressures at that composition. If the partial pressures are straight lines i.e. Raoult's law holds then the total pressure will be a straight line between 556 m for pure toluene and 1350 mm for pure benzene.

*Derivation*

Two liquids A and B are at constant temperature.

Liquid A is more volatile than B.

If Raoult's law holds for this binary mixture then from Raoult's law

$$p_A = P_A x \qquad (1)$$

$$\text{and } p_B = P_B (1 - x)$$

where $p_A$ and $p_B$ = partial pressure of A and B respectively $P_A$ and $P_B$ – vapor pressure of pure A and B x = mole fraction of A in the solution

If P represents the total pressure, then

$$P = p_A + p_B \qquad (2)$$

$$= P_A x + P_B (1 - x)$$

From Dalton's law

$$y = \frac{p_A}{p_A + p_B}$$

where y = mole fraction of A in vapour phase

$$= \frac{P_A x}{P}$$ [from (1) and (2)]

*Example*

The vapor pressures of benzene and toluene are as given in the table. Assuming that mixtures of benzene and toluene obey Raoult's law, calculate and plot the boiling point diagram for this pair of liquids at 760mm total pressure.

| Temp $^0$F | Vapor pressure, mm Hg | |
|---|---|---|
| | Benzene $P_A$ | Toluene $P_B$ |
| 176.2 | 760 | 314 |
| 180 | 811 | 345 |
| 185 | 882 | 378 |
| 190 | 957 | 414 |
| 195 | 1037 | 452 |
| 200 | 1123 | 494 |
| 205 | 1214 | 538 |
| 210 | 1310 | 585 |
| 215 | 1412 | 635 |
| 220 | 1520 | 689 |
| 225 | 1625 | 747 |
| 230 | 1756 | 760 |
| 231.1 | – | |

Solution: Let us take one temperature $180^0$F

So at $180^0$F, PA = 811 Hg

PB = 314 mm Hg

We have to calculate the mole fraction of benzene in liquid (x) and in vapor (y).

From the eqn.:

P = $P_A$x + $P_B$ (1 – x) or,

760 = 811 x + 314 (1 – x)

or, x = 0.897

$$y = \frac{P_A x}{P} = \frac{811 \times 0.897}{760} = 0.958$$

From eqn.

Similarly for all temperature values corresponding x and y values may be calculated:

| Temp. $^0$F | x | y |
|---|---|---|
| 185 | 0.773 | 0.897 |
| 190 | 0.659 | 0.831 |
| 195 | 0.555 | 0.757 |
| 200 | 0.459 | 0.678 |
| 205 | 0.370 | 0.591 |
| 210 | 0.288 | 0.496 |
| 215 | 0.211 | 0.393 |
| 220 | 0.141 | 0.281 |
| 225 | 0.075 | 0.161 |
| 230 | 0.013 | 0.031 |

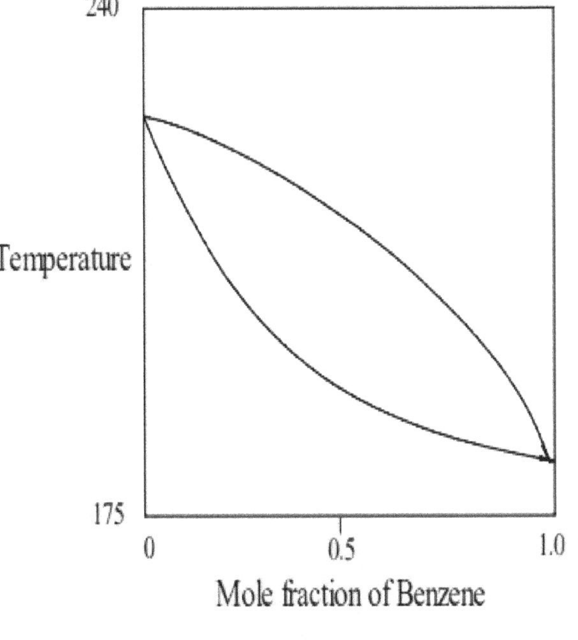

Boiling point diagram for benzene-toluene system at 1 atm pressure

## RELATIVE VOLATILITY

For a more volatile phase in equilibrium with a liquid phase, the relative volatility of component A (the more volatile component) with respect to component B is defined by the equation:

$$\alpha_{AB} = \frac{y_A / x_A}{y_B / x_B}$$

where

$\alpha AB$ = relative volatility of component A with respect to component B

y = mole fraction of component A in vapor phase

x – mole fraction of component in liquid phase

In case of binary system, $y_B = 1 - y_A$ and $x_B = 1 - x_A$.

Substituting,

$$\alpha_{AB} = \left(\frac{y_A}{1 - y_A}\right)\left(\frac{1 - x_A}{x_A}\right)$$

Rearranging we get

$$Y_A = \frac{\alpha_{AB} X_A}{1 + (\alpha_{AB} - 1) X_A}$$

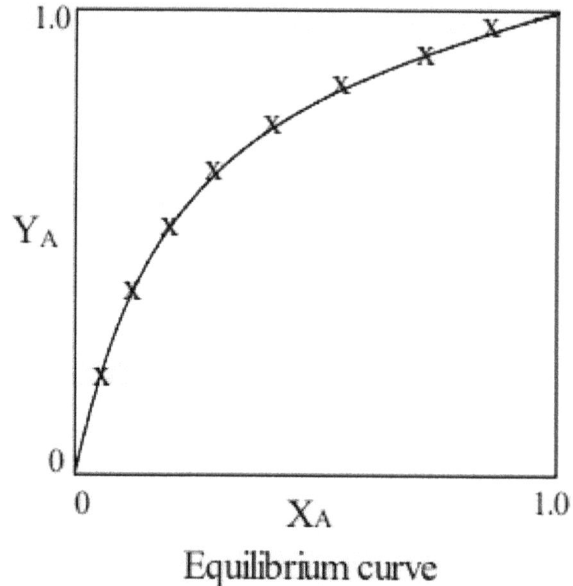

Equilibrium curve

*Equilibrium curve*

If $\alpha_{AB}$ is given then from the above equation a set of $X_A$ and $Y_A$ can be calculated. When $Y_A$ is plotted against $X_A$ the curve is called equilibrium curve. If the liquid phase obeys Raoult's law and the vapour phase obeys Dalton's law then,

$$y_A = \frac{P_A x_A}{P}$$

$$\alpha_{AB} = \frac{P_A x_A / P}{P_B (1-x_A)/P} \; \frac{1-x_A}{x_A} = \frac{P_A}{P_B}$$

So,

Example

Construct an equilibrium curve for binary system of benzene – toluene from the given data.

| Data | Boiling point at 1 atm | Vapor pressure of benzene ($P_A$) | Vapor pressure of toluene ($P_B$) | $\alpha_{AB} = P_A / P_B$ |
|---|---|---|---|---|
| Benzene | 80.1$^0$C | 760 mm | 270 mm | 2.81 |
| Toluene | 110.6$^0$C | 1780 mm | 760 mm | 2.34 |

Therefore, average relative volatility over the temperature range 80.1 to 110.6$^0$C

$$\alpha_{AB(avg)} = \frac{2.81 + 2.34}{2} = 2.57$$

Therefore,
$$Y_A = \frac{2.57 \, X_A}{1+(2.57-1) X_A} = \frac{2.57 \, X_A}{1+1.57 X_A}$$

| $X_A$ | 0.1 | 0.2 | 0.3 | 0.4 | 0.5 | 0.6 | 0.7 | 0.8 | 0.9 |
|---|---|---|---|---|---|---|---|---|---|
| $Y_A$ | 0.222 | 0.391 | 0.524 | 0.631 | 0.720 | 0.794 | 0.857 | 0.911 | 0.959 |

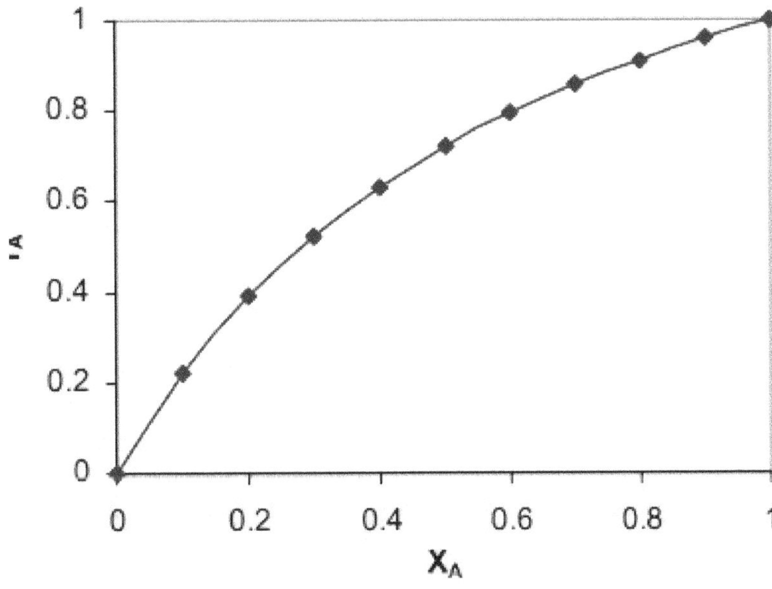


HENRY'S LAW

The partial pressure of a component over a solution is proportional to its mole fraction in the liquid . This can be expressed as

$$p_A = C\,x$$

where

$p_A$ = partial pressure of component A

$x$ = mole fraction of A in liquid phase

$C$ = Henry's law constant;

$C$ is constant only at constant temperature

N.B. Raoult's law is essentially a special case of Henry's law where the constant C in equation is the vapor pressure of the pure component.

## DISTILLATION METHODS

A. Distillation methods for miscible liquid systems

1. Equilibrium or Flash Distillation

2. Simple or Differential Distillation

3. Fractional Distillation

4. Distillation under reduced pressure (e.g. Molecular Distillation)

5. Special Distillation

Methods for non-ideal mixtures (a) Distillation of Azeotropic Mixtures (b) Extractive Distillation

B. Distillation of immiscible liquids (e.g. Steam Distillation)

1. EQUILIBRIUM DISTILLATION / FLASH DISTILLATION

There are two types of distillations that do not involve rectification

(a) Equilibrium distillation or flash distillation and

(b) Simple or differential distillation.

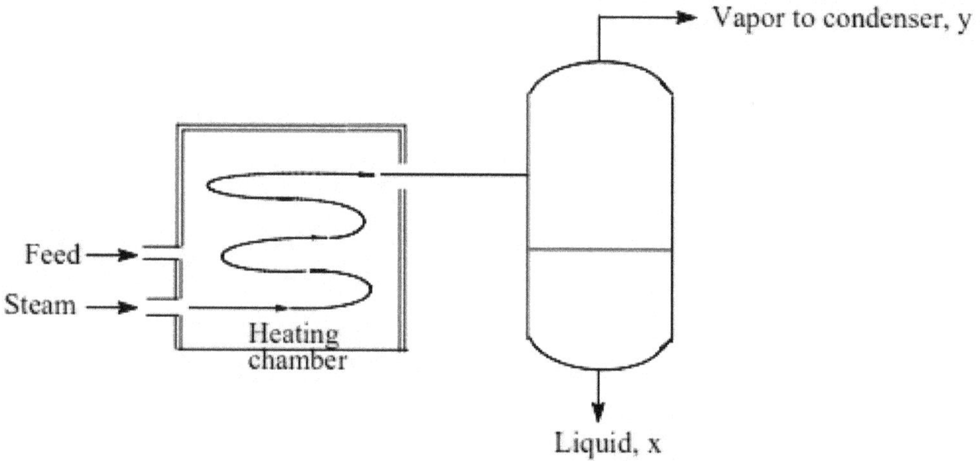


(a) Equilibrium distillation or flash distillation

This is a single stage operation where a liquid is partially vaporized, the vapors are allowed to come in equilibrium with the residual liquid and the resulting vapors and liquid are separated.

Use: This method is used only when the difference between volatilities of two components is very large

Let us consider a binary system whose components are A and B. A is more volatile.

• Feed: $W_F$ = number of moles of liquid fed $x_F$ = mole fraction of component A in feed

• Suppose V moles are vaporized in an equilibrium-distillation process.

Now in

Liquid phase

Number of moles left in liquid phase = $(W_F - V)$ moles

Let the composition of the residual liquid = x mole fraction of A

Vapor phase

Composition of vapor phase = y mole fraction of A

Number of moles gained = V

Form material balance equation with respect to A

Moles of A at start = Moles of A in vapor phase + Moles of A in liquid phase

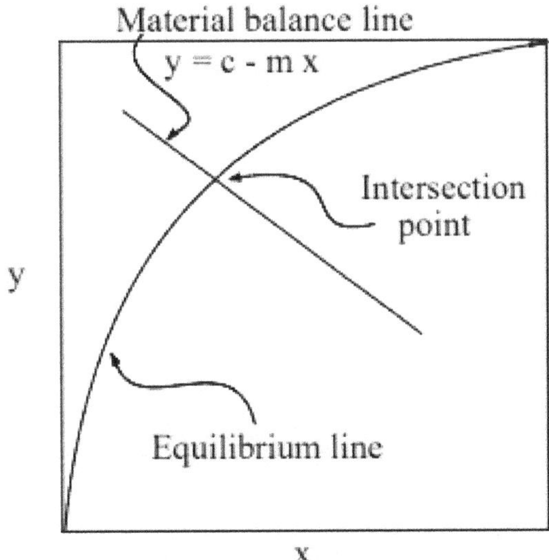



Equilibrium curve of A-B system

$$W_F \, x_F = V \, y + (W_F - V) \, x \qquad (i)$$

In this case all the parameters are known except x and y . 2nd equation required for solving is obtained from equilibrium curve of the A, B system. Eqn (i) is a straight line,

$$V \, y = W_F \, x_F - (W_F - V) \, x$$

$$\text{or,} \quad y = \left( \frac{W_F \, x_F}{V} \right) - \left( \frac{W_F - V}{V} \right) x$$

$$\text{or,} \quad y = c - m \, x$$

Plotting this equation in the equilibrium curve the point of intersection is obtained. The value of x and y can be obtained form the point of intersection.

## 2. SIMPLE / DIFFERENTIAL DISTILLATION

In this process vapor is removed from the system as soon as it is formed and condensed.

Use:

- This method is commonly used in laboratory

- In industries it is only used for systems having high relative volatilities.

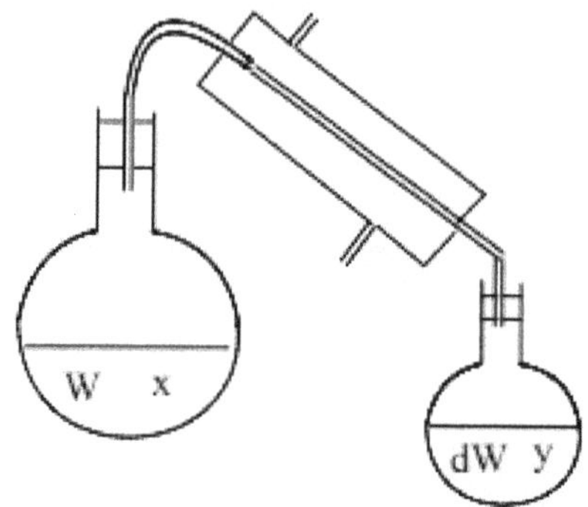


**Derivation of Raleigh's equation**

Let us consider a batch of W0 moles of liquid was taken at the beginning. Suppose at any given time during distillation there are W moles of liquid left in the still. At this time let the mole fraction of A in liquid is x. Suppose a very small amount of liquid dW is vaporized. In the vapor phase the mole fraction of component A is y.

|  | At a given time | After a moment |
|---|---|---|
| Total moles of liquid present | W | W – dW |
| Moles of A present in liquid | Wx | (W – dW)(x – dx) |
| Total moles of liquid removed |  | dW |
| Moles of A present in the vapor |  | y |

Therefore a material balance equation with respect to A will be

xW = (W – dW) (x – dx) + ydW or,

xW = xW – xdW – Wdx + dWdx + ydW

dWdx is very small hence ignoring the term the equation will be

ydW – xdW = Wdx or,

(y – x)dW = W dx

or,
$$\frac{dW}{W} = \frac{dx}{y-x}$$

Now, integrating between the limits

|  | Time = 0 | Time = $t_1$. |
|---|---|---|
| Amount of liquid in the still (moles) | $W_0$. | $W_1$. |
| Moles of component A in liquid | $x_0$. | $x_1$. |

$$\int_{W_0}^{W_1} \frac{dW}{W} = \int_{x_0}^{x_1} \frac{dx}{y-x} \qquad \text{or,} \qquad \boxed{\ln\frac{W_1}{W_0} = \int_{x_0}^{x_1} \frac{dx}{y-x}}$$

This equation is known as Raleigh's equation. It relates the amount of material distilled with instantaneous composition of the liquid at that moment

The function $\dfrac{dx}{y-x}$ can be integrated graphically from the equilibrium curve, since the curves gives the relationship between x and y.

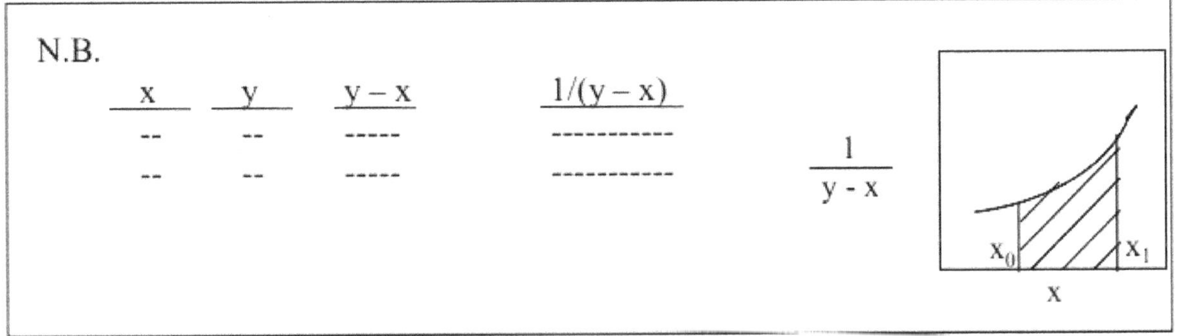


Application of Raleigh's Equation

1. By using the Raleigh's equation the effectiveness of simple distillation for a given system can be estimated.

2. It is used in determination of cut-off point when we can stop distillation as soon as the vapour composition falls below the required purity of the product.

## SIMPLE DISTILLATION

Objective

Simple distillation is the process of converting a liquid into its vapors which, are passed through a cooling surface to condense the vapors. The condensed vapors are reformed into liquid which, is collected in a receiver.

Apparatus for laboratory scale

It consists of a distillation flask with a side arm sloping downward that is connected to a condenser. The condensed vapors are collected in a flask called 'receiver'. The whole apparatus is made of glass. A thermometer is fitted in the distillation flask to note down the temperature at which, the vapors are distilled. Bumping is avoided by adding small pieces of porcelain or porous pot before distillation. Apparatus for preparation of purified water The boiler may be made of cast iron but the baffles and the condenser tubes that comes into contact with product are made of stainless steel or monel metal.

The cold water from the water tap enters the still through the inlet, which rises in the jacket fitted with a constant level device, the excess of water over flow through the outlet. A portion of hot water at 90 to $95^0$C enters into the boiler through a narrow opening – the level of water is maintained in the boiler up to overflow level.

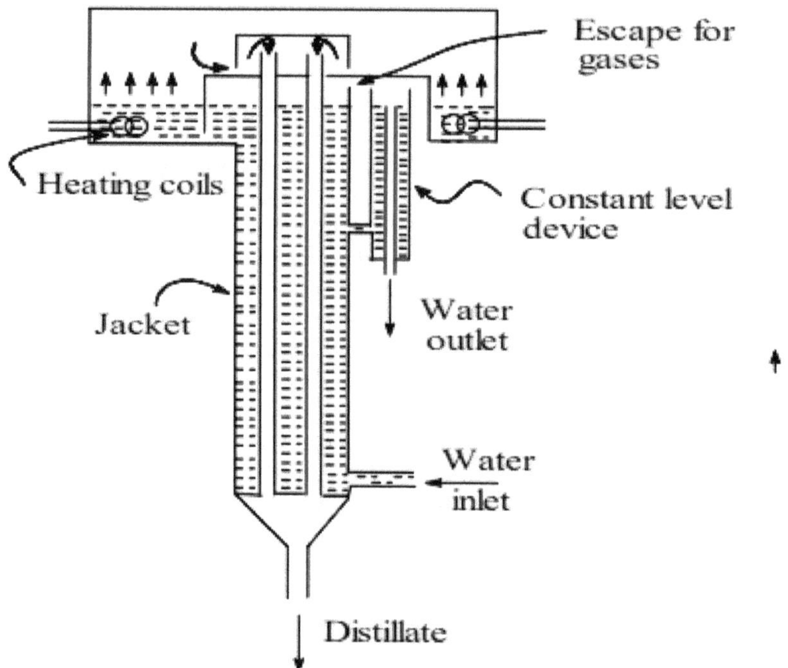


Fig.  Distillation unit for purified water

The water is boiled in the boiler by means of heating coils. On heating, the dissolved gases in the condenser are allowed to escape through a small opening and only the steam escapes into the condensing tubes. Since the dissolved gases are more volatile than water they escape in the first portion of the distillate, therefore, must be rejected. Similarly, the last portion may contain volatile portion of the dissolved solid substances in tap water – hence, discarded.

Application of simple distillation in pharmacy

I. It is used for the preparation of distilled water and water for injection.

II. Many volatile oils and aromatic waters are prepared by simple distillation e.g. Spirit of nitrous ether and Aromatic Spirit of Ammonia

III. Concentration of liquid and to separate non-volatile solid from volatile liquids such as alcohol and ether.

## 3. FRACTIONAL DISTILLATION / RECTIFICATION

A rectifying unit consists primarily of

(a) a still or reboiler, in which vapor is generated,

(b) a rectifying or fractionating column through which this vapor rises in countercurrent contact with a descending stream of liquid, and

(c) a condenser, which condenses all the vapor leaving the top of the column, sending part of this condensed liquid (the reflux) back to the column to descend counter to the rising vapors, and delivering the rest of the condensed liquid as product.

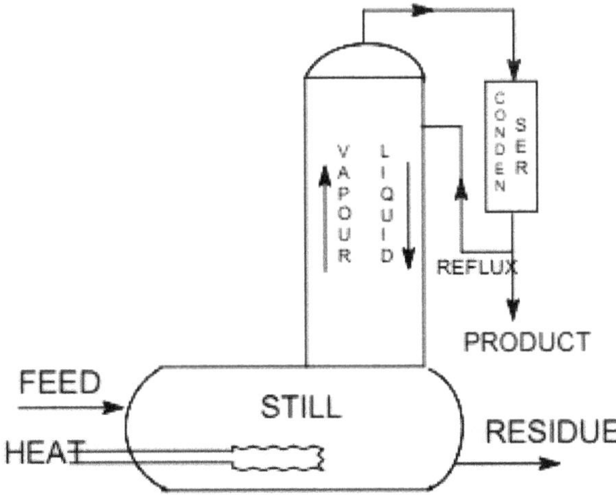

*Diagram of still and fractionating column*

As the liquid stream descends the column, it is progressively enriched with the less volatile constituent. The top of the column is cooler than the bottom, so that the liquid stream becomes progressively hotter as it descends and the vapor stream becomes progressively cooler as it rises. This heat transfer is accomplished by actual contact of liquid and vapor, and for this purpose effective contact is desirable.

CONSTRUCTION OF RECTIFYING COLUMN

There are different varieties of equipments for rectification

(a) Plate column (i) Bubble cap column (ii) Sieve-plate column

(b) Packed column

BUBBLE-CAP COLUMN

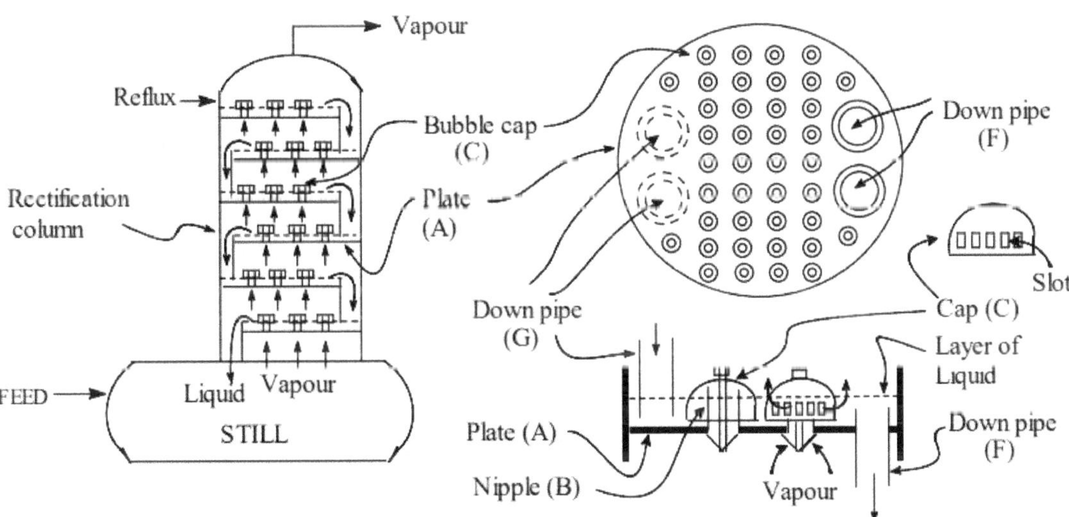


• The column is divided into sections by means of a series of horizontal plates A.

• Each plate carries a number of short nipples B (or riser). Each nipple is covered by a bellshaped cap C that is secured by a spider and bolt with the plate. The edge of the cap is serrated or the sides may be slotted.

• Vapor rises from the plate below through the nipple, is diverted downward by the cap, and bubbles out under the serration or through the slots.

• A layer of liquid is maintained on the plate by means of an overflow or down-pipe (F) and the depth of the liquid is such that the slots are submerged.

• The down-pipe, (G) from the plate above, is sealed by the liquid on the plate below, so that the vapor cannot enter the down-pipe.

• Ordinarily, the liquid is delivered at one end of a diameter by the down-pipe from the plate above, flows the other end of the same diameter.

Types of down-comers

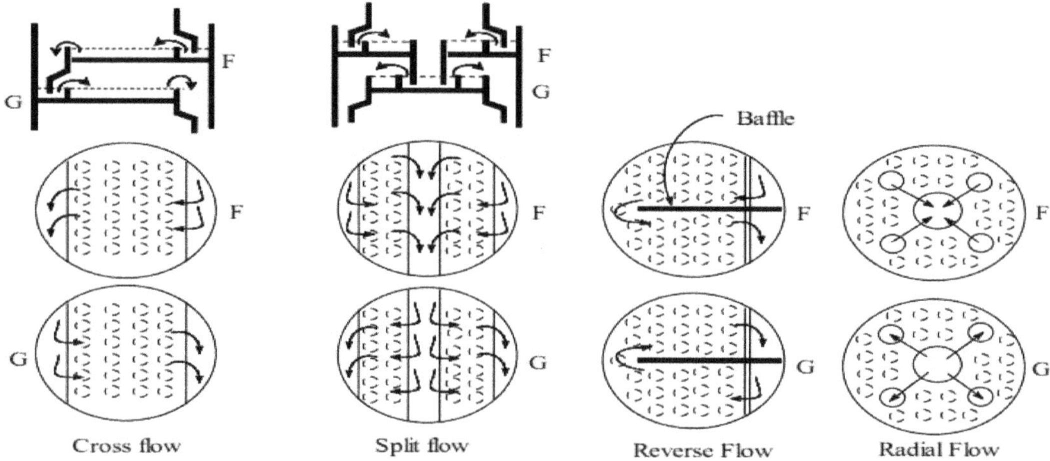


(a) Cross flow

The liquid flows across the plate from right to left on plate F and left to right on plate H and so on down the column.

(b) Split flow

On plate F the liquid flows form the two sides to the center. On plate H it flows from the center to the two sides and so on down the column. This arrangement is commonly known as split flow.

(c) Reverse flow

Liquid comes down the space on one side of the baffle and flows across the plate from right to left, around the end of the baffle, from left to right and down the space behind the weir. This arrangement is called reverse flow.

(d) Radial flow with circular down-take

One plate will have four or more down-comers around the circumference, and the next plate will have a down-comer at the center so that on the upper plate the flow is from the circumference towards center and on the next plate the flow is from the central down-take to the circumference.

Specification of bubble cap rectification column:

Column diameter 2 to 15 ft

Height few feet to over 100 ft

Bubble cap diameter 3 to 6 inches

Slots in a 3 inches bubble cap may be 1/8 to 3/32 inch wide

½ to 1 inch height

SIEVE PLATE COLUMNS

All the constructions are same as bubble cap columns. Instead of bubble cap plates, flat plates with a large number of relatively small perforations, drilled in them are used. These perforations are usually 3/16 to ¼ inch in diameter. The velocity of the vapor through these holes is sufficient to produce the liquid running down the holes.

PACKED COLUMNS

The column is entirely filled with some sorts of material that offers a large surface area supposedly wetted by the liquid. A large variety of materials are used among which Raschig rings are popular. A Raschig ring is a hollow cylinder whose length is equal to its diameter. This may be made of metal (by sawing sections off a pipe), stone ware, ceramics, carbon, plastics, or other materials. Raschig rings are usually dumped at random in the column.

## 4. DISTILLATION UNDER REDUCED PRESSURE / VACUUM DISTILLATION

Theroy

Liquid boils when its vapor pressure is equal to the atmospheric pressure. Liquids, which are decomposed at their boiling point under atmospheric pressure, can be distilled at a much lower temperature than its boiling point if the pressure is reduced on the surface of the liquid. Boiling under reduced pressure will also increase the rate of distillation.

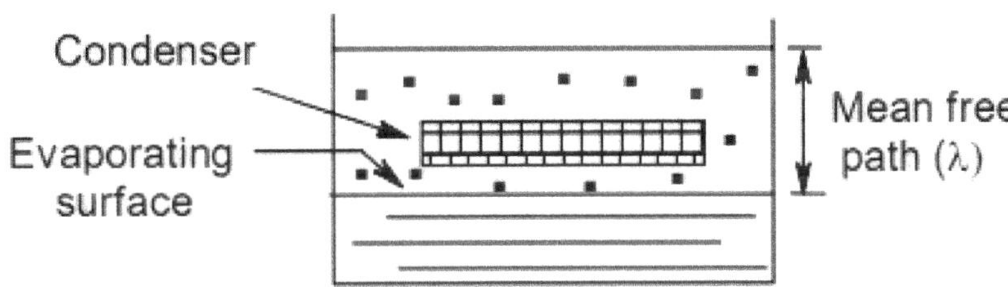


**Molecular Distillation**

*Theory / Principle of Molecular Distillation*

In a high vacuum distillation operation, where the material distills from an evaporating surface to a relatively cool condensing-surface. The conditions are such that, the mean free path of the distillating molecules is greater than the distance between the evaporating and condensing surface.

• The vacuum applied in these types of apparatus is about 1 μm Hg pressure or less.

Mean free path is defined as the average distance traveled by the molecules in a straight line without any collision. It can be calculated by Clausius law:

$$\lambda = \frac{1}{\sqrt{2\pi d^2 N}}$$

where,

$\lambda$ = mean free path (cm)

d = diameter of the molecules (cm)

N = number of molecules in 1 cm3 volume.

N.B.

| Temperature ($^0$C) | Volume (litre) | Pressure (mm Hg) | Number of molecules |
|---|---|---|---|
| 0 | 22.4 | 760 | $6.023 \times 10^{23}$. |
| 0 | 22.4 | $1 \times 10^{-3}$. | $7.9 \times 10^{17}$. |

It is clear from the above equation and chart that, mean free path can be increased, by reducing the number of molecules per cm$^3$ volume. The molecules evaporate from the surface and travel few cm without colliding with the molecules of the residual gas in the space above. If now the condensing surface is placed within distance, a major fraction of the molecules will condense and will not return to the distilland. Thus each molecule distills itself and hence called "Molecular Distillation".

*Characteristics of molecular distillation*

1. Molecules having molecular weight within the range of 300 to 1100 dalton can be distilled by this method. [N.B. Low molecular weight (below 300 dalton) molecules will re-evaporate again from the condenser surface. High molecular weight molecules (greater than 1100 dalton) will not have sufficient volatility.]

2. The molecules to be distilled should reach the surface and evaporate. The molecules at the bottom of the distilland have to overcome the pressure of the layer above, to come to the surface. Hence, the layer should be thin and should be in a state of turbulent motion to facilitate the molecules to reach the surface.

3. The distilland should be degassed before entering in the still, because at very low pressure the dissolved gas will occupy all the space and rate of distillation will be reduced.

**Falling Film Molecular Still**

The vessel has a diameter of the order of 1 m and the walls are heated suitably by a heating jacket. Vacuum pumps are connected by a large diameter pipe. The feed flows down the walls and is spread to a film by the polytetrafluoroethylene (PTFE) wipers which move about 3 m/s giving a film velocity of about 1.5 m/s. The residue is collected at the bottom of the vessel and it is re-circulated (through the feed line). The evaporated molecules are then condensed on the condenser surface. The condensate is taken out as product.

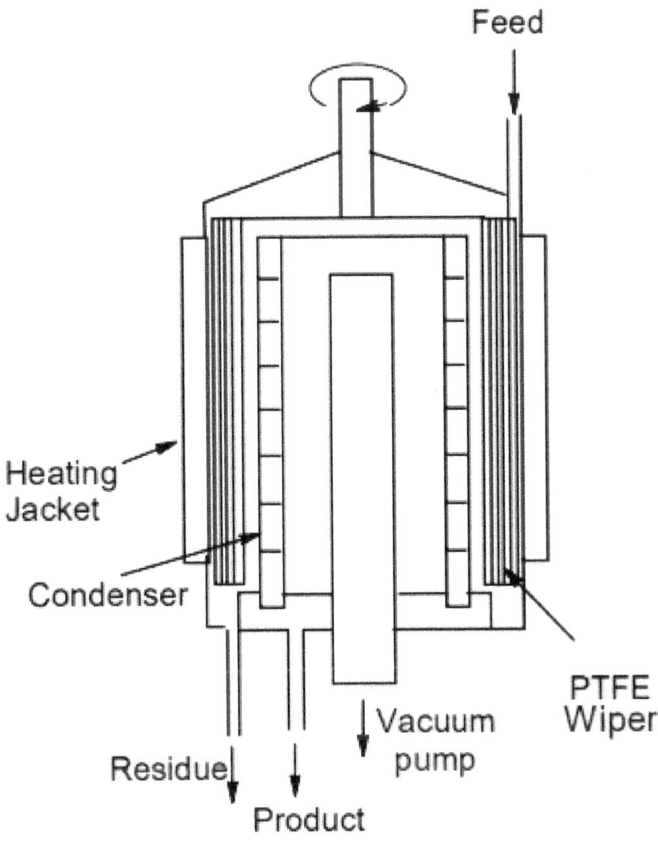


Fig. Falling film Molecular Still

**Centrifugal molecular still**

The distilland (feed) is introduced on to the center of a bucket-shaped vessel (1 to 1.5 m in diameter) that rotates at high speed. The film of liquid that is formed moves outwards over the surface of the vessel to the residuecollection pipe. The vessel is heated by radiant heaters. Condensers and a collection device are located close to the inner surface of the rotor.

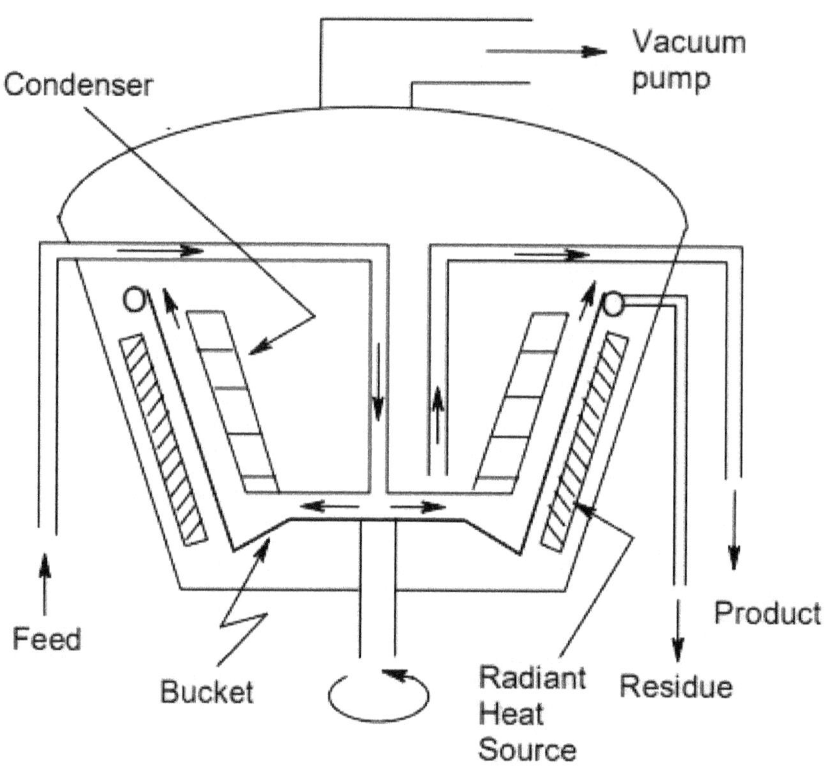


Fig. Centrifugal molecular stilll

*Application of vacuum distillation in pharmacy*

1. Vitamin concentrates

Vitamin A,D,E,K and tocopherols are obtained from vegetable and fish oils. The vitamin-A concentrate produced by molecular distillation is very pure and has good stability. As no chemical is used in this method which could split the ester linkage, the vitamins are retained in the natural ester form which is the most stable form of vitamin A. The stability of the concentrates is further enhanced by natural antioxidants distilling over from the original oil.

2. The fractionation of oil

The fractionation of oils into various components is carried out by molecular distillation.

| Components | Molecular Weight | Temperature Range |
|---|---|---|
| (a) Fatty acids, unsaponifiable matter of low molecular weight. | 150 – 300 | 50 – 140$^0$C |
| (b) Unsaponifiable matter like sterols, vitamins, dyes, waxy alcohols, monoglycerides | 300 – 600 | 150 – 190$^0$C |
| (c) Triglycerides, sterol esters, vitamin esters, resins, waxes | 600 – 900 | Above 190$^0$C |

3. Purification and fractionation of lanolin

It is used to get various fractions from Lanolin like, cetyl alcohol, cholesterol, ceryl alcohol, lanopalmitic acid, isocholesterol etc.

## 4. Separation of Poly Ethylene Glycol (PEG)

On laboratory scale it is used to separate PEG according to the degree of polymerization.

## 5. SPECIAL DISTILLATION METHODS FOR NON-IDEAL MIXTURES

Industrial scale distillation of Azeotropic Mixture

The liquor from fermentation process is a common source of ethanol and contains approximately 8–10% ethanol. After simple distillation an azeotrope will form containing 95.6% (96E+4W) ethanol and boiling at $78.15^0$C at atmospheric pressure. In this type of system a reboiler is used instead of boiler. The feed liquor is introduced into the system and must occur at a point where the equilibrium will not be disturbed. Hence, feed will take place, at a place part of the way up the column, where the equilibrium composition on the plate is similar to the feed composition. The plate below the feed plate form the stripping section where the rising vapor strips the more volatile component (ethanol) from the feed liquor while the upper section is known as the rectifying section. The binary azeotrope produced at this stage is freed from water by making use of ternary azeotrope – ethanol, benzene, and water. The ethanol/water azeotrope, with sufficient benzene (only required at start-up) is fed to column A and the pure ethanol is obtained as bottom product, since the ternary azeotrope takes off the water.

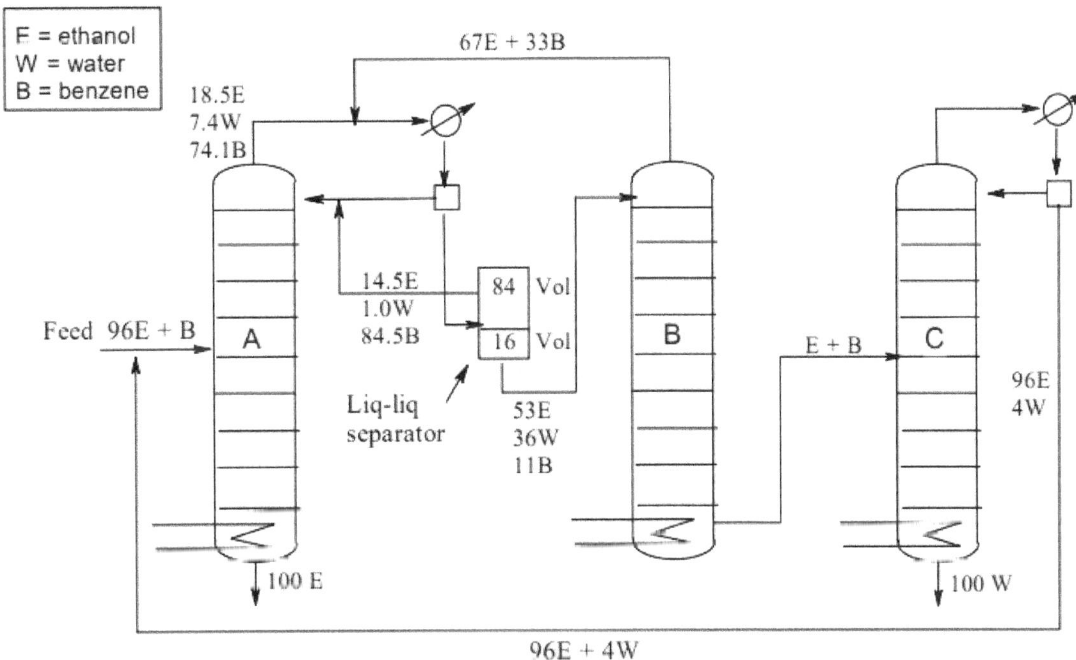


Fig. Plant for manufacture of Absolute ethanol (100% ethanol)

- The azeotrope (E+B+W) is taken from the top of the column A, condensed and separated (in liquid-liquid separator) into two layers, having the compositions given in the diagram.

- The upper layer predominates and, being rich in benzene (14.5E+1.0W+84.5B), is returned to column A. The lower layer (53E+36W+11B) is taken to column B, where the benzene is recovered as the ethanol/benzene binary azeotrope (67E+33B) and is mixed with the vapor from ethanol.

- The ethanol / water residue passes to column C, where the ethanol is recovered as the ethanol/water binary azeotrope (96E+4W), which can be incorporated with the original feed.

- The final product from column A is 100% ethanol and from column C is 100% water.

## 6. DISTILLATION OF IMMISCIBLE LIQUIDS

Steam distillation

Steam distillation is used for the distillation of two immiscible liquids one of which is water.

*Application:*

(i) Separation of volatile oil e.g. eucalyptus oil, rose oil, clove oil etc. and

(ii) Preparation of some aromatic water e.g. concentrated rose water.

*Theory*

Volatile oils are mixtures of high molecular weight compounds having low vapour pressure (i.e. high b.p.). To separate these from the natural sources like petals of flowers, barks etc. it is not possible to take them to their boiling points around $200^0C$. If these oils are distilled with water (low molecular weight but high vapour pressure i.e. low b.p.) then volatile oil will be distilled out at a temperature below $100^0C$.

$$\frac{\text{Weight of volatile oil in distillate}}{\text{Weight of water in distillate}} = \frac{M_V P_V}{M_W P_W}$$

Where, $M_W$ and $M_V$ are molecular weights of water and volatile oil respectively.

$P_W$ and $_{PV}$ are vapor pressure of water and volatile oil respectively.

- The aqueous phase of distillate that is collected is water saturated with volatile oil i.e. called aromatic water.

When a mixture of two practically immiscible liquids are heated, while being agitated to expose the surfaces of both liquids to the vapor phase, each component independently exerts its own vapor pressure as a function of temperature as if the other constituent was not present. Boiling begins and distillation may be effected when the sum of the partial pressures of the two immiscible liquids just exceeds the atmospheric pressure. An immiscible liquid and water independently boils at high temperature but when steam is passed through a mixture of these liquids (agitation) it boils at a much lower temperature than the boiling point of water. Example: Turpentine oil has a boiling point of about $160^0C$, when mixed with water it can be distilled at about $95.6^0C$ if steam is passed through it.

*Large scale apparatus*

This consists of a still having a mesh near the bottom. The steam is generated by boiling water below the mesh. The steam passes through the materials (to be extracted) packed over the mesh. The vapor containing volatile oil is then passed ot the condenser. The distillate is collected in Florentine receivers. Florentine receiver separates the oil and water depending on their densities. The aqueous phase may be re-circulated again to avoid loss of volatile oil in water.

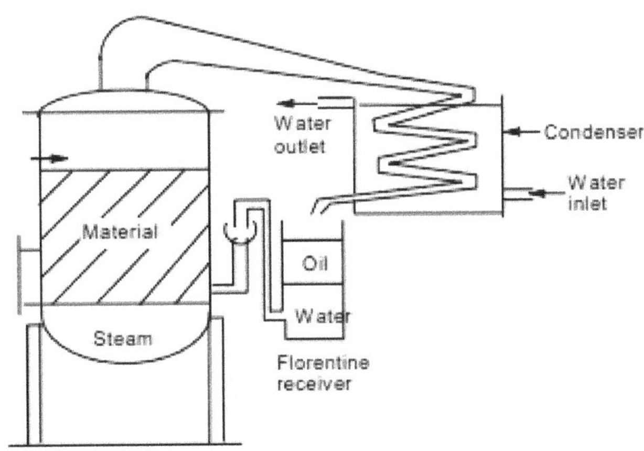



Fig . Steam distillaiton apparatus

Florentine Receiver

It is used for the separation of oil and water. Florentine receivers are of two types:

Type-I Used for separation of oil heavier than water.

Type-II Used for separation of oil lighter than water.

Type-I receiver has tow taps. The tap fitted near the bottom of the vessel is used for collecting oil, whereas the tap fitted near the top of the vessel is used for water to overflow.

Type-II receiver is fitted with siphon at the bottom that works when it gets filled with water whereas the tap fitted near the top is an outlet for the flow of oil.

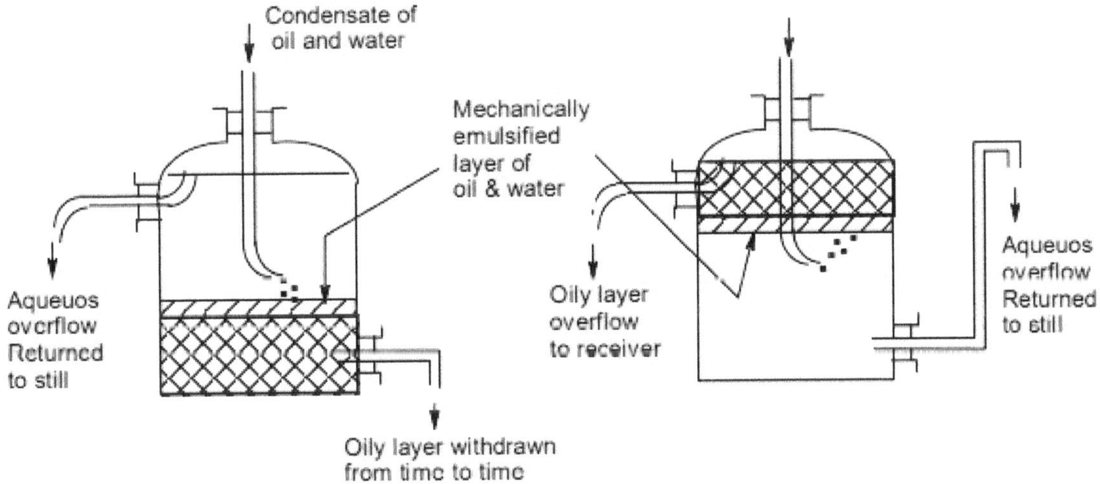



Fig  Florentine receiver for oils heavier than water      Fig. Florentine receiver for oils lighter than water

I. MCQs

1. In the heat interchanger, finned tubes are used for one of the following purposes.
a. Increasing the surface area
b. Introducing steam

c. Introducing the cold fluid

d. Reducing the size of apparatus

Answer: Increasing the surface area

2. The general equation for heat transfer rate, q, is expressed as:

a. $A\Delta t/U$

b. $U/A\Delta t$

c. $UA\Delta t$

d. $UA/\Delta t$

Answer: $UA\Delta t$

3. For heat insulation, one of the following is used

a. Al. wire

b. Cu foils

c. Glass wool

d. Fe Filings

Answer: Glass wool

4. In the double pipe heat exchanger, the two tubes are arranged in one of the following ways

a. Coaxial

b. Concentric

c. Parallel

d. Series

Answer: Coaxial

5. Which heat interchanger consists of bent tubes?

a. Double pipe heat exchanger

b. Floating head two-pass heater

c. Multi-pass heater

d. Tubular heater

Answer: Double pipe heat exchanger

6. Fourier's law is applicable to one of the following types of heat flow.

a. Conduction

b. Convection

c. Radiation

d. Emission

Answer: Conduction

7. The flow of heat is NOT applicable generally in one of the following unit operations

a. Centrifugation

b. Crystallization

c. Drying

d. Refrigeration

Answer: Crystallization

8. In the microwave oven, the heat flows in one of the following mechanisms.
a. Conduction
b. Convection
c. Diffusion
d. Radiation

Answer: Radiation

9. In the convection process for a liquid in a tube, one of the following offers great resistance.
a. Central layer of liquid
b. Liquid layer adhered to the metal wall
c. Metal wall
d. Stagnant liquid layer between viscous and turbulent flow

Answer: Stagnant liquid layer between viscous and turbulent flow

10. In forced convection, the rate of heat transfer is increased by:
a. Metal with high thermal conductivity
b. Metal with high thermal conductivity and mixing of fluid
c. Metal with high thermal conductivity, mixing of the fluid and low viscous fluid
d. Metal with high thermal conductivity, mixing of fluid, high viscous fluid and area of heating surface

Answer: Metal with high thermal conductivity, mixing of the fluid and low viscous fluid

11. Distillation operation involves one of the following steps
a. Vaporization
b. Vaporisation and condensation
c. Vaporisation, condensation and crystallization
d. Vaporisation, condensation, crystallization and drying

Answer: Vaporisation and condensation

12. The separation of liquid by distillation is based on one of the following principles
a. Boiling point
b. Miscibility
c. Vapor pressure
d. Viscosity

Answer: Vapor pressure

13. Absolute alcohol is prepared by one of the following methods
a. Azeotropic distillation
b. Simple distillation
c. Steam distillation
d. Vacuum distillation

Answer: Azeotropic distillation

14. One of the following theories is not applicable to distillation
a. Graham's law of diffusion
b. Law of conservation of energy

c. Law of conservation of matter

d. Raoult's law

Answer: Graham's law of diffusion

15. Distillation does not involve in one of the following processes

a. Evaporation

b. Extraction

c. Purification

d. Separation

Answer: Extraction

16. Raoult's law is applicable to one of the following types of distillation processes

a. Flash distillation

b. Fractional distillation

c. Molecular distillation

d. Simple distillation

Answer: Simple distillation

17. Which part in the distillation apparatus represents the heat exchanger?

a. Adapter

b. Condenser

c. Receiver

d. Still

Answer: Condenser

18. Which law satisfies the batch type distillation of binary system for separation

a. Dalton's law

b. Raoult's law

c. Rayleigh's law

d. Stokes law

Answer: Dalton's law

19. Which one of the methods is also known as differential distillation?

a. Azeotropic distillation

b. Molecular distillation

c. Simple distillation

d. Steam distillation

Answer: Simple distillation

20. Which distillation is known as dry distillation?

a. Compressive distillation

b. Destructive distillation

c. Evaporative distillation

d. Steam distillation

Answer: Destructive distillation

21. Which of the following conditions is correct for evaporation?

a. Constituents must be thermolabile

b. Liquids must be viscous

c. The solvent must be non-volatile

d. Solvent must be volatile

Answer: Solvent must be volatile

22. In the climbing film evaporator, the problem in the evaporation

a. Boiling point of liquid

b. Droplet formation

c. Entrainment of liquid

d. Film formation

Answer: Entrainment of liquid

23. Which is the factor that does not influence the rate of evaporation

a. Difference in vapour pressure

b. Melting points of solids

c. The surface area of the evaporator

d. The viscosity of the solution

Answer: Melting points of solids

24. Which condition of evaporation is used for the production of malt extract?

a. Atmospheric pressure

b. High-pressure

c. Normal pressure

d. Reduced pressure

Answer: Reduced pressure

25. Dry extract of belladonna is prepared by exposing the material to one of the following conditions

a. First to a higher temperature and then to a lower temperature

b. First to lower temperature and then to higher temperature

c. Higher temperature

d. Lower temperature

Answer: First to lower temperature and then to a higher temperature

26. Which equipment gives porous residue on evaporation

a. Film evaporator

b. Multiple effect evaporator

c. Open pan evaporator

d. Vacuum evaporator

Answer: Vacuum evaporator

27. Calandria consists of a number of

a. Baffles

b. Jackets

c. Outlets

d. Tubular surfaces

Answer: Tubular surfaces

28. Which operation is subsequent to evaporation?
a. Crystallization
b. Distillation
c. Drying
d. Extraction

Answer: Drying

29. Steam side film coefficients are increased by one of the following methods
a. Condensing liquid at low-temperature
b. Decreasing the velocity of liquid
c. Non-condensed gas in steam should be minimum
d. Temperature drop should be small

Answer: Non-condensed gas in steam should be minimum

30. The cost per square metre of the heating surface is usually high in one of the evaporators
a. Horizontal tube evaporator
b. Falling film evaporator
c. Steam jacketed kettle
d. Vertical tube evaporator

Answer: Horizontal tube evaporator

31. Which evaporator is used to concentrate insulin, liver extract and vitamins?
a. Climbing film evaporator
b. Falling film evaporator
c. Steam jacketed kettle
d. Vertical tube evaporator

Answer: Climbing film evaporator

32. In the climbing film evaporator, what is the purpose of the entrainment separator
a. Allowing the heat to transfer
b. Allowing the vapour to escape
c. Breaking the foam
d. Pulling the liquid up

Answer: Breaking the foam

33. What is the source of heat in most of the evaporators?
a. Coal
b. Hot water
c. Oil bath
d. Steam

Answer: Steam

34. In which type of evaporator, the formation of vapour film is assisted by gravity

a. Climbing film evaporator

b. Falling film evaporator

c. Steam jacketed kettle

d. Vertical tube evaporator

Answer: Falling film evaporator

35. From the following, select one which forms scales in an evaporator

a. Benzoic acid

b. Calcium sulphate

c. Salicylic acid

d. Sodium chloride

Answer: Sodium chloride

36. Evaporator which helps in growing of coarse crystals

a. Forced circulation evaporator

b. Long tube vertical evaporator

c. Multiple effect evaporator

d. Short tube vertical evaporator

Answer: Forced circulation evaporator

37. Triple effect evaporator uses one of the following types of evaporators

a. Climbing film evaporator

b. Falling film evaporator

c. Steam jacketed kettle

d. Vertical tube evaporator

Answer: Vertical tube evaporator

38. Which of the following is more heat sensitive during evaporation?

a. Alkaloids

b. Glycosides

c. Hormones

d. Volatile oils

Answer: Glycosides

39. Which type of evaporator is suitable for thermolabile substances and high viscous preparations

a. Forced circulation evaporator

b. Long tube vertical evaporator

c. Multiple effect evaporator

d. Short tube vertical evaporator

Answer: Short tube vertical evaporator

40. Which one of the following factors increases the efficiency of the evaporator?

a. High moisture content

b. High-velocity flow

c. The high viscosity of liquid
d. A high volume of liquid

Answer: High-velocity flow

41. Select the preferable evaporator suitable for a corrosive liquid that gives a crystalline product
a. Climbing film evaporator
b. Falling film evaporator
c. Forced circulation evaporator
d. Vertical tube evaporator

Answer: Forced circulation evaporator

42. Normally evaporation process is carried out at one of the following experimental conditions
a. Above the boiling temperature
b. At the boiling temperature
c. Below the boiling temperature
d. Room temperature

Answer: Below the boiling temperature

43. What is the purpose of a deflector in a forced circulation evaporator?
a. Creates large surface area
b. Facilitates pumping of liquid
c. Promotes separation of liquid and vapour
d. Provides heat to the evaporator

Answer: Promotes separation of liquid and vapour

44. Which of the following is TRUE about the Multiple effect evaporator?
a. It is suitable for batch operation
b. It is highly economical relative to a single effect
c. It cannot attach more than two evaporators
d. It utilizes a horizontal tube evaporator

Answer: It is highly economical relative to a single effect

45. The quantity of vapour produced per unit of steam admitted is called
a. efficiency of the evaporator
b. capacity of the evaporator
c. productivity of evaporator
d. economy of the evaporator

Answer: economy of the evaporator

46. The rate of evaporation reduces due to
a. films and deposits
b. high-temperature
c. large surface area
d. a longer time of exposure

Answer: films and deposits

# Unit III



Drying: Objectives, applications & mechanism of drying process, measurements & applications of Equilibrium Moisture content, rate of drying curve. principles, construction, working, uses, merits and demerits of Tray dryer, drum dryer spray dryer, fluidized bed dryer, vacuum dryer, freeze dryer.

Mixing: Objectives, applications & factors affecting mixing, Difference between solid and liquid mixing, mechanism of solid mixing, liquids mixing and semisolids mixing. Principles, Construction, Working, uses, Merits and Demerits of Double cone blender, twin shell blender, ribbon blender, Sigma blade mixer, planetary mixers, Propellers, Turbines, Paddles & Silverson Emulsifier.

## DRYING

Drying involves removal of water or another solvent by evaporation from a solid, semi-solid or liquid by application of heat and finally a liquid free solid product is obtained. In general, drying is accomplished by thermal techniques but non-thermal drying processes such as squeezing wetted sponge, adsorption by desiccant (desiccation) and extraction are also used. In bioproducts like food, grains, and pharmaceuticals like vaccines, the solvent to be removed is almost invariably water.

## OBJECTIVES OF DRYING

The main objectives of drying include to preserve foods and increase their shelf life by reducing the water content and water activity; avoid the need for use of refrigeration systems for transport and storage (expensive); reduce space requirements for storage and transport. In pharmaceutical technology, drying is carried out for one or more of the following reasons:

1. To avoid or eliminate moisture which may lead to corrosion and decrease the product or drug stability.

2. To improve or keep the good properties of a material like granules, e.g. Flowability, compressibility.

## APPLICATIONS OF DRYING

In pharmaceutical technology, drying is carried out for one or more of the following reasons:

1. Preparation of bulk drugs: In the preparation of bulk drugs, drying is the final stage of processing. A few examples are – dried aluminium hydroxide, spray dried lactose and powdered extracts.

2. Preservation of drug products: Drying is necessary in order to avoid deterioration. For examples protection of blood products, skin, tissues and crude drugs from microbial growth.

3. Improved characteristics: Drying produces materials of spherical shape, uniform size, free flowing and enhanced solubility.

4. Improved handling: To reduce the cost of transportation of large volume materials. To make the materials easy or more stable for handling. Drying reduces moisture content.

5. Drying as final step: Drying is the final step in evaporation, filtration, and crystallization.

## MECHANISM OF DRYING PROCESS

Drying does not mean only removal of the moisture but during the process, physical structure as well as the appearance has to be preserved. Drying is basically governed by the principles of transport of heat and mass. When a moist solid is heated to an appropriate temperature, moisture vaporizes at or near the solid surface and the heat required for evaporating moisture from the drying product is supplied by the external drying medium, usually air or a hot gas. Drying is a diffusional process in which the transfer of moisture to the surrounding medium takes place by the evaporation of surface moisture, as soon as some of the surface moisture vaporizes, more moisture is transported from interior of the solid to its surface. This transport of moisture within a solid takes place by a variety of mechanisms depending upon the nature and type of the solid and its state of aggregation. Different types of solids may have to be handled for drying crystalline, granular, beads, powders, sheets, slabs, filter-cakes etc. The mechanism of moisture transport in different solids may be broadly classified into (i) transport by liquid or vapour diffusion (ii) capillary section, and (iii) pressure induced transport. The mechanism that dominates depends on the nature of the solid, its pore structure and the rate of drying. Different mechanisms may come into play and dominate at different stages of drying of the same material.

The following terms are commonly used in Designing of Drying Systems:

Bound Water: Moisture content of a substance which exerts as equilibrium vapour pressure less than of the pure liquid at the same temperature is referred to as bound moisture or bound wated.

Unbound Water: Moisture content of the solid which exerts an equilibrium vapour pressure equal to that of pure liquid at the given temperature is the unbound moisture or unbound water.

Free Moisture Content (FMC): The moisture content of solid in excess of the equilibrium moisture content is referred as free moisture. During drying, only free moisture can be evaporated. The free moisture content of a solid depends upon the vapour concentration in the gas.

Equilibrium Moisture Content (EMC): The moisture contents of solid when it is in equilibrium with given partial pressure of vapour in gas phase is called as equilibrium moisture content. The EMC of a hygroscopic material surrounded at least partially by air is the moisture content at which the material is neither gaining nor losing moisture. The value of the EMC depends on the material and the relative humidity and temperature of the air with which it is in contact.

Critical Moisture Content (CMC): Similarly, the moisture content at which the constant rate drying period ends and the falling rate drying period starts is called critical moisture content. Constant Rate Drying Period: During the constant rate drying period, the moisture evaporated per unit time per unit area of drying surface remains constant.

Falling Rate Drying Period: In falling rate drying period the amount of moisture evaporated per unit time per unit area of drying surface continuously decreases.

Rate Relationships:

Percentage Moisture Content:

$$\% \ Moisture \ content = \frac{Weight \ of \ water \ in \ sample}{Weight \ of \ dry \ sample} \times 100$$

Rate of Drying:

$$Drying\ Rate\ = \frac{Weight\ of\ water\ in\ sample\ (kg)}{Time\ (h) \times Weight\ of\ dry\ solid\ (kg)}$$

Loss on Drying:

$$Loss\ on\ drying\ (\%) = \frac{Mass\ of\ water\ in\ sample\ (kg)}{Total\ mass\ of\ wet\ sample\ (kg)} \times 100$$

## RATE OF DRYING CURVE

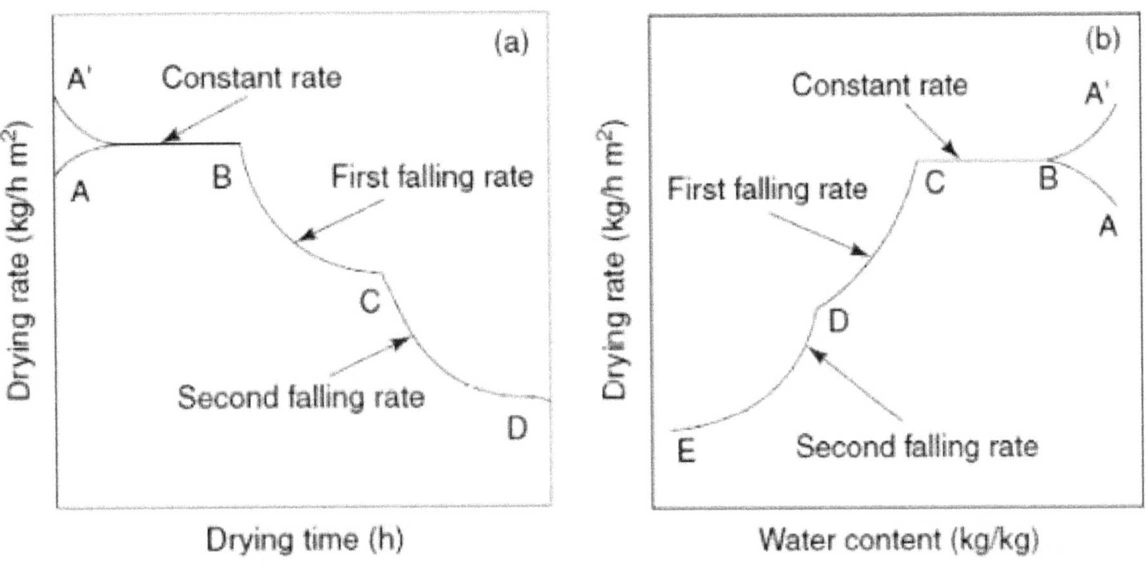


Fig. 1: Typical drying rate curves: (a) drying rate versus drying time and (b) drying rate versus water content

- Drying curve usually plots the drying rate versus drying time or moisture contents.

- Three major stages of drying can be observed in the drying curve.

1. Transient early stage, during which the product is heating up (transient period)

2. Constant rate period, in which moisture is comparatively easy to remove

3. Falling rate period, in which moisture is bound or held within the solid matrix

Critical moisture content: The moisture content at the point when the drying period changes from a constant to a falling rate. The drying behaviours of food materials depend on the porosity, homogeneity, and hygroscopic properties. Hygroscopic food materials enter into the falling rate faster compared to nonhygroscopic food materials.

## CLASSIFICATION OF DRYERS

Drying equipment is classified in different ways, according to following design and operating features. It can be classified based on mode of operation such as batch or continuous, In case of batch dryer the material is loaded in the drying equipment and drying proceeds for a given period of time, whereas, in case of continuous mode the material is continuously added to the dryer and dried material continuously removed. In some cases, vacuum may be used to reduce the drying temperature. Some dryers can handle almost any kind of material, whereas others are severely limited in the style of feed they can accept. Drying processes can also be categorized according to the physical state of the feed such as wet solid, liquid, and slurry. Type of heating system i.e. conduction, convection, radiation is another way of categorizing the drying process. Heat may be supplied by direct contact with hot air at atmospheric pressure, and the water vaporized is removed by the air flowing. Heat may also be supplied indirectly through the wall of the dryer from a hot gas flowing outside the wall or by radiation. Dryers exposing the solids to a hot surface with which the solid is in contact are called adiabatic or direct dryers, while when heat is transferred from an external medium it is known as non-adiabatic or indirect dryers. Dryers heated by dielectric, radiant or microwave energy are also non adiabatic. Some units combine adiabatic and non-adiabatic drying; they are known as direct-indirect dryers. To reduce heat losses most of the commercial dryers are insulated and hot air is recirculated to save energy. Now many designs have energy-saving devices, which recover heat from the exhaust air or automatically control the air humidity. Computer control of dryers in sophisticated driers also results in important savings in energy.

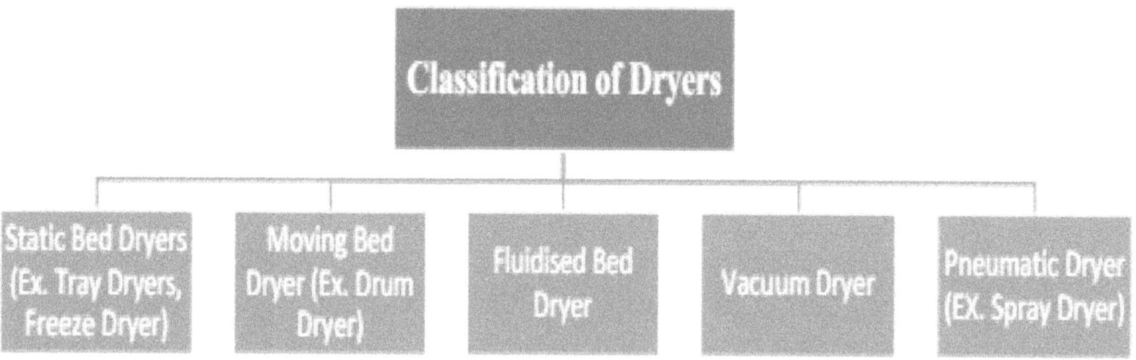


## TRAY DRYER

Principle of Tray Dryer: The basic working principle of this incredible machine is the continuous circulation of hot air. In the tray dryer, moisture is removed from the solids that are placed in the tray by a forced convectional heating. The moist air is removed is partially but in a simultaneous fashion.

Construction of Tray Dryer: Tray Dryer is used for the best drying results in conventional process. It is a double walled cabinet with Single or Two doors. The gap between two walls is filled with high density fibre glass wool insulation material to avoid heat transfer. Doors are provided with gaskets. Stainless steel trays are placed on the movable trolleys. Tray Dryer is provided with control panel board, process timer, Digital temperature controller cum indicator etc. Tray Dryer is available in capacities ranging from 6, 12, 24, 48, 96, 192 trays.

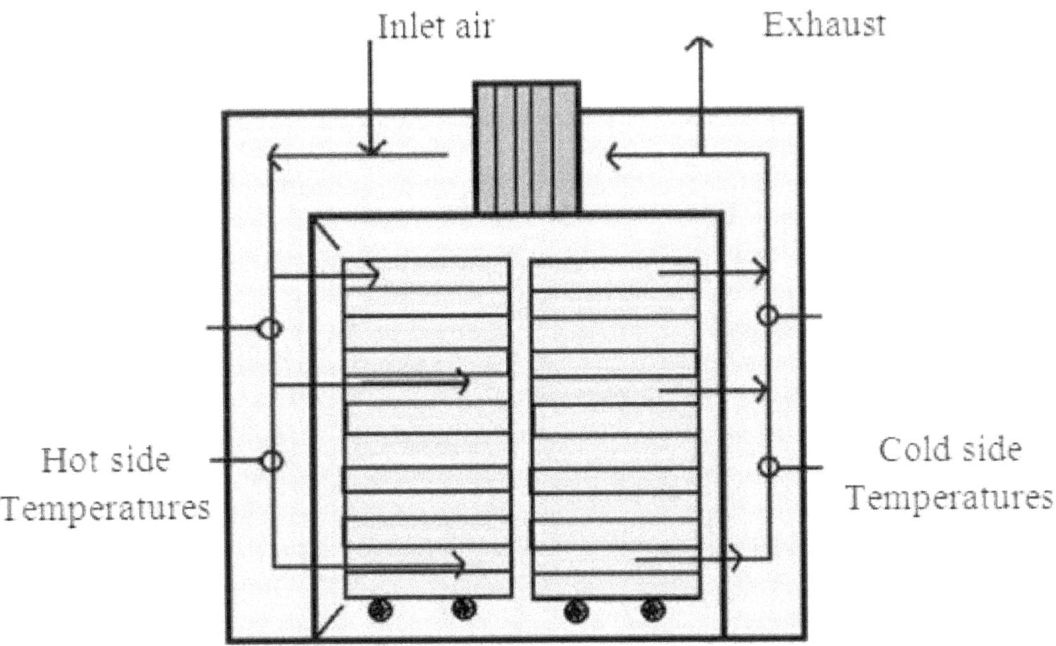



Fig. 2: Tray Dryer

**Working of Tray Dryer:**

• In tray dryer hot air is continuously circulated. Forced convection heating takes place to remove moister from the solids placed in trays.

• Simultaneously the moist air is removed partially.

• Wet solid is loaded in to the trays. Trays are placed in the chamber.

• Fresh air is introduced through in let, which passes through the heaters and gets heated up.

• The hot air is circulated by means of fans at 2 to 5 metre per second.

• Turbulent flow lowers the partial vapour pressure in the atmosphere and also reduces the thickness of the air boundary layer.

• The water is picked up by the air. As the water evaporates from the surface, the water diffuses from the interior of the solids by the capillary action.

• These events occur in a single pass of air. The time of contact is short and amount of water picked up in a single pass is small.

• Therefore, the discharged air to the tune of 80 to 90 % is circulated back through the fans. Only 10 to 20% of fresh air is introduced.

• Moist air is discharged through outlet. Thus, constant temperature and uniform air flow over the materials can be maintained for achieving uniform drying.

• In case of the wet granules as in tablets and capsules drying is continued until the desired moister content is obtained.

• At the end of the drying trays or trucks are pulled out of the chamber and taken to a tray dumping station.

**Advantages of Tray Dryer:**

- Each batch is handled as a separate entity.

- It is more efficient in fuel consumption.

- It is operated batch-wise.

- It is simple to use.

- It provides tendency to over-dry the lower trays.

- It requires little labour costs – merely load and then unload.

**Disadvantages of Tray Dryer:**

- The process is time-consuming.

- It requires extra cost.

- Not suitable for oxidizable and thermolabile substances.

**Pharmaceutical Uses of Tray Dryer:**

- Tray dryer is used in the drying of the sticky materials.

- It is used in the drying of the granular mass or crystalline materials.

- Plastic substances can be dried by the tray dryers.

- Wet mass preparations and pastes can be dried in a tray dryer.

- In the tray dryers the crude drugs, chemicals, powders and tablet granules are also dried to obtain free flowing materials.

- Some types of equipments can be dried in the tray dryers.

**Variants:**

Tray dryer may be operated under vacuum called vacuum tray dryers. Another is Tunnel dryer. In this type, trucks are loaded with wet materials at one end of the tunnel. The tunnel comprised of a number of units, each of which is electro-statically controlled. The solids get dried and the product is discharged at the other end of the tunnel.

## DRUM DRYER OR ROLL DRYER

**Principle of Drum Dryer:**

In drum drying, the heated surface is the envelope of a rotating horizontal metal cylinder. The cylinder is heated by steam condensing inside, at a pressure in the range of 200 to 500 kPa bringing the temperature of the cylinder wall to 120–155°C.

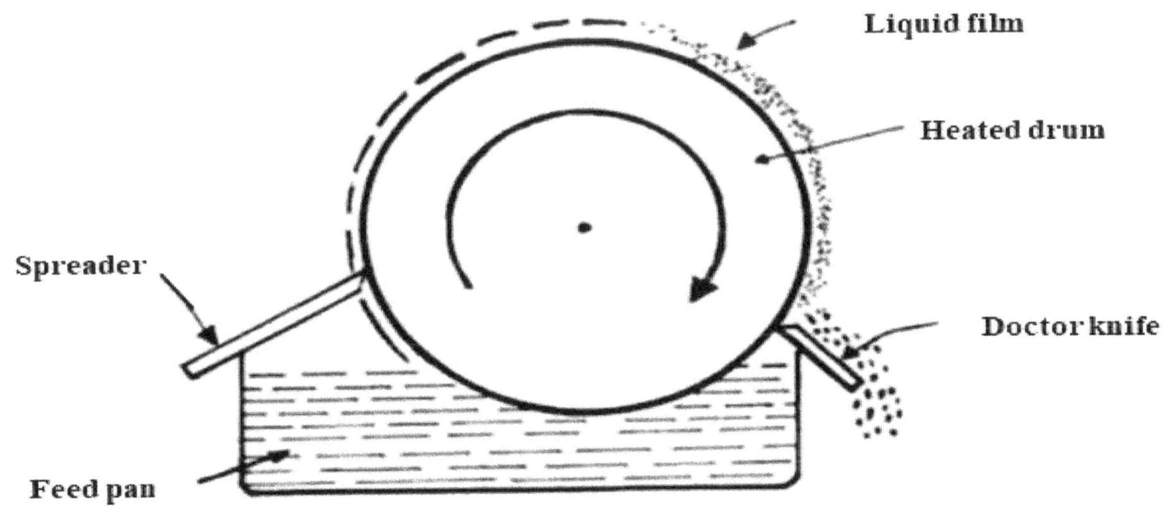



**Fig. : Drum Dryer or Roll Dryer**

## Construction of Drum Dryer or Roll Dryer:

A drum dryer consists of one or two horizontally mounted hollow cylinder(s) or drums of about 0.75-1.5 m in diameter and 2-4 m in length, made of high-grade cast iron or stainless steel, a supporting frame, a product feeding system, a scraper, and auxiliaries. The drum is heated internally by steam, and rotated on its longitudinal axis. The external surface of the drum is polished. Liquid or slurry is placed as feed in a pan. The drum is partially dipped in pan. The spreader is used to spread liquid film evenly on roller. The rotation of the drum adjusted so that all of the liquid is fully vaporized. The drum is rotated continuously. The dried deposits can be scrapped off with the help of doctor knife.

## Working of Drum Dryer or Roll Dryer:

As the drum rotates, the liquid material gets adhere to external surface of drum. The liquid is spread as film on to the surface. The drying of the material is done by process of steam when passed in to the drum. By the mechanism of conduction, the heat gets transferred in to drum and drying process takes place. The material is completely dried during whole process during its revolution. The dried material is scrapped by the knife and that fall in to the bin.

## Advantages of Drum Dryer or Roll Dryer:

- Drying takes place in less time.
- It is suitable for thermosensitive drugs.
- It occupies less space.
- In order to reduce the temperature of drying the drum can be enclosed in a vacuum chamber.
- Rapid drying takes place due to rapid heat and mass transfer.

## Disadvantages of Drum Dryer or Roll Dryer:

- Maintenance cost is high.

- Skilled operations are essential to control thickness of film.

- It is not suitable for less solubility products.

- The operating conditions are critical. It is necessary to introduce careful control on feed rate, film thickness, speed of drum rotation and drum temperature.

**Pharmaceutical Uses of Drum Dryer or Roll Dryer:**

- Drum dryer takes viscous liquids, slurries, suspensions, and pastes as input material to be dried and produces the output as powders or flakes.

- Drum dryers find application majorly in Food & Dairy industry and Chemical &Pharmaceutical Industries for drying various types of pasts and slurries.

Variants:

- A vacuum drum dryer encloses both drum and feed line in a vacuum chamber to facilitates drying of heat sensitive materials.

- In large scale, instead of one drum, two drums are set in parallel, rotating in opposite direction with a common feed inlet.

## SPRAY DRYER

Principle of Spray Dryer: Spray drying is an industrial process for dehydration of a liquid feed containing dissolved and/or dispersed solids, by transforming that liquid into a spray of small droplets and exposing these droplets to a flow of hot air.

**Construction of Spray Dryer:**

A spray dryer is composed of a feed pump, atomizer, air heating unit, air dispenser, drying chamber (diameter of the drying chamber ranges between 2.5 to 9.0 m and height is 25 m or more) and also systems for exhaust air cleansing and also powder recovery/separator. The spray disk atomizer is about 300 millimetres in diameter and rotates at a speed of 3,000 to 50,000 revolutions per minutes. In the spray dryer the liquid to be dried is atomised into the good droplets, that are tossed radially into a relocating stream of warm gas.

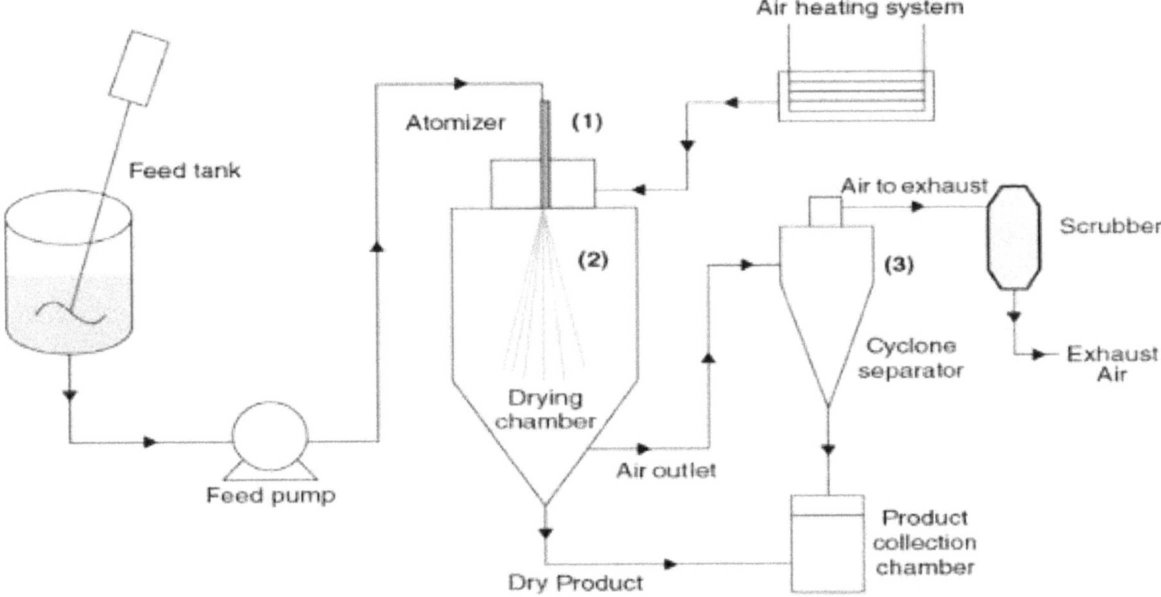


Fig: Spray Dryer

**Working of Spray Dryer:**

A spray dryer takes a liquid stream and separates the solute or suspension as a solid and the solvent into a vapor. The solid is usually collected in a drum or cyclone. The liquid input stream is sprayed through a nozzle into a hot vapor stream and vaporized. Solids form as moisture quickly leaves the droplets.

The three stages that occur in a spray dryer before drying is accomplished include:

- Atomization

- Spray-air mixing and moisture evaporation.

- Dry product separation from the exit air

The nature of the final product obtained after drying in a spray dryer depends on;

- The design and operation of the spray dryer.

- The physicochemical properties of the feed.

**Advantages of Spray Drying:**

- Product quality and properties can be effectively controlled and maintained through the entire drying operation.

- Thermolabile products/ pharmaceuticals can be dried at atmospheric pressure and low temperature.

- Spray dryer permits high- tonnage production in continuous operation adaptable to conventional PLC control (Programmable Logic Controller) and it is relatively simple to operate.

- Feedstock in solution, slurry, emulsion, paste, and melt form can be dried if pumpable.

- Corrosion problem is minimal and the selection of materials of construction of spray dryer is simplified since the dried material comes in contact with the equipment surfaces in an anhydrous condition.

• Spray dryer produces dry powder particles of controllable particle size, shape, form, moisture content, and other specific properties irrespective of dryer capacity and heat sensitivity.

• Spray dryer handles a wide range of production rates and provides extensive flexibility in its design that is product specification are readily met through the selection of appropriate spray dryer design and its operation from a wide range of available design.

• It is energy-intensive equipment because specific heat of evaporation can be supplied in a short time. The temperature difference across the drying chamber is relatively small and an appreciable amount of heat is lost with exhaust air.

**Disadvantages of Spray Drying:**

• Spray dryer is bulky and also expensive to install.

• It is difficult to clean after use.

• It has a low thermal efficiency that is a lot of heat is wasted during operation.

• Solid materials cannot be dried using spray dryers.

• Product degradation or fire hazard may result from product deposit on the drying chamber.

**Pharmaceutical Uses of Spray Dryer:**

• Spray dryer is used in drying pharmaceuticals like penicillin, blood products, enzymes, vaccines, etc.

• It is used in the production of excipients and co-processed excipients with increased flowability, compatibility, and tablet disintegration.

• To improve drug compressibility and reduce capping tendencies in crystals.

• It is equally used in the preparation of matrix microcapsule containing drug substances and a biodegradable polymer in order to obtain controlled drug release formulation.

• It is employed in enhancing solubility and dissolution rates of poorly soluble drugs by formation of pharmaceutical complexes or via the development of solid dispersion thus increasing bioavailability.

• It is used in the production of dry powder formulation/dry powder aerosol and thermolabile materials.

• Apart from its applications in the pharmaceutical industries, spray dryers also find use in; Chemical industries, Ceramic industries, Food industries, etc.

• Biochemical industries e.g. algae, fodder antibiotics, yeast extracts, enzymes, etc.

• Environmental pollution control e.g. flue gas desulfurization, black liquor from papermaking etc.

**Variants:**

• Spray dryer can be constructed in such a way as to suit sterile products.

• It can be operated under closed conditions to recover solvents.

• It can be operated under oxygen free environment.

• The same equipment can be used for spray congealing.

• It is useful for encapsulation (coating) of solid and liquid particles.

## FLUIDIZED BED DRYER (FBD)

### Principle of Fluidized Bed Dryer (FBD):

The equipment works on a principle of fluidization of the feed materials. In fluidization process, hot air is introduced at high pressure through a perforated bed of moist solid particulate. The wet solids are lifted from the bottom and suspended in a stream of air (fluidized state).

### Construction of Fluidized Bed Dryer (FBD):

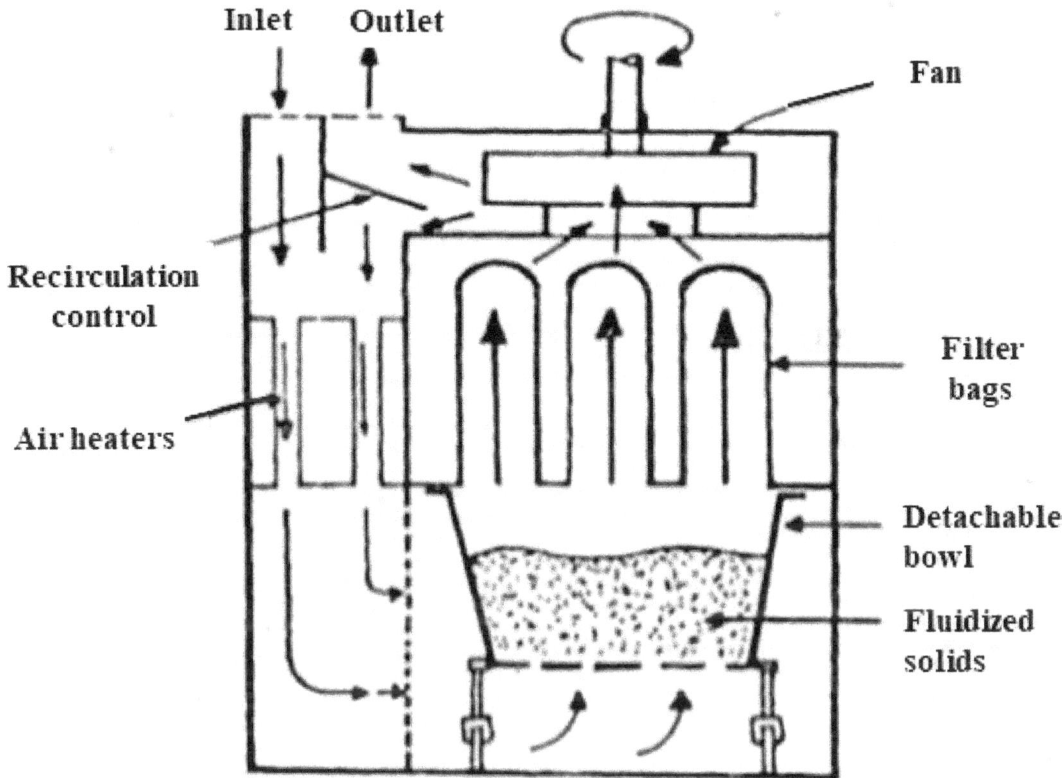


Fig. : Fluidized Bed Dryer

• The dryer is made up of stainless steel or plastic.

• A detachable bowel is placed at the bottom of the dryer, which is used for charging and discharging.

• The bowel has a perforated bottom with a wire mesh support for placing materials to be dried.

• A fan is mounted in the upper part for circulating hot air.

• Fresh air inlet, prefilter and heat exchanger are connected serially to heat the air to the required temperature.

• The temperature of hot air and exit air are monitored.

• Bag filters are placed above the drying bowl for the recovery of fines.

### Working of Fluidized Bed Dryer:

• The wet granules to be dried are placed in a detachable bowl. The bowl is inserted in the drier.

- Fresh air can pass trough a prefilter, which is then heated when passing trough a heat exchanger.

- Hot air flows through the bottom of the bowl.

- At the same time, fan start to rotate.

- The air speed increases gradually.

- When the velocity of air is greater than the sedimentation rate of the granules, the granules remain suspended in the gas stream.

- After specific time, a pressure point is reached in which the friction drag on a particle is equal to the force of gravity.

- The granules rise in the container due to high gas velocity of 1.5 to 7.5 meter per minute and then fall back. This state is known as fluidized state.

- The gas surround to each granule do dry them completely.

- The air comes out of the dryer passing through the filters in the bag.

- The entrained particles remain adhered to the interior surface of bags.

- Periodically bags are shaken to remove entrained particles.

**Advantages of Fluidized Bed Dryer:**

- It takes less time to complete drying as compared to other dryer.

- Drying is achieved at constant rate.

- Handling time is also short.

- It is available at different sizes with different drying capacity.

- The equipment is simple and less labour cost required.

- More thermal efficiency.

- Drying capacity is more than other dryer.

- It facilitates the drying of thermolabile substances since the contact time of drying is short.

- It is batch type or continuous type process.

**Disadvantages of Fluidized Bed Dryer:**

- Many organic powders develop electrostatic charge during drying. To avoid this efficient electrical grounding of the dryer is essential.

- Chances of attrition of some materials resulting in production of fines.

**Pharmaceutical applications of Fluidized Bed Dryer:**

- It is used for drying of granules in the production of tablets.

- It is used for coating of granules.

- It can be used for three operations such as mixing, granulation and drying.

**Variants:**

Plug flow dryer: It is a rectangular fluid bed dryer having different compartments for fluidisation. The material is made to move from inlet through different compartments to outlet. Different drying condition can be maintained in the compartments. Often the last compartment is fluidised with cold gas to cool the solids before discharge.

## VACUUM DRYER

Principle of Vacuum Dryer: Vacuum drying is generally used for the drying of substances which are hygroscopic and heat sensitive, and is based on the principle of creating a vacuum to decrease the chamber pressure below the vapour pressure of the water, causing it to boil. Hence, water evaporates faster. The heat transfer becomes, i.e., rate of drying enhances substantially.

**Construction of Vacuum Dryer:**

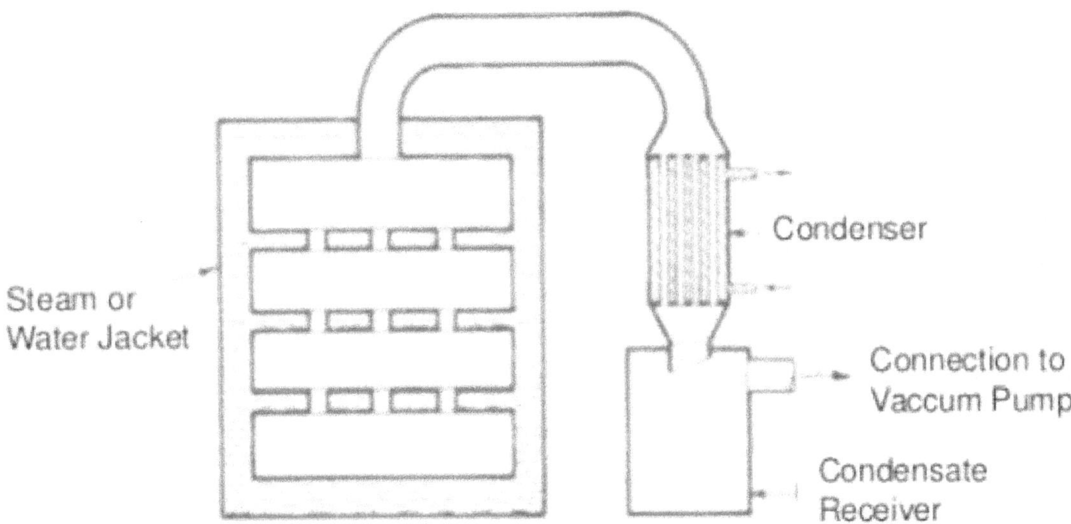


Fig. : Vacuum Dryer

The oven is divided into hollow trays which increases the surface area for heat conduction. The oven door is locked air tight and is connected to vacuum pump to reduce the pressure. The materials to be dried are kept on the trays inside the vacuum dryer and pressure is reduced by means of vacuum pump. The enclosed space (approximately 1.5 meter cube ) is divided in to a number of portions by means of 20 hollow shelves, which are part of the jacket. These shelves provide larger surface area (about 45 to 50 meter square) for conduction of heat. Over the shelves, metal trays are placed for keeping the material. The oven door can be locked tightly to give an air tight seal. The oven is connected to a vacuum pump by placing condenser in between.

**Working of Vacuum Dryer:**

• The tray that are present in the dryer are used to dry the material that are placed in the shelves and the pressure is reduced to 30 to 60 Kps by vacuum pump.

• The door closes firmly and steam passes through the jacket space and the shelves.

• So the heat transfer is carried out by the conduction mechanism.

• When evaporating under vacuum, the water is evaporated from the material at 25 - 30°C.

- The vapour goes to the condenser.

- After drying vacuum line is disconnected.

- Then the materials are collected from the tray.

**Advantages of Vacuum Dryer:**

- Material handling is easy.

- Hollow shelves which are electrically heated can be used.

- It provides large surface area. So the heat can be easily transfer through the body of the dryer and last drying action takes place.

- Hot water can be supplied through the dryer, which help in drying process at the desired temperature.

**Disadvantages of Vacuum Dryer:**

- Dryer is a batch type process.

- It has low efficiency.

- It is more expensive.

- Labour cost is too high.

- Needs high maintenance.

- There is a danger of overheating due to vacuum.

**Uses of Vacuum Dryer:**

Vacuum dryer can be used for drying of following:

- Heat sensitive materials, which undergo decomposition.

- Dusty and hygroscopic material.

- Drugs containing toxic solvents. These can be separated in to closed containers.

- Feed containing valuable solvents. These are recovered by condensation.

- Drugs which are required as porous end products.

- Friable dry extracts.

## FREEZE DRYER

Principle of Freeze Dryer: Freeze drying or lyophilisation is a drying process used to convert solutions or suspensions of labile materials into solids of sufficient stability for distribution and storage. The fundamental principle in freeze-drying is sublimation, the shift from a solid directly into a gas. Just like evaporation, sublimation occurs when a molecule gains enough energy to break free from the molecules around it. Drying is achieved by subjecting the materials to temperature and pressures below the triple point.

**Construction of Freeze Dryer:**

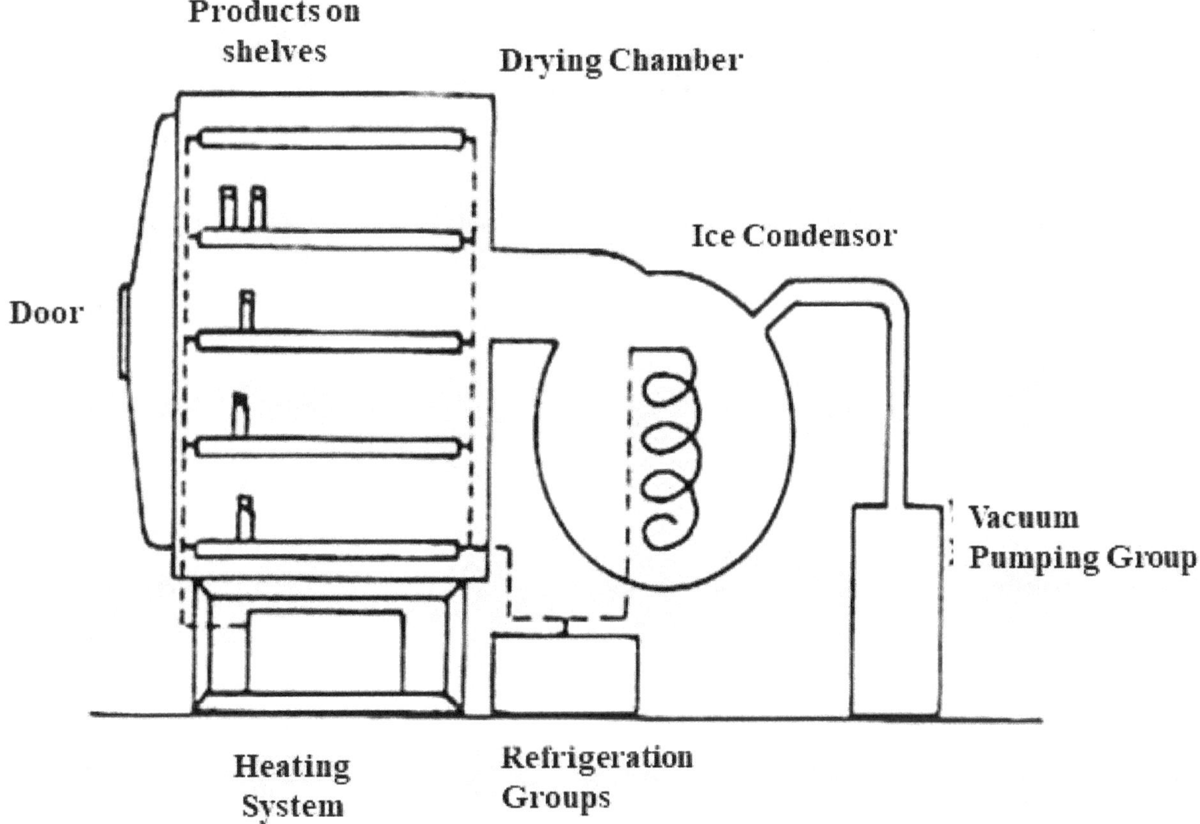


Fig. : Freeze Dryer

The construction of freeze dryer is shown in figure.

It consists of

- Drying chamber in which trays are loaded.

- Heat supply in radiation source, heating coils.

- Vapour condensing or adsorption system.

- Vacuum pump or stream ejector or both.

The chamber for vacuum drying is generally designed for batch operation. It consists of shelves for keeping the material. The distance between subliming and condenser must be less than the mean path of molecules. This increases the rate of drying. The condenser consists of relatively large surface cooled by solid carbon dioxide slurred with acetone or ethanol. The temperature of condenser must be much lower than evaporated surface of frozen substance. In order to maintain this condition, the condenser surface is cleaned repeatedly.

**Working of Freeze Dryer:**

The following steps are involved in the working of freeze dryer

Pretreatment includes any method of treating the product prior to freezing. This may include concentrating the product, formulation revision (i.e., addition of components to increase stability, preserve appearance, and/or improve processing), decreasing a high-vaporpressure solvent, or increasing the surface area. This reduces the actual drying by 8 to 10 times. The final product becomes more porous.

During pre-freezing, the freeze dryer works as a freezer in that no vacuum is applied. Vials, ampoules or bottle in which the aqueous solutions are packed or frozen in cold shelves (about -50°C). During this stage, cabinet is maintained at low temperature and atmospheric pressure. The normal cooling rate is about 1 to 3 kelvin per minute so that large ice crystals with relatively large holes are formed on sublimation of ice. This is also responsible for giving a porous product.

Primary drying (sublimation of ice under vacuum): In this step, the material to be dried is spread as much large surface as possible for sublimation. The temperature and pressure should be below the triple point of water, i.e., 0.0098°C and 0.533 Kilopascal, (4.58 mmHg) for the sublimation, when water alone is present. When a solution of solid is dried, the depression of freezing point of water occurs. Hence it is essential that the temperature be brought bellow the eutectic point. The pressure and temperature at which the frozen solid vaporises without conversion to a liquid is referred to as the eutectic point. Depending on the drug substance dissolved in water, the eutectic point is determined. The usual range is from -10°C to 30°C. The condition of 1 to 8 K bellow eutectic point is sufficient. Vacuum is applied to the tune of about 3 mmHg (0.4 Kilopascals) on the frozen sample. The temperature is linearly increased to about 30°C in a span of 2 hours.

Heat (about 2900 Kilojoules per kg) is supplied which transfers as latent heat and ice sublimes directly into vapour state. The heat controls the movement of ice layer inwards. It has to be controlled in such a manner so as to get highest possible water vapour at ice surface without melting the material. As soon as the vapour molecules are formed, these are removed. The overall driving force is the temperature difference (also vapour pressure difference) between evaporating surface and condenser. As the drying proceeds, the thickness of frozen layer decreases and thickness of partially dried solids increases. Primary drying stage removes easily removable moisture. During this stage, about 98% to 99% water is removed. Till traces of moisture is present in the sample.

Secondary drying (removal of residual moisture under high vacuum): During this stage traces of moisture is removed. The temperature of solid is raised to as high as 50 to 60°C, but vacuum is lowered bellow that is used in primary drying (50 mmHg). The rate of drying is very low and it takes about 10 to 20 hours.

Primary drying is a top-down process with a well-defined sublimation front moving through the product as it dries. Above the ice surface interface is dried product, or "cake"; below the interface is product with ice crystals still remaining to be sublimed. After primary freeze-drying is complete and all ice has sublimed, in the area where ice has been removed, desorption of water from the cake occurs. This process is called secondary drying and has started in the primary drying phase. The product appears to be dry but the residual moisture content may be as high as 7–8%. Packing is done by replacing vacuum with inert gas, bottles and vials are closed.

**Advantages of Freeze Dryer:**

- It is suitable for drying heat sensitive products

- Freeze dried products is porous and easy to dehydrated and instantly dissolved.

- Drying takes place at very low temperature, so that enzyme action is inhibited and chemical decomposition, particularly hydrolysis, is minimized.

- Denaturation of protein does not occur.

- Loss of volatile material is less.

- Sterility can be maintained.

**Disadvantages of Freeze Dryer:**

- The process is very slow.

- Expensive process.

- It is not a general method of drying, but it is limited to certain type of valuable products that cannot be dried by any other means.

- The period of drying is high.

- The product is prone to oxidation, due to the high porosity and large surface area. Therefore, the product must be vacuum packed or with an inert gas or in container.

**Uses of Freeze Dryer:**

- It is used in production of injection, solutions, and suspension.

- It is also used for production of blood plasma and its fractionated products, bacterial and viral cultures, antibiotics and plant extracts, steroids, vitamins and enzymes.

- Food product like mushroom, meat products can be dried by this method.

- Coffee and tea concentrates and citrus fruit juices are also dried by this method.

- Pharmaceutical companies often use freeze-drying to increase the shelf life of products, such as vaccines and other injectable.

- By removing the water from the material and sealing the material in a vial, the material can be easily stored, shipped and later reconstituted to its original form for injection.

**MIXING**

**OBJECTIVES OF MIXING**

The main objective of this mixing is to produce a bulk mixture which when divide into different doses, every unit of divided doses must contain the correct proportion of each ingredient. It is critical process because the quality of the final product and its attributes are derived by the quality of the mixing.

**APPLICATIONS OF MIXING**

• Mixing is an intermediate step in production of tablet or capsule. Mixing of powders in different proportion prior to granulation or tableting.

• Dry mixing of materials for direct compression in to tablets.

• Dry mixing of powder or composites powders in capsule and insufflations respectively.

• Blending of powders are also important in preparation of cosmetic products such as facial powder or dental powder.

• In case of potent drugs where dose is low, mixing is critical factor. Otherwise it will affect content uniformity of tablet.

**FACTORS AFFECTING MIXING**

These factors include the following:

1. Nature of product: For effective mixing particle surface should be smooth.

2. Particle size: It is easier to mix powder of same particle size. Increasing the difference in particle size will lead to segregation.

3. Particle shape: Particle should be spherical in shape to get a uniform mixture.

4. Particle charge: some particle due to electrostatic charge exerts attractive force which leads to separation.

5. Proportion of material: It is easier to mix powders if available in same quantities.

6. Relative density: If the components have a different density, the denser material will sink through lighter material.

7. Viscosity: An increase in viscosity reduces the extent of mixing.

8. Surface tension of liquids: High surface tension reduces the extension of mixing.

9. Temperature: Temperature also affects the mixing because viscosity changes with increase in temperature.

10. Mixture volume: Mixing efficiency depends on mixture volume.

11. Agitator type: The shape, size, location and type of agitator also affect affects the degree of mixing.

12. Speed/rpm of the impeller: Mixing at less rpm is more homogenous than at higher rpm.

13. Mixing time: Mixing time is also very important for appropriate mixing

**DIFFERENCE BETWEEN SOLID AND LIQUID MIXING**

The difference between solid and liquid mixing has been shown in Table below.

| Solid Mixing | Liquids Mixing |
|---|---|
| In solid mixing two or more substances are intermingled by continuous movement of particles. | This is achieved by mixing elements of suitable shape to act as impeller to produce appropriate flow pattern in mixing vessel. |
| This is used for mixing of dry powders. | This is used in preparation of emulsion, suspension and mixtures. |
| Large sample size is required. | Small sample size is sufficient. |
| High power required for mixing. | Less power required for mixing. |

## MECHANISM OF MIXING

Mechanism of Solid Mixing: Mechanism in involved in solid mixing are

Convective mixing, In which group of particles move from one position to another. It also referred to as macromixing.

Shear mixing, In this, shearing force is created within the mass of material by the use of a stirring arm or a burst of air.

Diffusive mixing, During this mixing, gravitational forces cause the upper layers of material to slip and random motion of individual particles take place on newly developed surfaces. Also known as micro mixing.

### Mechanism of Liquid Mixing:

Mechanism of liquid mixing are

Bulk transport: It is the movement of large portion of material from one location to another location. The movement is done by rotating blades or paddles.

Turbulent mixing: In this mixing is due to turbulence. Turbulence is a function of velocity gradient between two adjacent layers of a liquid.

Laminar mixing/Streamline mixing: When two dissimilar liquid are mixed through a laminar flow, the shear that is generated stretches the interface between them. In this mechanism layers folds on themselves. As a result, the number of layers, and therefore interfacial area between them, increases exponentially with time.

Molecular diffusion: The mechanism responsible for mixing at molecular level is the diffusion resulting from thermal movement of molecules. Primary mechanism responsible for mixing at the molecular level is the thermal motion of molecules. Governed by Fick's fist law of diffusion,

$$dm/dt = - DA \, dc/dx$$

Where,

$dm/dt$ – rate of transport of mass across a surface area

$D$ – Diffusion Co-efficient

$A$ – Area across which diffusion is occurring

$dc/dx$ – Concentration gradient

**Mechanisms of Semi-Solid Mixing:**

The mechanisms involved in mixing semi solids depend on the character of the material which may show considerable variation. Many semi solids form neutral mixtures having no tendency to segregate although sedimentation may occur. Three most commonly used semi solid mixers are

(a) Sigma blade mixer – Contains two blades which operate in a mixing vessel which has a double trough shape, the blades moving at different speeds towards each other. Used for products like granulation masses and ointments.

(b) Triple-roller mill – The differential speed and narrow clearance between the roller develop high shear over small volumes of material. The roller mills are generally used to grind and complete the homogeneity of ointments.

(c) Planetary mixers – it utilizes a mixing arm rotating about its own axis and also about a common axis usually the centre of the mixing wheel. The blades provide the kneading action, while the narrow passage between the blades and the wall of the can provides shear.

## MIXER SELECTION

Factors to be taken into consideration while selecting a mixing equipment include,

(a) Physical properties of materials to be mixed such as density, viscosity and miscibility

(b) Economic considerations – operating efficiency, cost and maintenance

One of the first things to determine is if the process is intended to be a batch or a continuous process, each of which can have its advantages and drawbacks depending on the load to be used. Size is considered keeping in mind the optimal working volume, fill level and residence time. The optimal working volume would depend on the construction of the mixer. It generally lies between 50 to 70 percent of the maximum. Similarly, too much of fill would lead to low mixing and hence fill level becomes important. Residence time which is defined as the amount of time ingredients are in the mixer and is a particularly important determinant of the size of a continuous mixer. Choice of agitators determines the efficiency in breaking up lumps/agglomerates and serves to add shear aiding the final dispersion. A brief table showing various agitator types and their respective uses in shown below:

1.Ribbon - For Powders, granules, some slurries, mainly free flowing

2. Paddle - For Powders, granules, some slurries, free flowing, light pastes

3. Sigma - For Sticky materials, thick pastes and slurries

## MIXING INDICES

The selection of a mixer depends on the mixing index or degree of mixing. Mixing index involves the comparison of standard deviation of sample of a mixer under study with estimated standard deviation of a completely random mixture.

Mixing index is expressed by Lacey. Two of them are

$$Mixing\ index, M = \frac{Standard\ deviation\ of\ random\ blend}{Standard\ deviation\ of\ the\ sample\ blend} = \frac{\sigma_R}{\sigma}$$

$$Mixing\ index, M = \frac{\sigma_0 - \sigma}{\sigma_0 - \sigma_R}$$

Where $\sigma_0$ = *standard deviation of unmixed powde*. The ratio will be less than 1. The higher the M value, the greater the homogeneity. The above equations are used to determine homogeneity in a mixture depending on the objectives at hand. The selection of a particular equation is essential when the mechanism of mixing is being results of practical use can be achieved by using statistical analysis.

The differences may indicate poor or inadequate sampling, inappropriate mixing operation, improper handling of the powder sample, unsuitably of the mixer, operational condition etc. Before mixing has begun, the material in the mixer exists in two layers, one of which contains no tracer material and one of which is tracer only. Under these conditions, the standard deviation at zero time $\sigma_0$ may be expressed as:

$$\sigma_0 = \sqrt{a(1-a)}$$

Where $a$ = *overall fraction of tracer in the mixture.*

**DOUBLE CONE BLENDER**

**Principles of Double Cone Blender:**

The Double Cone Blenders design is most often used for the intimate dry blending of free flowing solids. The solids being blended in these units can vary in bulk density and in percentage of the total mixture. Materials being blended are constantly being intermixed as the Double Cone rotates. Normal cycle times are typically in the range of 10 minutes; however, they can be less depending on the difficulty of blending. The slant double cone design eliminates dead spots which occasionally occur in conventional double cone mixer. The conical shape at both end enables uniform mixing and easy discharge.

**Construction of Double Cone Blender:**

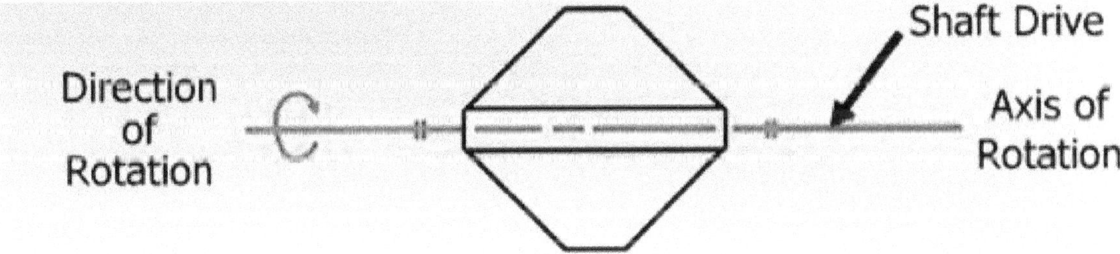


Fig. : Double Cone Blender

- The conical shape at both ends enables uniform mixing and easy discharge.

- The cone is statically balanced which protects the gear box and motor from any excessive load.

- Powder is loaded into the cone through a wide opening and discharged through a butterfly or a Slide valve.

- Depending upon the characteristic of the product, paddle type baffles can be provided on the shaft.

- Flame proof electricals can be provided as optional.

- 'Slant' design (off centre) CLIN CONE BLENDER are also used.

- Dust free bin charging system ensures minimum material handling.

- Mixing, uniform blending and de-agglomeration.

**Working of Double Cone Blender:**

- Double Cone Blenders are most often used for dry blending of free flowing solids. The solids being blended in these units can vary in bulk density and in percentage of the total mixture.

- Materials being blended are constantly being intermixed as the Double Cone rotates.

**Uses of Double Cone Blender:**

- Double cone blender is used to produce homogeneous solid-solid mixture.

- It is used for effective mixing of powder and granules.

- The double cone blender machine is of canonical shape at both ends that provide uniform mixing of granules in bulk.

**Merits of Double Cone Blender:**

- If fragile granules are to be blended, double cone blender is suitable because of minimum attrition.

- They handle large capacities.

- Easy to clean, load, and unload.

- This equipment requires minimum maintenance.

**Demerits of Double Cone Blender:**

- Double cone blender needs high head space for installation.

- It is not suitable for fine particulate system or ingredients of large difference in particle size distribution, because not enough shear is applied.

- If powders are free flowing, serial dilution is required for the addition of low dose active ingredients.

**TWIN SHELL BLENDER OR V CONE BLENDER**

**Principle of Twin Shell Blender:**

The mixing occurs due to tumbling motion.

**Construction of Twin Shell Blender:**

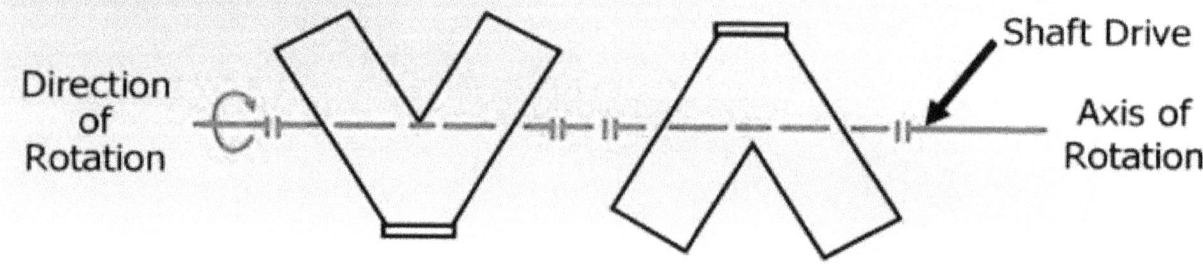

Fig. : Twin Shell Blender

• Twin shell blenders have two connected blending shells that are connected to form a V-shape. Intensifier bars are designed to break up clumps of solids while the product is separated in the two ends of the V (when the twin shell blender is upside down).

• It consists of horizontal shaft rotated about an axis causing the particles within the mixer to tumble over each other onto the mixture surface.

• The charging of materials into the V-Blender is through either of the two ends.

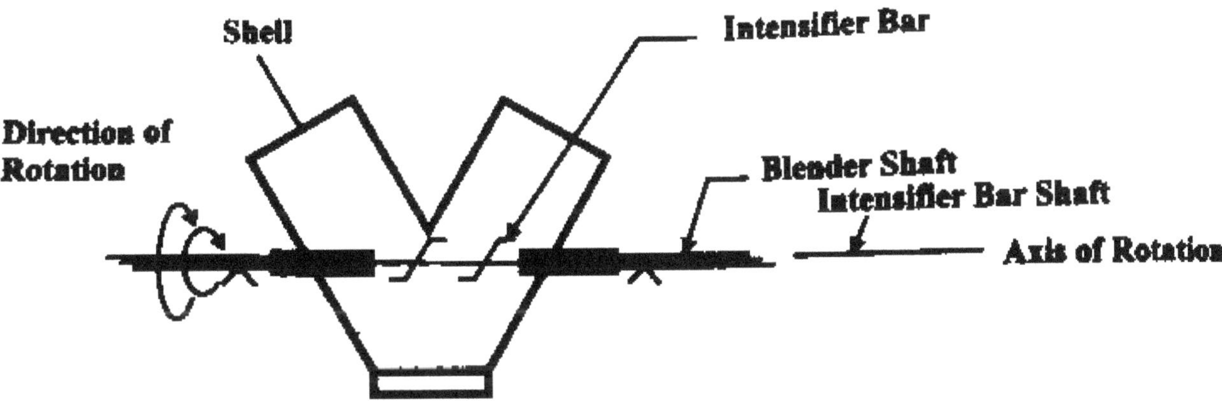


Fig. : V Blender with Intensifier Bar

• Twin shell blenders have two connected blending shells that are connected to form a V-shape. Intensifier bars are designed to break up clumps of solids while the product is separated in the two ends of the V (when the twin shell blender is upside down).

• It consists of horizontal shaft rotated about an axis causing the particles within the mixer to tumble over each other onto the mixture surface.

• The charging of materials into the V-Blender is through either of the two ends.

• Batches from 20 kg to 1 tonne can be loaded for mixing depending upon the size of the equipments.

Working of Twin Shell Blender:

• The V-Blender (also known as a twin shell blender) is one of the most commonly used tumbling blenders.

• The material is loaded into the blender.

• As the V-blender tumbles, the material continuously splits and recombines, with the mixing occurring as the material free-falls randomly inside the vessel.

• Tumble blenders rely upon the action of gravity to cause the powder to cascade within a rotating vessel.

• The recommended filled-up volume for the V-Blender is 50 to 60% of the total blender volume.

• The product is collected from the bottom of V.

• Normal blend times are typically in the range of 5 to 15 minutes depending on the properties of materials to be blended.

**Marist of Twin Shell Blender or V Cone Blender:**

**V Cone Blender without Baffle-**

- Have large capacities

- Easy handling

- Minimum maintenance

**V Cone Blender with Baffle-**

- Wet and dry mixing

- High shearing force

- Serial dilution is not required

**Uses of Twin Shell Blender or V Cone Blender:**

- V blenders are used for dry mixing.

- It provides efficient blending in short time.

- This blender is often used for pharmaceuticals. But not suitable for very soft powders or granules.

- V blenders are generally used for the food products, milk products, dry flavors, pesticides and herbicides, animal feed, spice blends, baby foods and cosmetics.

**RIBBON BLENDER**

**Principle of Ribbon Blender:**

- The mechanism of mixing is shear which is transferred by moving blades (ribbon shaped) in a fixed (non-movable) shell.

- Convective mixing is the macro movement of large portions of the solids.

- Convection mixing occurs when the solids are turned over along the horizontal axis of the agitator assembly.

- High shear rates are effective in breaking lumps and aggregates. An equilibrium state of mixing can be achieved.

**Construction of Ribbon Blender:**

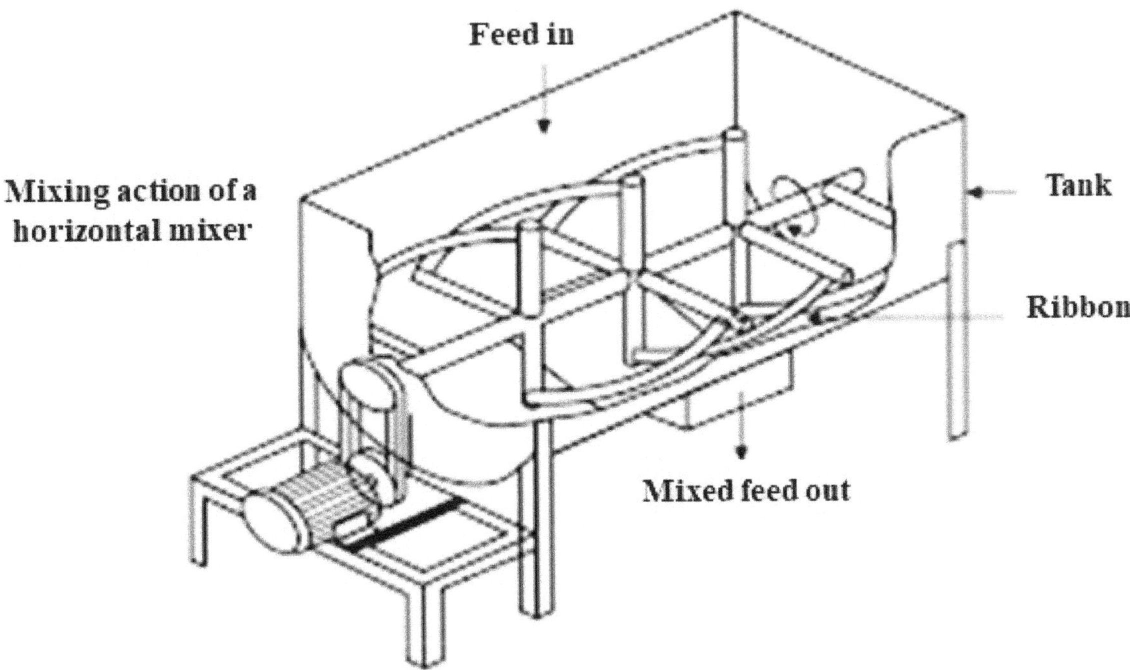


Fig. : Ribbon Blender

• A ribbon blender consists of a U-shaped horizontal trough (shell) containing a double helical ribbon agitator that rotates within.

• The agitator's shaft is positioned in the centre of the trough and has welded spokes on which the helical ribbons (also known as spirals) are welded.

• The blades have both right- and left-hand twists.

• The blades are connected to a fixed speed drive.

• The ribbon blender is top loading with a bottom discharge port.

• The trough can be closed with a lid.

**Working of Ribbon Blender:**

• Different powders are introduced from the top of the trough.

• The outer ribbon of agitator moves the material from the ends to centre while the inner ribbon moves the material from the centre to end.

• Through the fixed speed drive, ribbons are allowed to rotate.

• Radial movement is achieved because of the rotational motion of the ribbons.

• The difference in the peripheral speeds of the outer and inner ribbon results in axial movement, homogenous blending is achieved in short time.

• The powders are lifted by a centrally located vertical screw and allowed to cascade to the bottom of the container (tumbling action).

• The counter acting blades set up high shear fend are effective in breaking up lumps or aggregates.

- Helical blades move the powders from one end to another.

- The blend is discharged from the bottom opening.

**Merits of Ribbon Blender:**

- The Ribbon mixer has price savings as a result of the thermal treatment is accomplished among a similar time and liner being utilized for combining step.

- Correct management of batch thermal treatment time. Low opportunity cost because the drying is accomplished within the same time and vessel getting used for transferring and combining.

- One of the most important benefits of using a ribbon mixer for any industrial project is that it blends nearly any material completely with nearly no flaws.

- This comes in handy for producing any material that must be mixed well like paint, concrete, and foods.

- These mixers are usually utilized in bakeries that require to blend large amounts of ingredients at only once. They will additionally mix materials fairly quickly, although the ribbons themselves inch.

- Finally, the common ribbon mixer features a very large trough, thus it's ideal for big projects.

- High shear is also applied by exploitation perforated baffles that create a rubbing and breakdown aggregates. Headroom needs less aera.

- Protect the motor and ribbon mixer from overload.

- Once the load is just too massive to the drum and rotates, the operating liquid is ejected from the liquid plug to separate the operating machine and therefore the load, in order that the motor and instrumentality won't be broken once beginning and overloading.

- The speed distinction caused by the impact is going to be mitigated by coupling.

**Demerits of Ribbon Blender:**

- The hydraulic mechanical device isn't loaded with the electrical converter generally, and may not modify the rotating speed of the ribbon mixer effectively, because the loading of hydraulic couplings is simple to make multiple transfer mechanical energy, leading to power consumption, thus it can't improve the start-up performance of the ribbon mixer.

- It is a poor mixer as a result of the movement of particles is two dimensional.

- Shearing action is a smaller amount than in planetary mixer.

- It has a set speed drive.

- Rate of mixing is greater at the surface, causing local differences in mixture composition.

- Attrition of particles may occur at the wall due to the higher forces present there.

- Prone to dead spots, especially near the discharge valve, and along the central axis.

- There aren't many downsides to using a ribbon mixer to combine ingredients. the sole major disadvantage that you simply may realize is that a ribbon mixer takes large amounts of power to work properly, thus you must positively detain mind your energy desires if you're about to use one in every of these machines.

**Uses of Ribbon Blender:**

- Ribbon blender is used to mix finely divided solids, wet solid mass, sticky and plastic solids.

- Uniform size and density material can be easily mixed.

- It is used for liquid-solid and solid-solid mixing.

## SIGMA BLADE MIXER

Principle of Sigma Blade Mixer:

- The mechanism of mixing is shearing.

- The inter meshing of sigma shaped blades creates high shear and kneading actions.

- The mixing action is a combination of bulk movement, shearing, stretching, folding, dividing, and recombining as the material is pulled and squeezed against blades, saddle, and side walls.

- This is used for high viscosity material.

**Construction of Sigma Blade Mixer:**

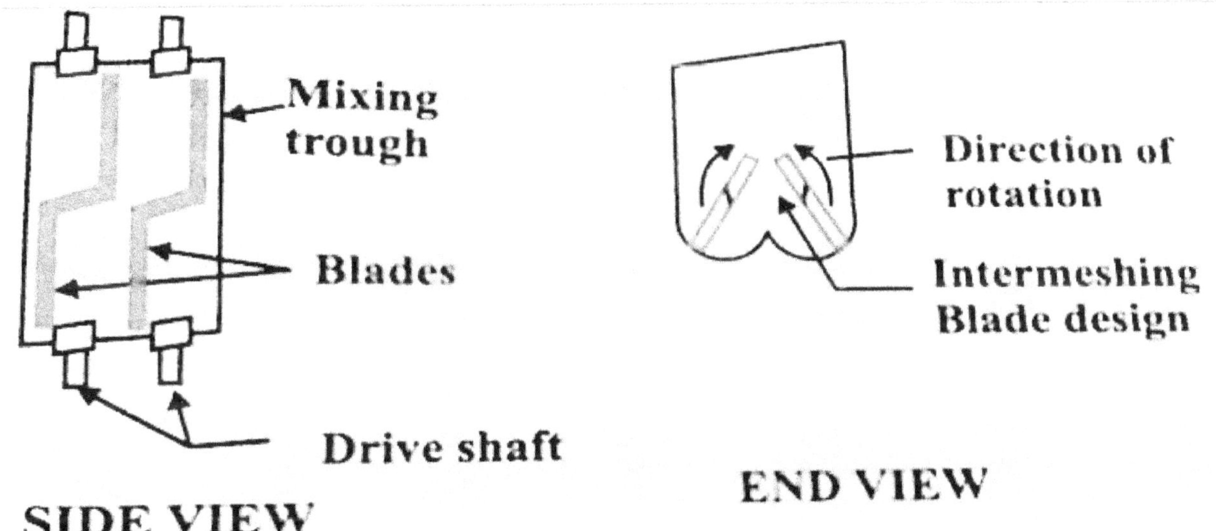


Fig. : Construction of Sigma Blade Mixer

- A ribbon blender consists of a u-shaped horizontal trough or shell containing a helical double ribbon agitator that rotates inside.

- The shaft of agitator is positioned in the centre of the trough on which the helical ribbons are welded.

- Since the ribbon stirrer consists of a set of internal and external helical ribbons, it is also called a double helical ribbon agitator.

- The ribbon blenders are powered by a drive system consisting of a motor, a gear box and couplings.

- These are powered by 10 HP to 15HP motor for 100Kg of product mass to be blended.

- The specific power ranges from 3 to 12 $KW/M^3$ according to the products to be mixed.

**Working of Sigma Blade Mixer:**

- Different powders are introduced from the top of the trough.

- The body is covered because considerable dust may be involved during dry blending and granulating solution may evaporate during wet granulation.

- Through the fixed speed drive, the sigma blades are allowed to rotate.

- The blade moves at different speeds.

**Merits of Sigma Blade Mixer:**

- Sigma blade mixture creates a minimum a dead space during mixing.

- Ideal for mixing, kneading of high viscous mass, sticky and dough like products.

- Extruding.

- These mixers and their variants are capable of handling viscosities as high as 10 centipoises.

**Demerits of Sigma Blade Mixer:**

- Sigma blade mixer works at a fixed speed.

- Power consumption in double arm kneader is very high compared to other type of mixer and range from 45 to 75 KW/m$^3$ of mix material.

**Uses of Sigma Blade Mixer:**

- The sigma blade mixer is a commonly used mixer for high viscosity materials.

- Sigma blade mixer is used for wet granulation process in manufacturing of tablets, pill masses and ointments.

- It is primarily used for solid-liquid mixing and also for solid-solid mixing.

**PLANETARY MIXER**

**Principle of Planetary Mixer:**

The principle of planetary mixers is very simple, which usually have two or three multihinged blades, when the paddles are revolution and rotation running at the same time, so that the material will flows up and down as well as around the inner cylinder, which can reach the mixing effect in a very short time. It is also known as change can mixer.

**Construction of Planetary Mixer:**

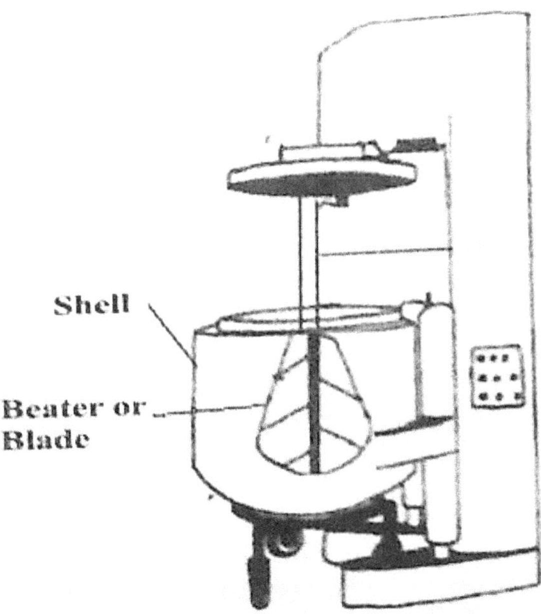


Fig. : Construction of Planetary Mixer

• It consists of a vertical cylindrical shell, which can be removed either by lowering it beneath the blade or raising the blade above the bowl.

• The mixing blade is mounted from the top of the bowl.

• The mixing shaft if driven by a planetary gear train.

• It rotates around the ring gear, which further rotates round the mixer blade.

• It is normally built with a variable speed drive.

**Working of Planetary Mixer:**

• The material to be mixed is loaded in mixing bowl.

• The blade rotates on their own axis when they orbit the mixing bowl on a common axis. Therefore, there is no dead space in the mixing and high shear is applied for mixing.

• After mixing, the material is discharged through a bottom valve, or by manual scooping of the material from the bowl.

**Merits of Planetary Mixer:**

• Simple construction, operation, and relatively low cost.

• No dead spot in the mixing.

• Rotation speed of the blade can be varied.

• Used for wet granulation process.

• High mixing efficiency.

• After mixing, the material is discharged through a bottom valve, or by manual scooping of the material from the bowl.

**Merits of Planetary Mixer:**

- Simple construction, operation, and relatively low cost.

- No dead spot in the mixing.

- Rotation speed of the blade can be varied.

- Used for wet granulation process.

- High mixing efficiency.

**Demerits of Planetary Mixer:**

- Requires high power.

- Heat build-up within powder mix.

**Uses of Planetary Mixer:**

- Planetary mixture produces precise blends in addition to breaking down of agglomerates rapidly.

- Low speeds are used for dry blending and kneading action is required in wet granulation.

- Steam jacketed bowls are used in manufacture of sustained released products and ointments.

## PROPELLERS

Propellers are the mechanical device that are used to mix liquid materials using blades A three bladed design is generally used for liquids.

**Principle of Propeller Mixer:**

- The propeller mixer mainly works on the principle of shearing force.

**Construction of Propeller Mixer:**

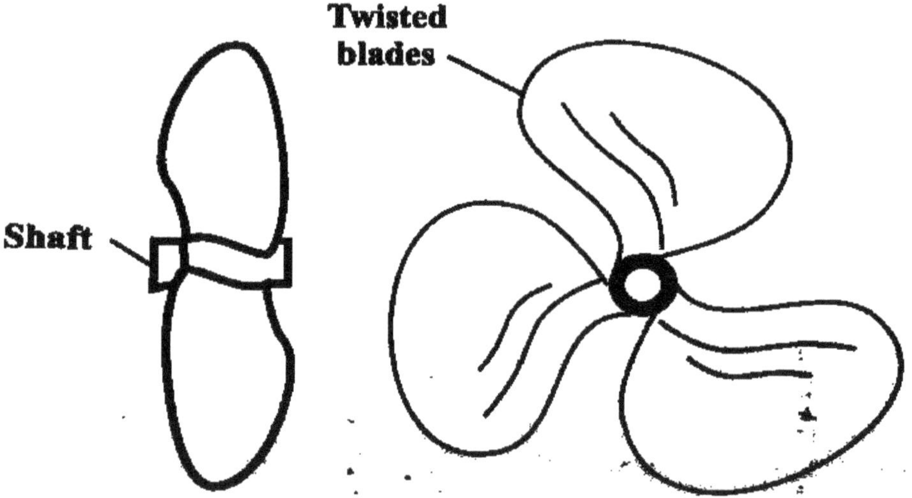


Fig. : Three Bladed Design Propeller

Fig. : Marine type propeller

It consists of vessel and propeller.

**Working of Propeller Mixer:**

• A vortex forms when a centrifugal force is imparted to the liquid by the propeller blades cause it to backup ground the sides of the vessel and creates a depression at the shaft.

• As the speed of the rotation is increased air may be sucked in to the fluid by the formation of a vortex this causes frothing and possible oxidation.

• Another method supressing vortex is to fit vertical baffles in to the vessel.

• Installation of vertical propeller reduces the vortex to considerable extent.

• Vertical propeller mixer consists of three blades (4 ft long). A propeller has angled blades, which cause the fluid to circulate in both an axial and radial direction. Size of the propeller is small and many increases up to 0.5meters depending on size of tank. Small size propeller can rotate up to 8000 rpm.

• Horizontal or Inclined Propeller or Marine Propeller are also used on side entry mixers. They are mounted with the impeller shaft inclined at an angle to the vessel axis to improve the process results. They provide good blending capability in small batches of low to medium viscosity.

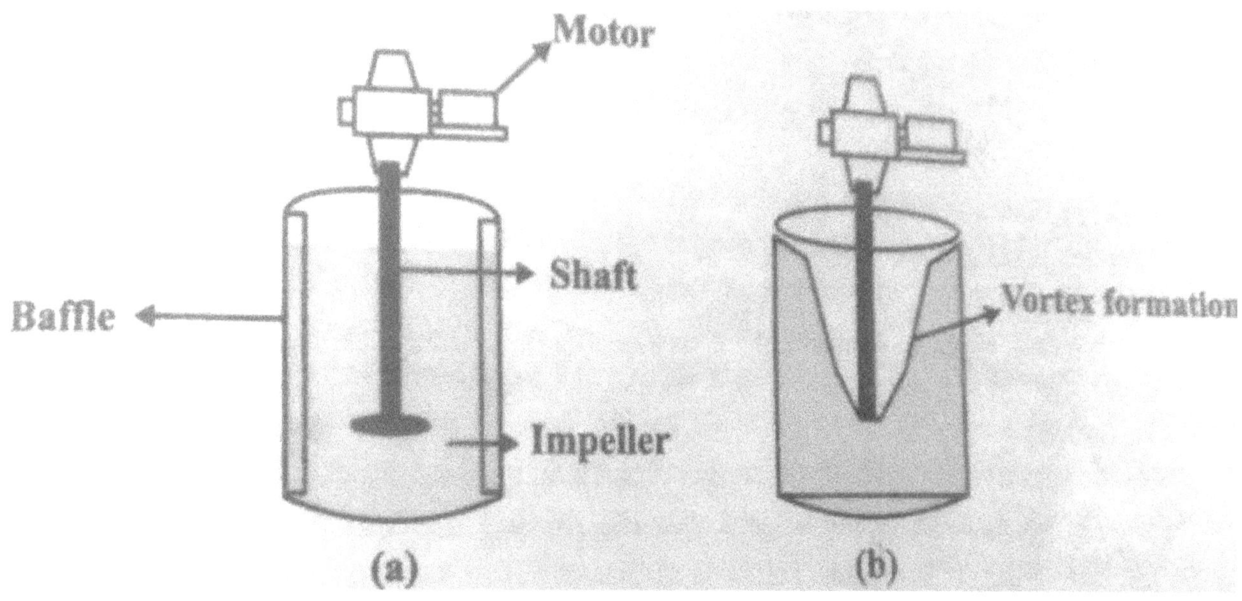


Fig. : (a) Baffled tank with no vortex formation; (b) Unbaffled tank having vortex formation

**Merits of Propeller Mixer:**

• Propeller is effective when high mixing capacity is required.

**Demerits of Propeller Mixer:**

• Propellers are not effective for liquids having viscosity greater than 5.0 Pascal second. • Equipment cost is high.

**Uses of Propeller Mixer:**

• Propeller mixer used for mixing liquid having maximum viscosity of 2.0 pascal second, for mixing of low viscosity emulsions and also used in mixing suspensions with particle size up to 0.1 to 0.5 mm.

**TURBINES**

**Principle of Turbine Mixer:**

A turbine mixer is a mechanical device that is used in mixing different type of liquids. The turbine mixer works mainly on the principle of shearing action.

**Construction of Turbine Mixer:**

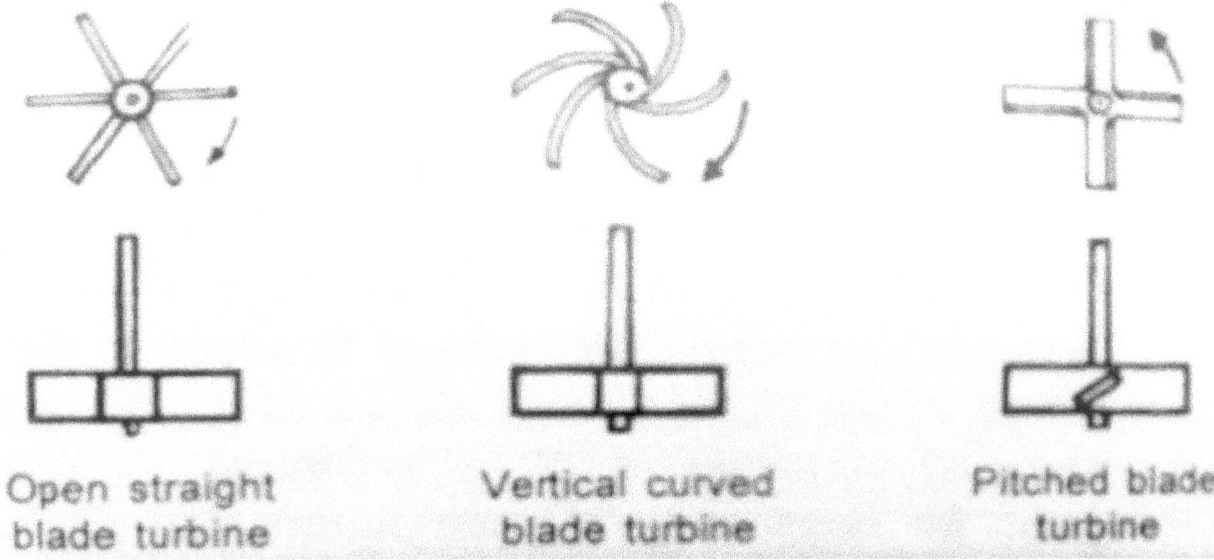



Fig. : Different types Turbines

- Turbine consists of number of blades attached to the circular disk.

- The blades used in the mixture are of various types: flat blades, disk-type flat blades, inclined blades, curved blades, arrow headed blades, and so on.

- The diameter of turbine varies from 30 to 50 percentage of the diameter of vessel.

- As compared to propeller turbines rotates at lower speed.

**Working of Turbine Mixer:**

When turbine mixer operates at sufficiently at high rotational speeds, the radial tangential flow becomes pronounced with the formation of vortex. It is necessary to install baffles in the vessel for the mixing process for uniform mixing. The radial flow of the impeller impinges on vessel walls, where it slits in to two streams.

**Merits of Turbine Mixer:**

- Turbines give greater shearing force than propeller.

- Therefore, turbines are suitable for emulsification.

**Demerits of Turbine Mixer:**

- Turbines have less pumping rate.

**Uses of Turbine Mixer:**

- A turbine mixer suitable for viscous fluids (7.0 pascal-second).

- Turbines used for thin paste and emulsification.

- Turbines can also be used to handle slurries with 60 percentage solids.

- Mainly used for semisolid materials.

**PADDLES**

**Principle of Paddles:**

- Paddles consist of two long flat blades attached vertically to a shaft.

- It rotates at low speed.

- Paddle mixer is suitable to mix viscous liquids or semisolids.

**Construction of Paddles:**

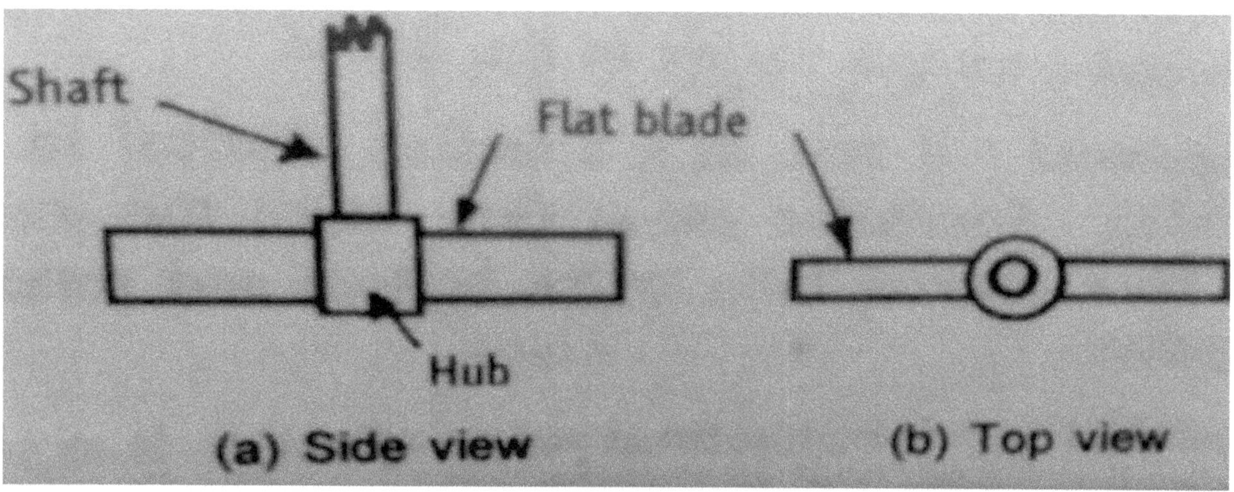


Fig. : Paddle type of Agitator or Impeller

- Blades used in this mixer are dished or hemispherical in shape.

- The diameter of paddle is 50-80 percentage of inside diameter of vessel.

**Working of Paddles:**

- Paddles push liquid radially and tangentially.

- There is no axial movement of flow during mixing.

**Merits of Paddles:**

- Vortex formation is not possible.

- It has low speed.

- Mixing efficiency is better.

- No dead spots and deposited solids.

**Demerits of Paddles:**

- Here suspension mixing is poor.

- Baffled tanks are required.

**Uses of Paddles:**

- Paddles are used in the manufacture of antacid suspensions (aluminium hydroxide gel and magnesium hydroxide), agar and pectin related purgative, antidiarroheal mixtures such as bismuth-kaolin.

**SILVERSON EMULSIFIER**

Principle of Silverson Emulsifier:

The silverson homogenizer works on the principle that the large globules in a course emulsion are broken in to smaller globules by intensive shearing forces and turbulence by high speed rotors.

**Construction of Silverson Emulsifier:**

- It consists of emulsifier head.

- The emulsifier head consist of a number of turbine blades.

- The blades are surrounded by mesh which is enclosed by cover having perforations.

- The blades are rotated by using electric motor fitted at the top.

- There is also one shaft whose one end is connected to motor and other end is connected to head.

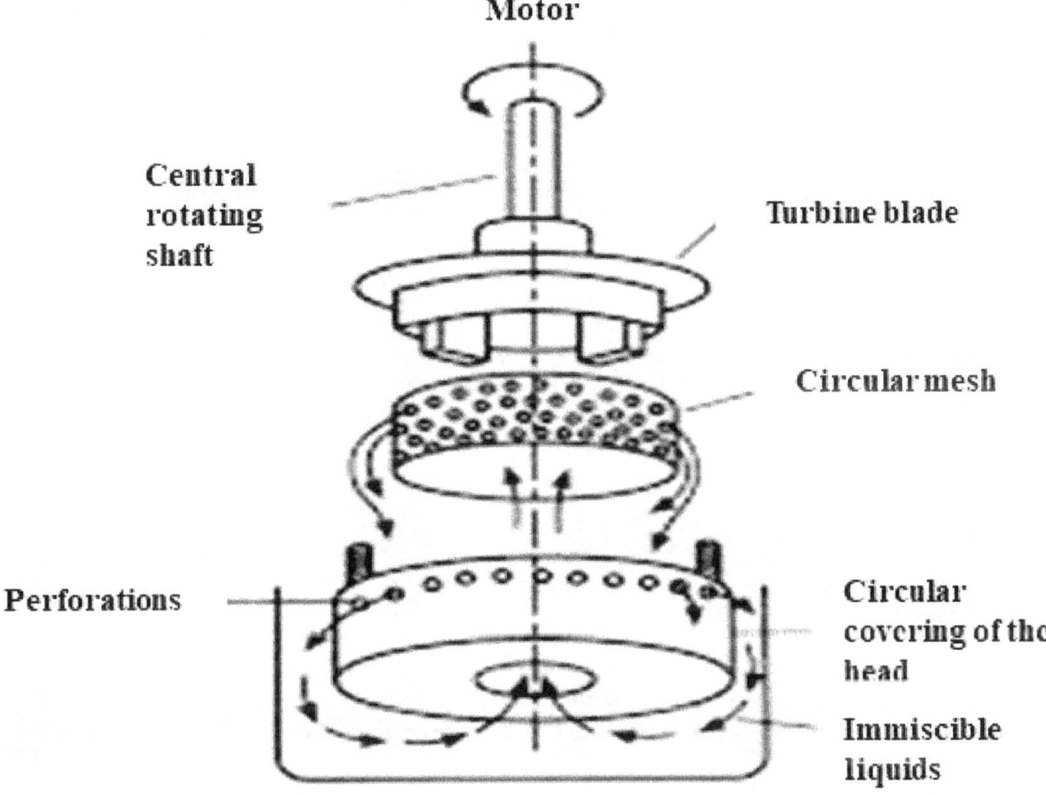


Fig. : Silverson Emulsifier

**Working of Silverson Emulsifier:**

- The emulsifier head is dipped in to the vessel containing immiscible liquids.

- When the motor is started, shaft rotates the head.

- Therefore, turbines blades also rotate at very high speed.

- The liquids are sucked trough the fine holes.

- The complex flow pattern can cause droplet break up under either laminar or turbulent conditions

- Centrifugal force expels the content through mesh and then to cover and subjects them to mechanical shear.

- This is followed by intense hydraulic shear.

- The oil is reduced in to globules quickly resulting in a homogenous uniform product.

- Then the fine emulsion emerge trough opening of cover.

- As a result, bigger globules rapidly break in to smaller globules

**Merits of Silverson Emulsifier:**

- Fast and efficient.

- They are used to get a fine droplet or particle size (2-5 microns).

- Process efficiency is good.

- Low operating cost.

**Demerits of Silverson Emulsifier:**

- Chance of chocking of pores of mesh.

**Uses of Silverson Emulsifier:**

- Used in preparation of creams, ointments, pharmaceutical suspension and emulsion of fine particle size.


MCQs

1. Drying is essential after one of the following unit operations
a. Crystallisation
b. Evaporation
c. Mixing
d. Size reduction

Answer: Crystallisation

2. For fixing the effective drying conditions, which processing factor is essential?
a. Height
b. Humidity
c. Pressure
d. Temperature

Answer: Humidity

3. At a given temperature and humidity, if the moisture content of a material is greater than equilibrium moisture content, then the following process takes place
a. Absorption
b. Adsorption

c. Desorption

d. Sorption

Answer: Desorption

4. Fluidised bed dryer has one of the following advantages?

a. Attrition is not observed

b. Entire material is continuously exposed to a heat source

c. Fluffy mass is formed

d. Humidity can be increased

Answer: Entire material is continuously exposed to a heat source

5. Which one of the following dryer is known as lyophiliser?

a. Fluidised bed dryer

b. Freeze dryer

c. Spray dryer

d. Vacuum dryer

Answer: Freeze dryer

6. Talc has EMC of practically equal to

a. High

b. One

c. Variable

d. Zero

Answer: Zero

7. Which equipment is used for drying methylcellulose?

a. Drum dryer

b. Spray dryer

c. Tray dryer

d. Vacuum dryer

Answer: Spray dryer

8. Migration of salts & solutes does not occur in one of the following equipment for drying

a. Freeze dryer

b. Spray dryer

c. Tray dryer

d. Vacuum dryer

Answer: Freeze dryer

9. Which one of the following types of products is having an EMC of practically zero?

a. Non-porous & insoluble

b. Non-porous & soluble

c. Porous & insoluble

d. Porous & soluble

Answer: Non-porous & insoluble

10. Which product is not dried by a spray dryer?
a. Bacterial & viral cultures
b. Fruit juice
c. Lactose
d. Serum

Answer: Bacterial & viral culture

11. Which of the following produces randomization during the Mixing operation?
a. Dissimilar charges
b. Dissimilar forces
c. Dissimilar ions
d. Dissimilar particles

Answer: Dissimilar particles

12. Mixing must be done at a lower speed for semisolids, as some of them may exhibit one of the following rheological behaviour.
a. Dilatant flow
b. Plastic flow
c. Pseudoplastic flow
d. Thixotropy

Answer: Dilatant flow

13. Which of the following arrangements are involved in a static mixer?
a.  Shell and blade are stationary
b.  Shell and blade rotate
c.  Shell is stationary and blade rotates
d.  Shell rotates and blade is stationary

Answer: Shell is stationary and blade rotates

14. In which type of mixer, the trough is stationary?
a.  Barrel mixer
b. Double cone blender
c.  Ribbon mixer
d. Zigzag mixer

Answer: Ribbon mixer

15. When the paddle is used for the mixing of liquids, the flow pattern of fluid is.
a. axial and tangential
b. axial or tangential
c. radial and tangential
d. radial or tangential

Answer: radial and tangential

16. Which of the following forces aids the tumbling action for promoting inter-particle movement?
a.  Electrostatic force

b. Gravitational force

c. Surface force

d. Van der Walls force

Answer: Gravitational force

17. Which one of the following rates (kinetic orders) is observed in the mixing of solids?

a. First order

b. Pseudo-first order

c. Second-order

d. Zero order

Answer: First order

18. Which type of particle-particle interactions is experienced on account of surface charges produced during mixing?

a. Attraction

b. Collisions

c. Diffusion

d. Repulsion

Answer: Repulsion

19. Which one of the following is NOT an example for inertial forces?

a. Electrostatic forces

b. London forces

c. Surface forces

d. Van der Waals forces

Answer: Surface forces

20. In dispensing, which one of the following terms is NOT used for mixing?

a. Sizing

b. Spatulation

c. Trituration

d. Tumbling

Answer: Sizing

# Unit IV

*Syllabus*

• Filtration: Objectives, applications, Theories & Factors influencing filtration, filter aids, filter medias. Principle, Construction, Working, Uses, Merits and demerits of plate & frame filter, filter leaf, rotary drum filter, Meta filter &Cartridge filter, membrane filters and Seidtz filter.

• Centrifugation: Objectives, principle & applications of Centrifugation, principles, construction, working, uses, merits and demerits of Perforated basket centrifuge, Non-perforated basket centrifuge, semi continuous centrifuge & super centrifuge.

## FILTRATION

**Filtration:** It may be defined as a process of separation of solids from a fluid by passing the same through a porous medium that retains the solids but allows the fluid to pass through.

Clarification: When solid are present in very lowv concentration, i.e., not exceeding 1.0% w/v, the process of its separation from liquid is called clarification.

### Terms used in Filtration

- Slurry - Suspension to be filtered

- Filter medium - porous medium used to retain solid

- Filter cake - Accumulated solids on the filter

- Filtrate - Clear liquid passing through the filter

### Process of filtration

- Pores of filter medium are smaller than size of particles to be separate.

- Filter medium (filter paper) is placed on a support (mesh)

- Slurry is placed over the filter medium

- Due to pressure difference across the filter, fluid flows through the filter medium

- Gravity is acting over the liquid medium

- So, solids are trapped on the surface of the filter medium

### Applications of filtration

- Production of sterile products

- Production of bulk drugs

- Production of liquid dosage formulation

    i. Dewaxing of oils

    ii. Removing suspended oils from aqueous solutions

iii.  Removing of undesirable solids

iv.  Clarifying the potable water

- Effluents and waste water treatment

**Mechanism of filtration**

The mechanism whereby particles are retained by a filter is significant only in initial stages of filtration.

1. Straining - Similar to sieving, i.e., particles of larger size can't pass through smaller pore size of filter medium.

2. Impingement - Solids having the momentum move along the path of streaming flow and strike (impinge) the filter medium. Thus the solids are retained on the filter medium.

3. Entanglement - Particles become entwined (entangled) in the masses of fibres (of cloths with fine hairy surface or porous felt) due to smaller size of particles than the pore size. Thus solids are retained within filter medium.

4. Attractive forces - Solids are retained on the filter medium as a result of attractive force between particles and filter medium, as in case of electrostatic filtration.

**Types of filtrations**

1. Surface/ screen filtration –

- It is a screening action by which pores or holes of medium prevent the passage of solids.
- Mechanism involved: straining and impingement
- For this, plates with holes or woven sieves are used.

2. Depth filtration –

- In this slurry penetrates to a point where the diameter of solid particles is greater than that of the tortuous void or channel.
- Mechanism: Entanglement
- The solids are retained with a gradient density structure by physical restriction or by adsorption properties of medium.

**Theories of filtration**

- The flow of liquid through a filter follows the basic rules that govern the flow of any liquid through the medium offering resistance.
- The rate of flow may be expressed as- Rate = driving force / resistance
- The rate of filtration may be expressed as volume (litres) per unity time (dv/dt).
- Driving force = pressure upstream – pressure downstream
- Resistance is not constant.
- It increases with an increase in the deposition of solids on the filter medium.
- Therefore, filtration is not a steady state.

- The rate of flow will be greatest at the beginning of filtration process, since the resistance is minimum.

- After forming of filter cake, its surface acts as filter medium and$v$ solids continuously deposit adding to thickness of the cake.

Resistance to movement= {pressure upstream- pressure downstream}/ length of capillaries

1. Poiseuille's Equation

- Poiseuille considered that filtration is similar to the streamline flow of liquid under pressure through capillaries.

- Poiseuille's Equation is-

$$V= \pi \Delta P r4/8L\eta$$

Where, V = rate of flow, m3 /s (l/s)

$\Delta P$= Pressure difference across the filter, Pa

r = radius of capillary in the filter bed, m

L = thickness of filter cake (capillary length), m

$\eta$ = viscosity of filtrate, Pa.s

- If the cake is composed of bulky mass of particles and the liquid flows through the interstice, then flow of liquids through these may be expressed by this equation.

2. Darcy's Equation

- Poiseuille's law assumes that the capillaries found in the filter are highly irregular and nonuniform.

- Therefore, if the length of capillary is taken as the thickness of bed, a correction factor for radius is applied so that the rate is closely approximated and simplified.

- The factors influencing the rate of filtration has been incorporated into an equation by Darcy, which is:

$$V= KA\Delta P/\eta L$$

Where, K = permeability coefficient of cake, m2

A = surface area of porous bed (filter medium), m2

K depends on characteristics of cake, such as porosity, specific$v$ surface area and compressibility.

- Permeability may be defined quantitatively as the flow rate of a liquid of unit viscosity across a unit area of cake having unit thickness under a pressure gradient of unity.

- This equation is valid for liquids flowing through sand, glass$v$ beds and various porous media.

- This model is applied to filter beds or cakes and other types of depth filter.

- This equation is further modified by including characteristics of K by Kozeny-Carman.

3. Kozeny-Carman (K-C) equation

- Kozeny-Carman equation is widely used for filtration.

$$V = A/\eta S^2 * \Delta P/KL * \epsilon 3/(1-\epsilon)^2$$

Where, $\epsilon$ = porosity of cake (bed)

S = specific surface area of particles comprising the cake m2 / m3

K = Kozeny constant (usually taken as 5)

Limitations:

- It does not consider the fact that depth of granular bed is lesser than the actual path traversed by the fluid.

- The actual path is not same throughout the bed, but it is sinuous or tortuous.

**Factors influencing filtration**

1. Surface area of filter medium –

- Rate of filtration is Inversely proportional to specific surface of filter bed (According to K-C equation)

- Directly proportional to surface area of filter medium (According to Darcy's equation)

- Rate can be increased either using large filter or connecting a number of small units in parallel. Filter press works on principle of connecting units in parallel.

2. Pressure drop across the filter medium

- According to K-C equation the rate of filtration is proportional to the overall pressure drop across both the filter medium and filter cake.

- The pressure drop can be achieved in a number of ways:

    a. Gravity- A pressure difference could be obtained by maintaining a head of slurry above the filter medium. The pressure developed will depend on the density of the slurry

    b. Vacuum (Reducing pressure) - The pressure below the filter medium may be reduced below atmospheric pressure by connecting the filtrate receiver to a vacuum pump and creating a pressure difference across the filter.

    c. Pressure  The simplest method being to pump the slurry into the filter under pressure

    d. Centrifugal force - The gravitational force could be replaced by centrifugal force in particle separation

3. Viscosity of filtrate

According to K-C equation rate of filtration is inversely proportional to the viscosity of the fluid.

This is an increase in the viscosity of the filtrate will increase the resistance of flow.

This problem can be overcome by two methods:

    a) The rate of filtration may be increased by raising the temperature of the liquid, which lowers its viscosity. However, it is not practicable if thermolabile materials are involved or if the filtrate is volatile.

b) Dilution is another alternative but the rate must be doubled.

Filter Media

- The surface upon which solids are deposited in a filter is calledv the "Filter medium"

- Properties of ideal filter medium are as follows

- It should

    a) Be capable of delivering a clear filtrate at a suitable production rate.

    b) Have sufficient mechanical strength. o Be inert. o Retain the solids without plugging at the start of filtration.

    c) Not absorb dissolve material.

    d) Sterile filtration imposes a special requirement since the pore size must not exceed the dimension of bacteria or spores.

**Material used as filter media**

1. Woven material

    - Made up of wool, silk, metal or synthetic fibres (rayon, nylon etc.).

    - These include a- wire screening and b- fabrics of cotton, wool, nylon.

    - Wire screening e.g. stainless steel is durable, resistance to plugging and easily cleaned.

    - Cotton is a common filter, however, Nylon is superior for pharmaceutical use, since it is unaffected by Mold, fungus or bacteria and has negligible absorption properties.

    - The choice of fibre depends on chemical reactivity with the slurry

2. Perforated sheet metal

    - Stainless steel plates have pores which act as channels as in case of meta filters.

3. Bed of granular solid built up on supporting medium

    - In some processes, a bed of graded solids may be formed to reduce resistance of flow.

    - Ex. Of granular solids are gravel, sand, asbestos, paper pulp and keiselgur.

    - Choice of solids depends on size of solids in process.

4. Membrane filter media •

    - These are cartridge units and are economical and available in pore size of 100 μm to even less than 0.2 μm.

    - Can be either surface cartridges or depth type cartridges.

Surface cartridges: –

    - These are corrugated and resin treated papers and used in hydraulic lines.

    - Ceramic cartridges and porcelain filter candles are examples.

- Can be reuse after cleaning.

Depth type cartridges: -

- Made up of cotton, asbestos or cellulose.

- These are disposable items, since cleaning is not feasible.

**Filter Aids**

- The objective of filter aid is to prevent the medium from becoming blocked and to form an open, porous cake, hence, reducing the resistance to flow of the filtrate.

- Filter aid forms a surface deposit which screens out the solids and also prevents the plugging of supporting filter medium.

**Characteristics of filter aids:**

- Chemically inert and free from impurities.

- Low specific gravity, so remain suspended in liquids.

- Porous rather than dense, so that pervious cake can be formed.

- Recoverable.

**Disadvantages:**

- Remove the coloured substances by absorbing them.

- Sometimes active principles such as alkaloids are absorbed on filter aid.

- Rarely, filters are source of contamination such as soluble iron salts, which can provoke degradation of sensitive ingredient

**Handling of filter aids**

- Filter aids may be used in either or both two ways:

  a) Pre- coating technique: by forming a pre-coat over the filter medium by filtering a suspension of the filter aid.

  b) Body- mix technique: A small proportion of the filter aid (0.1- 0.5 %) is added to the slurry to be filtered. This slurry is recirculated through the filter until a clear filtrate is obtained, filtration then proceeds to completion.

- Different flow rates can be achieved depending on grade of aid o Low flow rate: fine grade filter aids- mainly used for clarity o Fast flow rate: coarse grade filter aids- acceptable filtrate.

**Examples of filter aids**

- Diatomite (Kieselguhr), obtained from natural siliceous deposits.

- Perlite, it is an aluminium silicate.

- Cellulose, Asbestos, charcoal, talc, bentonite, fullers earth etc.

**Classification of filtration equipment's**

Based on application of external force:

- Pressure filter – Plate and frame filter press, meta filter
- Vacuum filters – Filter leaf
- Centrifugal filters

**Based on operation of filtration**

- Continuous filtration - Discharge and filtrate are separated steadily and uninterrupted
- Discontinuous filtration - Discharge of filtered solid is intermittent. Filtrate is removed continuously. Operation should be stopped to collect solid.

**Based on nature of filtration**

- Cake filters - Remove large amount of solids
- Clarifying filters - Remove small amounts of solids
- Cross-flow filters - Feed of suspension flows under pressure at fairly high velocity across the filter medium

EQUIPMENTS: -

Plate and frame filter press

**Principle:**

- Mechanism is surface filtration.
- The slurry enters the frame by pressure and flows through filter medium.
- The filtrate is collected on the plates and send to outlet.
- A number of frames and plates are used so that surface areav increases and consequently large volumes of slurry can be processed simultaneously with or without washing.

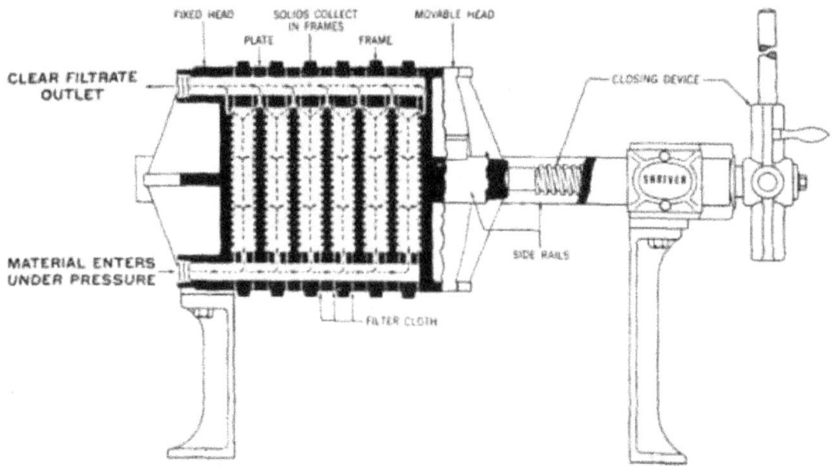


**Construction**

- The Filter press is made of two types of units, plate and frames.

- Usually made of aluminium alloy.
- Sometimes, these are also lacquered for protection against corrosive chemicals and made suitable for steam sterilization.

**Frame-**

- It contains an open space inside wherein the slurry reservoir is maintained for filtration and an inlet to receive the slurry.
- It is indicated by two dots in description.
- Frames of different thickness are available.
- It is selected based on the thickness of cake formed during filtration.
- Optimum thickness of frame should be chosen.

**Plate**

- The plate has a studded or grooved surface to support the filter cloth and an outlet.
- It is indicated by one dot in description.
- Plate supports the filter medium, receiving the filtrate and outlet.
- The filter medium usually cloth is interposed between plate and frame.
- Plate, filter medium, frame, filter medium and plate are arranged in sequence and clamed to a supporting structure.
- It is normally described by dots as 1.2.1.2.1 so on.
- A number of plates and frames are employed so that the filtration area is as large as necessary.
- Number of filtration units are operated in parallel.
- Channels for slurry inlet and filtrate outlet can be arranged by fitting eyes to the plates and frames, these join together to form a channel.
- In some types only one inlet channel is formed, while each platev is having individual outlets controlled by valves.

**Working**

Working can be divided into two steps

1. Filtration operation

- Frame- marked by 2 dots
- Plate – marked by 1 dot
- Slurry enters the frame from the feed channel and passes through the filter medium on the surface of the plate
- The solid forms a filter cake and remain in the frame

- The thickness of the cake is half of the frame thickness, because on each side of frame filtration occurs

- Thus, two filter cakes are formed, which meet eventually in the centre of the frame

- The filtrate drains between the projections of the surface of the plate and escape from the outlet

- As filtration proceeds, the resistance of the cake increases and filtration rate decrease

- At a certain point process is stopped and press is emptied and cycle is restarted.

2. Washing of cake (if desirable)

- When washing of cake is also required modified plate and frame filter is used.

- For this purpose, an additional channel is included called as washing plate and are identified by 3 dots.

- In the half of the washing plate, there is a connection from washv water cannel to the surface of plate.

- The sequence of arrangement of plates and frames can be represented by dots as 1.2.3.2.1.2.3.2.1 so on (between 1 and 1, 2.3.2 must be arranged.

**Procedure for washing the press**

- Filtration proceeds in the ordinary way until the frames are filled with cake.

- To wash the filter cake, the outlets of washing plates are closed.

- Wash water is pumped in the washing channel. The water enters through the inlets on the surface of washing plate.

- Water passes through the filter cloth and enters frame which contains the cake. Then water washes the cake, passes through the filter cloth and enters the plate down the surface

- Finally washed water escapes through the outlet of that plate.

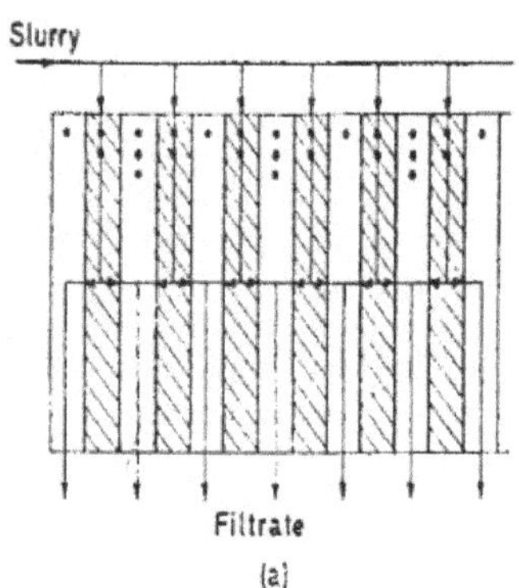


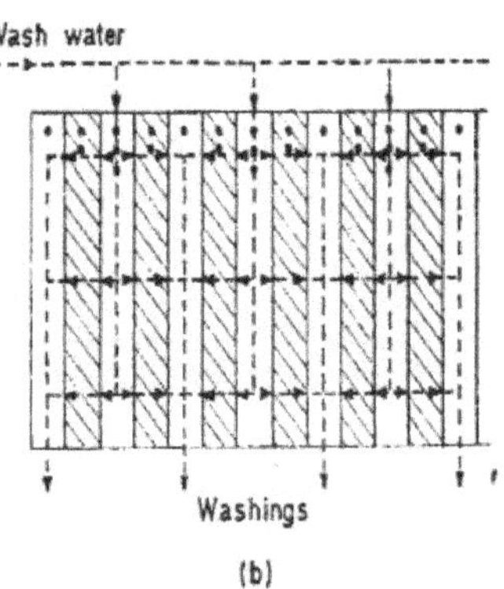


**Special provisions:**

- Any possible contamination can be observed by passing the filtrate through a glass tube or sight glass from the outlet on each plate.

- This permits the inspection of quality of filtrate. The filtrate goes through the control valves to an outlet channel.

- The filtration process from each plate can be seen. In the event of broken cloth, the faulty plate can be isolated and filtration can be continued with one plate less.

**Uses:**

- Sterile filtrate can by obtain by using asbestos and cellulosev filter sheet (for this, whole filter press and filter medium have been sterilized previously).
- Filtration of viscous liquid can also be done by incorporatingv heating/cooling coils in the press.

**Advantages**

- Construction of filter press is very simple and a variety of materials can be used.
- Provide large filtration area in relatively small floor space.
- The capacity being variable according to thickness of frames and number used.
- Sturdy construction permits the use of considerable pressurev difference. (2000 Kilopascals normally used)
- Efficient washing of cake is possible.
- Operation and maintenance are easy.
- It produces dry cake in form of slab.

**Disadvantages**

- It is a batch filter, so it is a time consuming.
- The filter press is an expensive filter, the emptying time, the labour involved, and the wear and tear on the cloths resulting in high costs.
- Operation is critical, as the frames should be full, otherwisev washing is inefficient and the cake is difficult to remove.
- The filter press is used for slurries containing less about 5 %v solids In view of the high labour costs it is most suitable for expensive materials e.g. the removal of precipitated proteins from insulin liquors.

**Filter leaf**

**Principle:**

- It is an apparatus consisting of a longitudinal drainage screen covered with a filter cloth.
- The mechanism is surface filtration and acts as sieve or strainer.
- Vacuum or pressure can be applied to increase the rate of filtration.

**Construction:**

- The leaf filter is consisting of a frame enclosing a drainage screen or grooved plate.
- The frame may be any shape circular, square or rectangular.
- The whole unites being covered with filter cloth.
- The outlet for the filtrate connects to the inside of the frame through suction.

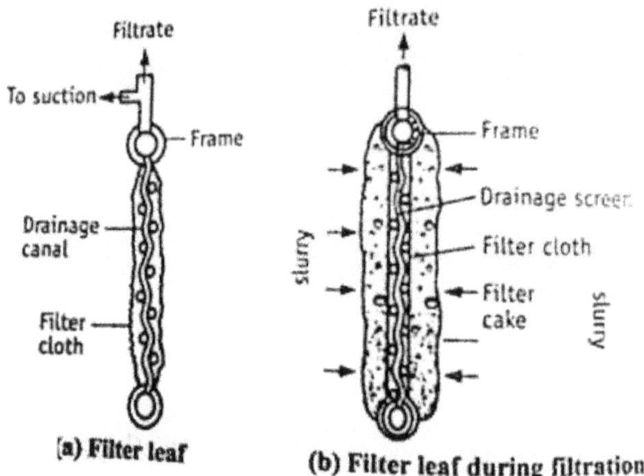



## Working

- The filter leaf is immersed in the slurry
- Vacuum system is connected to the outlet
- The slurry passes through the filter cloth
- Finally filtrate enters the drainage canal and goes through the outlet into receiver
- Air is passed to flow in reverse direction which facilitates removal of cake

## Use:

- Use for the filtration of slurry which do not contain high solid content, about 5%, i.e. dilute suspensions.

## Advantages

- Simplest form of filter used for batch process.
- A number of units can be connected in parallel to increase the surface area of filtration.
- Pressure difference can be obtained either with vacuum or using pressure up to the order of 800 kilopascals.
- Labour costs for operating the filter leaf are fairly moderate.
- The efficiency of washing is high.
- The slurry can be filtered from any vessel.
- The cake can be washed simply by immersing the filter in a vessel of Water.

## Sweetland filter (variant of filter leaf)

- An alternative method is to enclose the filter leaf in a special vessel into which the slurry is pumped under pressure.
- A number of leaves are connected to a common outlet, to provide a large area for filtration.

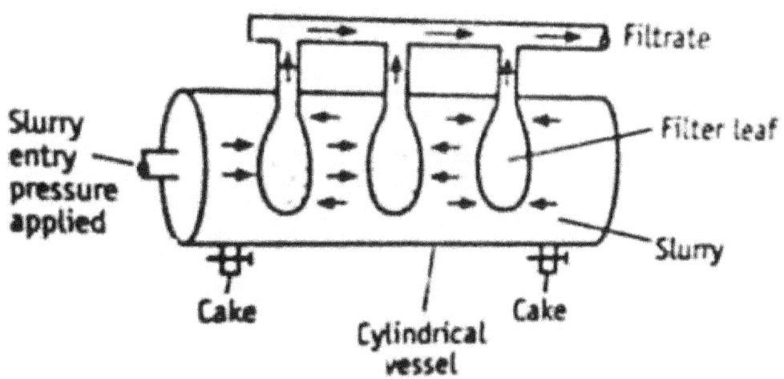



**Sweetland filter**

Meta filter

## Principle:

• Mechanism is surface filtration.

• In this, metal rings contain semicircular projections, which are arranged as a nest to form channels on the edges.

• This channel offers resistance (strainer) to the flow of solids (coarse particles).

• The clear liquid is collected into receiver from the top.

## Construction

• Meta filter consists of a series of metal rings.

• These are threaded so that a channel is formed on the edges.

• It contains a grooved drainage column on which a series of metal rings are packed.

• These rings are usually made up of stainless steel and have dimensions of about 15.0 mm internal diameter and 22.0 mm external diameter.

• Each metal ring has a number of semicircular projections (0.8 mm in thickness) on one side of surface.

• The projections are arranged as a nest to form channels on the edges.

• These rings are tightened on the drainage column with a nut.

• Metafilters are also known as edge filters.

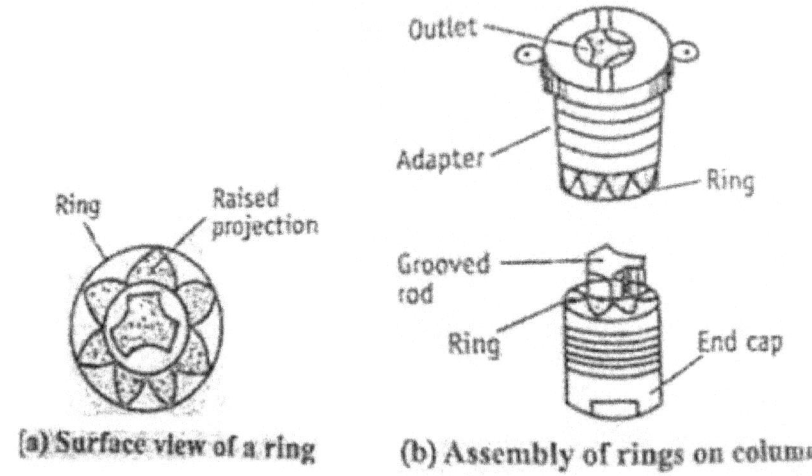



Metafilter

## Working

- Filters are placed in a vessel

- Slurry is pumped under pressure or occasionally by applying reduced pressure to the outlet side

- Slurry passes through the channels formed on the edges between the rings

- The clear liquid rises up and collected from the outlet into receiver

- For separation of fine particles, a bed of suitable materials such kieselguhr is first built up.

- The pack of rings serves essentially as a base on which the true filter medium is supported.

## Uses

Meta filters can be used for-

- Clarification of syrups

- Filtration of injection solutions

- Clarification of insulin liquors

- Filtration of viscous liquids can be achieved by applying pressure.

## Advantages

- Can be used under high pressures, without any danger of bursting the filter medium.

- Running cost is low, as separate filter medium is not used.

- Can be constructed from a material that can provide excellent resistance to corrosion and avoid contamination of sensitive products.

- It is extremely versatile filter because fine as well as large both type of particles can be separated.

- Removal of cake can be carried out by simply back- flushing with water.

• Change over from one batch to another or one product to another is easy.

• Sterile products can be handled.

**Cartridge filter**

**Principle:**

- It is a thin porous membrane in which pre filter and membrane filter are combined in a single unit.

- The filtration action is mainly sieve like and particles are retained on the surface.

**Construction:**

- It has cylindrical configuration made with disposable or changeable filter media.

- Made up of either plastic or metal.

- Consist of two membrane filters (sieve like) made of polypropylene: prefilter and actual filter for filtration.

- A protective layer surrounds them.

- The cartridge is housed in a holder and a number of cartridges can be placed in a same housing.

- The housing is closed with the lid.

- Housing has provisions for slurry inlet and outlets.

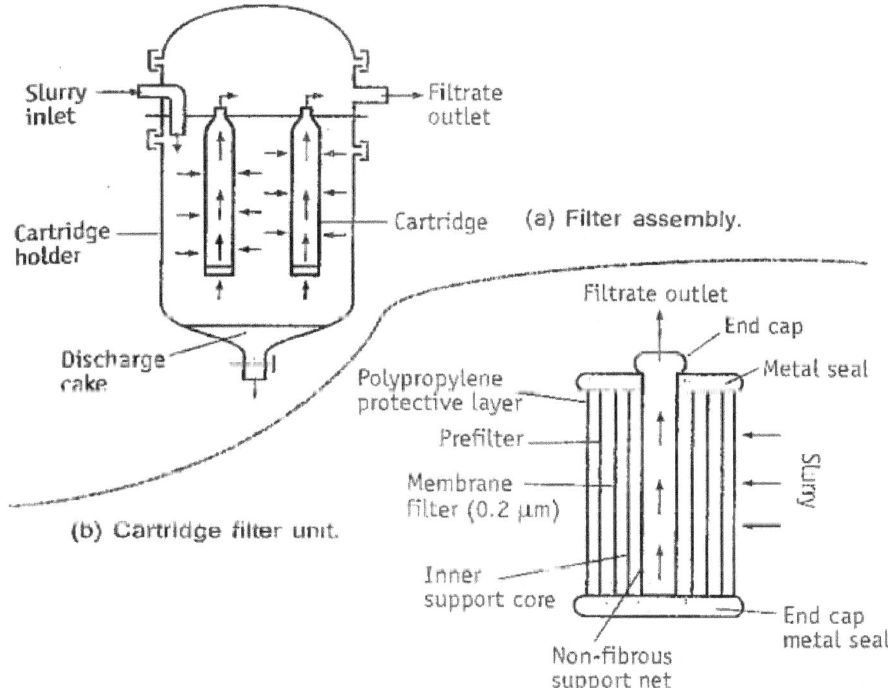


**Working:**

- Slurry is pumped into cartridge holder

- It passes through cartridge filter unit by straining

- The clear liquid passes through the centre

- Moves up to collect through outlet

- Uses:

- Particularly useful for preparation of particulate free solutions for parenterals and ophthalmic uses.

- This filter holder will process 1000 – 15000 litres of sterile solution per hour.

**Advantages:**

- Autoclaving can be done for sterile operations due to stainless steel construction.

- Cartridges with self-cleaning devices are advantageous.

- Rapid disassembling as well as reusing of filter medium is possible.

- Cartridges are not brittle, when they are dry.

- Used as in-line continuous filtration, this reduces handling of solution. It minimizes chances of contaminations.

**Disadvantages:**

- A number of manufactures provide the components, which are generally not interchangeable between suppliers.

- Cost of disposable elements offsets the labour saving in terms of assembly and cleaning of cartridge clarifiers.

**Rotary drum filter**

**Principle:**

- Slurry filtered through sieve like mechanism on the rotation drum surface, under the condition of vacuum.

- In addition, compression, drying (using hot air), and removing the filter cake (using knife) are possible.

**Construction:**

- It consists of a metal cylinder mounted horizontally.

- The drum may be up to 3 meters in diameter and 3.5 meters in length and gives surface area of 20-meter square.

- The curved surface being a perforated plate, supporting a filter cloth.

- Internally, it is divided into several sectors and a separate connection is made between each sector and a special rotary valve.

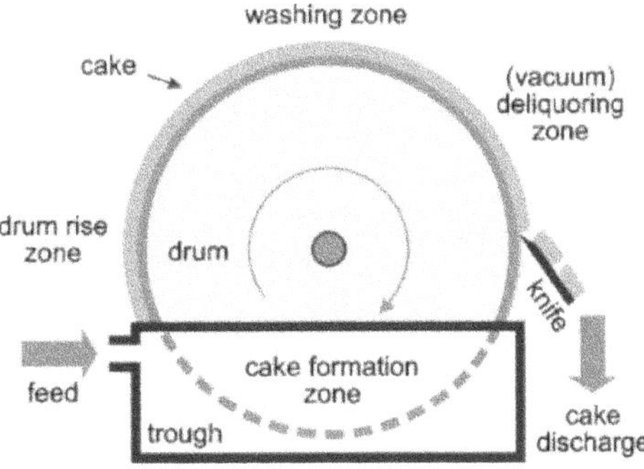



**Working**

- The drum is dipped into the slurry and vacuum applied to the outlet, which is connected to the filtrate receiver.

- When the cake has formed, the cake drained or partially dried by vacuum.

- The drum is sprayed with water to wash the cake.

- Retaining the vacuum connection drains the cake and produces partial dryness then, removed by a doctor knife.

- When the solids of the slurry are too much that the filter cloth becomes blocked with the particles, a pre-coat filter may be used.

- A pre-coat of filter aid is deposited on the drum prior to the filtration process.

**Uses**

- The rotary filter for continuous operation on large quantities of slurry.

- Suitable for slurry contains considerable amounts of solids in the range 15-30%.

- Examples of pharmaceutical application includes the collection of calcium carbonate, magnesium carbonate, and starch.

- The separation of the mycelium from the fermentation liquor in the manufacture of antibiotics.

**Advantages**

- The rotary filter is automatic and is continuous in operation, so that the labour costs are very low.

- The filter has a large capacity, so it is suitable for the filtration of highly concentrated solutions.

- Variation of the speed of rotation enables the cake thickness to be controlled.

- Pre-coat of filter aid could used to accelerate the filtration rate.

- Filter has large surface area.

**Disadvantages**

- The rotary filter is a complex piece of equipment, with many moving parts and is very expensive.

- In addition to the filter itself, some accessories are connected, e.g., a vacuum pump, vacuum receivers, slurry pumps and agitators are required.

- The cake tends to crack due to the air drawn through by the vacuum system, so that washing and drying are not efficient.

- Being a vacuum filter, the pressure difference is limited to 1 bar and hot filtrates may boil. • It is suitable only for straight- forward slurries

## Membrane filters

Membrane filters act as a barrier to separate contaminants from water, or they remove the particles contaminating the water. Reverse osmosis, ultrafiltration, and nanofiltration all use a membrane in their different filtration processes.

## Construction

- Membrane filters are made of thin and flat membranes of cellulose derivatives, such as, cellulose acetate and cellulose nitrate.

- These filters are brittle when in dry condition and can be stored for an indefinite period.

- The filters are between 50 and 150 $\mu$ thick and are available in sizes up to 60 cm$^2$

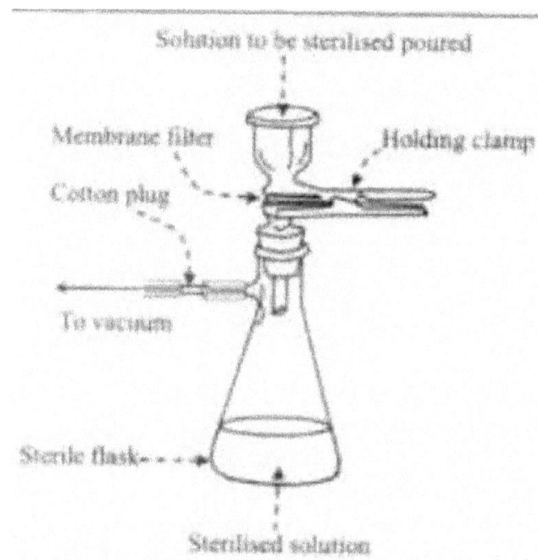


## Working

• A membrane filter has 400 to 500 million pores per square centimetre of filter surface.

• The pores are absolutely uniform in size and occupy about 80% of filter volume.

• To avoid rapid clogging of a membrane, pre-filtration is often required.

• The selection of a membrane filter for a particular application depends on the particles to be removed.

Uses

• These filters are mainly used for sterilization of both aqueous and oily liquids.

• The membrane filters cannot be used for filtration of organic solvents, such as alcohols, ketones, esters and chloroform.

## SEITZ FILTER

**Principle**

- It is based on filtration of asbestos pad filter disc Construction

- It consists of two parts. Lower part fitted with a perforated plate over which compressed asbestos pad is placed.

- Upper part has a value through which pressure can be applied.

- Both parts joined together by winged nuts.

- A valve is present on the upper part through which vacuum is applied

- The asbestos pads may yield alkali and cause precipitation of alkaloids

- It may shed fibres into the filtrate and absorb drug from solution.

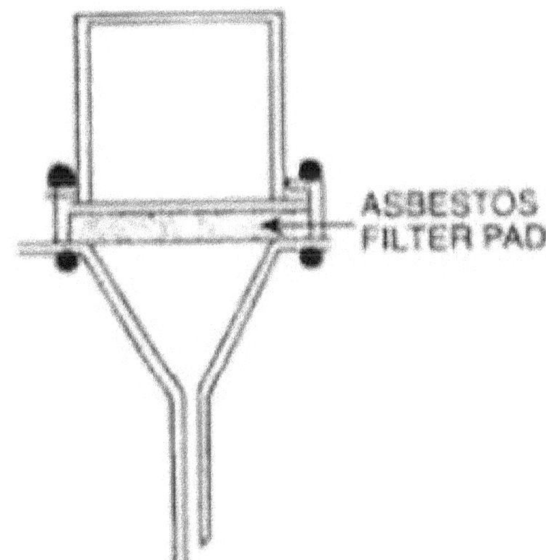


**Advantages:**

- No risk of contaminating the filtrate.

- Apparatus is very simple to use.

- For viscous solution they are more suitable.

**Disadvantages:**

- Asbestos may shed loose fibres.

- Pad may absorb sufficient amount of medicament

## CENTRIFUGATION

Centrifugation is a process which involves the use of the centrifugal force for the sedimentation of heterogeneous mixtures with a centrifuge, used in industry and in laboratory settings.

- This process is used to separate two immiscible liquids.

- More-dense components of the mixture migrate away from the axis of the centrifuge, while less dense components of the mixture migrate towards the axis.

- Centrifuge is a device for separating particles from a solution according to their size, shape, density, viscosity of the medium1.

**Applications of centrifugation**

- Production of bulk drugs

- Production of biological products

- Biopharmaceutical analysis of drugs

- Evaluation of suspensions and emulsions

- Determination of molecular weight of colloids

**Theory of centrifugation**

- The centrifuge works on sedimentation. Spinning sample at a high speed. The component of a mixture is subjected to centrifugal force. Dense particle migrates away from axis of rotation and lighter ones towards it.

- **Relative Centrifugal Force (RCF)**

- RCF is the ratio of the centrifugal acceleration at a specified radius and the speed to the standard acceleration of gravity.

- Relative Centrifugal force is defined as $\qquad$ **f=Mω2 r**

Where, F= intensity of centrifugal force

M= mass of particle

ω= angular velocity of rotation

R= distance of migrating particles from central axis of rotation.

The RCF value for any centrifuge may be calculated from the following equation:

RCF = $1.18 \times r \times (rpm) 2 \times 10^{-5}$

Where, $1.18 \times 10\text{-}5$ = An empirical factor

r is the radius in cm from the centre of the centrifuge shaft to the external tip of centrifuge tube.

rpm is the number of revolutions per minute of the centrifuge rotor

- The time required to separate particles depends on the rotor speed, radius of rotor and effective path length travelled by sedimented particles.

- The following formula useful for the calculation of the speed required for a rotor with a radius that differ from the radius with which a prescribed,

R.P.M. = $1000 \times \sqrt{RCF}/1.18 \times r$

- The length of time of centrifugation also can be calculated so, that running with an alternative rotor of a different size is equivalent to running with a original rotor.

# CLASSIFICATION OF CENTRIFUGES

Sedimentation centrifuge

It is a centrifuge that produces sedimentation of solids based on the difference in the densities of two or more phases of the mixture

Filtration centrifuge It is a centrifuge in which solids pass through the porous medium based on the difference in the densities of the solid and liquid phases

EQUIPMENT

PERFORATED BASKET CENTRIFUGE

Principle:

- Perforated basket (bowl) centrifuge is a filtration centrifuge.

- The separation is through a perforated wall based on the difference in the densities of solid and liquid phases. The bowl contains a perforated side-wall.

- During centrifugation, the liquid phase passes through the perforated wall, while solid phase is retained in the bowl.

- The solid is removed after cutting the sediment by a blade after stopping the centrifuge.

Construction:

- It consists of a basket, made of steel (sometimes covered with vulcanite or lead) or copper or Monel or any other suitable metal.

- The basket may have a diameter of 0.90 metres and a capacity of 0.085 metre cube.

- The basket is suspended on vertical shaft and is driven by a motor using suitable power systems such as belt pulleys, water turbines and electric motors.

- Surrounding the basket, a casing stationary is provided which collects the filtrate and discharges it at the outlet.

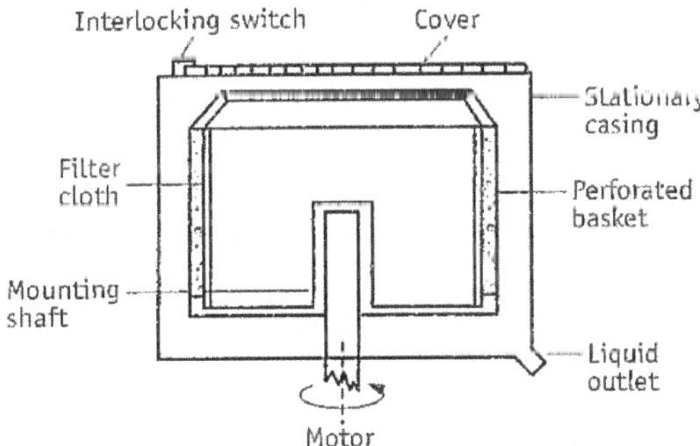



**Working:**

- The material is kept in the basket when the basket is stationary.

- Power is applied to rotate the basket and maximum speed must be attained quickly. The basket runs at 1000 revolutions per minute.

- During centrifugation, the liquid passes through the perforated wall, while the solid phase retains in the basket. The liquid leaves the basket and is collected at the outlet.

- The cake is then spun to dry as much as possible.

- After a definite period of time, the power is turned off. By applying a brake the centrifuge is stopped.

- The basket is brought to rest. The solid cake is cut using a blade and then unloaded manually.

**Uses:**

- Performed basket centrifuge is extensively used for separating crystalline drugs (such as aspirin) front the mother liquor. Free flowing product can be obtained because mother liquor is removed completely.

- It is also used for removing unwanted solids from a liquid. For example, precipitated proteins arc removed from insulin.

**Advantages:**

- The centrifuge is very compact and it occupies very little floor space.

- It can handle slurries with a high proportion of solids and even those having paste like consistency.

- The final product has very low moisture content.

- In this method, the dissolved solids are separated from the cake.

- The process is rapid.

**Disadvantages:**

- The entire cycle is complicated resulting in considerable labour costs.

- It is a batch process.

- If the machine is adapted for prolonged operation, there is considerable wear and tear of the equipment.

## NON-PERFORATED BASKET CENTRIFUGE

Principle:

- This is a sedimentation centrifuge.

- The separation is based on the difference in the densities of solid and liquid phases without a porous barrier.

- The bowl contains a non-perforated side-wall.

- During centrifugation, solid phase is retained on the sides of the basket, while the liquid remains at the top, which is removed by a skimming tube.

Construction:

- It consists of a basket, which may be made of steel or any other suitable metal.

- The basket is suspended on vertical shaft and is driven by a motor using a suitable power system.

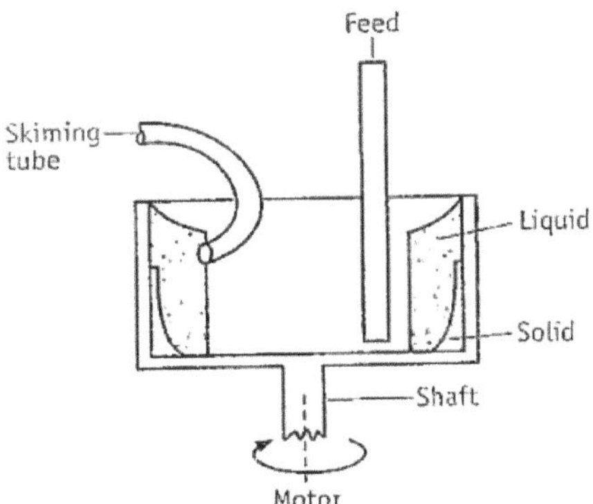


Working:

- The suspension is fed continuously into the basket.

- During centrifugation, solid phase is retained on the sides of the basket, while liquid remains on the top.

- The liquid is removed over a weir or through a skimming tube.

- When a suitable depth of solids has been deposited on the walls of the basket, the operation is stooped.

- The solids are then scraped off by hand or using a scraper blade.

Uses:

- Non-perforated basket centrifuge is useful when the deposited solids offer high resistance to the flow of liquid.

## SEMI-CONTINUOUS CENTRIFUGE OR SHORT CYCLE AUTOMATIC BATCH CENTRIFUGE

Principle:

- It is a filtration centrifuge.

- The separation is through a perforated wall based on the difference in the densities of solid and liquid phases.

- The bowl contains a perforated side-wall. During centrifugation, the liquid phase passes through the perforated wall, while solid phase retains in the bowl, the solid is washed and removed by cutting the sediment using a blade.

- It is a short cycle automatic batch centrifuge.

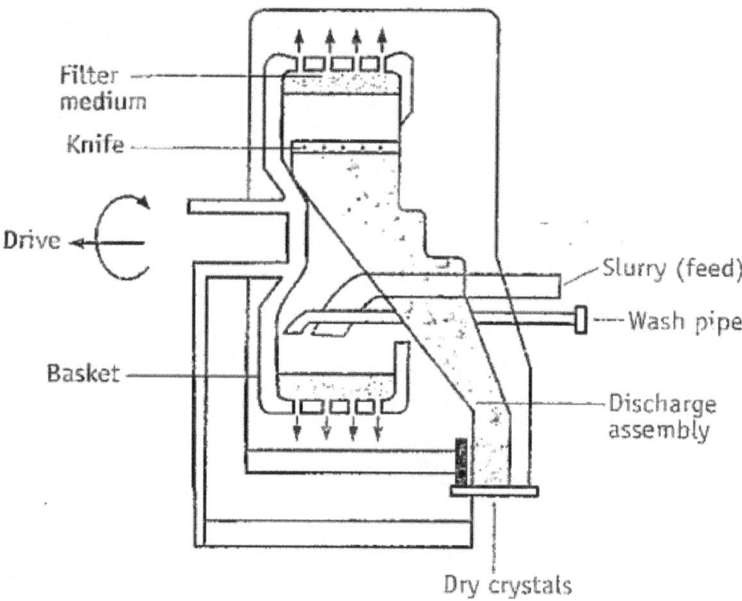



Construction:

- It consists of a vertical perforated basket, which is supported from a horizontal shaft driven by a motor.

- From the open side of the basket, provisions are made at the centre to introduce feed and wash pipe through horizontal tubes.

- A feeler rides over the feed, which is connected to diaphragm valve through air supply.

- The feeler controls the thickness of the feed. Hydraulic cylinder attachment is made in such a manner that the discharge chute enters from the sides of basket, when discharge of crystals is desirable.

Working:

- The perforated basket is allowed to rotate and slurry is introduced from the side pipe.

- During centrifugation, the slurry passes through the perforated wall. The solids are retained in the basket, while filtrate leaves the basket, which is collected at outlet.

- Further, the cake is washed with water.

- The wash escapes from the basket through the filtrate outlet

- After achieving the desired thickness (50 to 70 millimetres), the feeler cuts off the air supply to a diaphragm valve that automatically shuts off the entry of slurry.

- The hydraulic cylinder is actuated, which lifts the knife along with the discharge chute.

- The knife does not cut the cake completely down to the screen, but leaves a layer of crystals that acts as a filter medium for further separation in the next cycle.

- The residual crystals may be given a brief wash before starting the next cycle.

- Therefore, the entire cycle is semiautomatic.

Advantages:

- Short-cycle automatic batch centrifuge is used when solids can be drained fast from the bowl.

Disadvantage:

- During discharge, considerable breakage of crystals is possible.
- Construction and functioning are complicated.

## SUPERCENTRIFUGE

Super centrifuge is a continuous centrifuge used for separating two immiscible liquid phases.

Principle:

- It is a sedimentation centrifuge.
- The separation is based on the difference in the densities between two immiscible liquids. Centrifugation is done in the bowl of small centrifuge.
- During centrifugation, the heavier liquid is thrown against the wall, while the lighter liquid remains as an inner layer.
- The two layers are simultaneously separated using modified weirs.

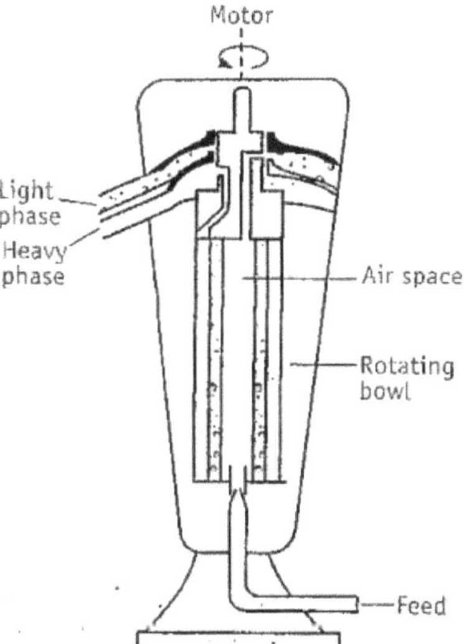


Construction:

- It consists of a long hollow cylindrical bowl of small diameter.
- It is suspended from a flexible spindle at the top and guided at the bottom by loose-fit bushing.
- Two liquid outlets are provided at different heights at the top of the bowl, for simultaneous recovery of the separated liquids using modified weirs.

Working:

- The centrifuge is allowed to rotate on its longitudinal axis at a high frequency usually about 2000 revolutions per minute with the help of drive-assembly.
- The feed is introduced from the bottom of the centrifuge using a pressure system.

- During centrifugation, two liquid phases separate based on the difference in their densities.

- The heavier liquid is thrown against the wall, while the lighter liquid forms an inner layer. Both liquids rise to the top of the vertical bowl.

- The liquid-liquid interface (the so-called neutral zone) is maintained by an hydraulic balance.

- These two layers are simultaneously separately removed from different heights through modified weirs.

- Thus. the super centrifuge can work for continuous separation of immiscible liquid phases.

Uses

• It is used for separating liquid phases of emulsions in food and pharmaceuticals.


**QUESTION BANK**

**Filtration:**

1. Filtration is a unit operation that is commonly used for collecting:

    a. filtrate B. particulate matter C. precipitate D. slurry

2. In clarification process, which is the factor more important?

    a. Depth of the media B. Pore size of the filter media C. Surface area of filter D. Volume of slurry

3. Who has proposed that the filtration process is similar to the streamline flow of a liquid under pressure through capillaries?

    a. Camian B. Darcy C. Kozeny D. Poiseuilli

4. The fluid flows through the filter medium by virtue of:

    a. potential difference across the filter

    b. pressure difference across the filter

    c. temperature difference across the filter

    d. volume difference across the filter

5. Filter aids are mainly used when: -

    a. liquid is required as product

    b. filter medium is not available

    c. solid and liquid are required as products

    d. solid is required as product

6. On what aspect of pressure does the filter leaf work?

    a. Atmospheric pressure

b. Negative pressure

c. Normal pressure

d. Pressure is zero

7. Which one of the following is NOT a mechanism of filtration?

a. Entanglement

b. Impact

c. Impingement

d. Straining

8. Cellulose membrane filter is an example for which type of filtration?

a. Cake filtration

b. Decantation filtration

c. Depth filtration

d. Screen filtration

9. Which of the following acts as a mechanical support for the filter cake and is also responsible for the collection of solids?

a. Feed

b. Filter aid

c. Filter medium

d. Funnel J

10. The efficiency of filtration increases if:

a. compressibility of solids is high

b. filter aid is added to the slurry

c. filter medium is used

d. size distribution of solids is wide in slurry

SHORT ANSWER:

1. Explain the mechanisms of filtration.

2. What are filter aids? Name the filter aids commonly used in pharmacy practice.

3. Describe the construction and working of a rotary continuous filter.

LONG ANSWER: -

1. With a neat diagram, describe the construction and working of a suitable industrial filter for handling of high solid containing slurries.

2. With a neat diagram, describe the construction and working of an industrial filter suitable for clarification of syrups.

3. With a neat labelled diagram, describe the construction and working of a chamber press.


<u>**Centrifugation:**</u>

**MULTIPLE CHOICE QUESTIONS**

1. Centrifugal method is used for one of the following processes.

    A. Mixing B. Purification C. Separation D. Sizing

2. Centrifugal effect counter-acts one of the following forces.

    A. Brownian forces B. Cohesive forces C. Electrostatic forces D. Gravitational forces

3. Which of the following centrifuges works against the gravitation acceleration?

    A. Conical disc centrifuge B. Continuous horizontal centrifuge C. Perforated basket centrifuge D. Semi-continuous centrifuge

4. The solid that has high specific gravity remains in one of the following states in the centrifuge tube, once centrifugation is completed.

    A. Bottom B. Middle C. Top D. Uniform

5. Which one of the following forces greatly enhances the separation forces?

    A. Brownian forces B. Centrifugal forces C. Gravitational forces D. Van der Waals forces

6. Centrifugal effect is expressed in one of the following ratios.

    A. Centrifugal force to density of liquid B. Centrifugal force to gravitational force C. Centrifugal force to sedimentation force D. Gravitation force to sedimentation force

7. What are the two factors responsible for separation by centrifugation?

    A. Density and sedimentation force B. Density and speed of rotation C. Diameter and speed of rotation D. Speed of rotation and sedimentation force

8. Centrifugation is useful in one of the following types of dispersions.

    A. Coarse dispersions B. Colloidal dispersions C. Molecular dispersions D. Multi-size dispersions

9. For a sedimentation type, the centrifuge has one of the following conditions.

    A. Basket is non-perforated B. Basket is perforated C. Containing filter aid D. Containing filter medium

10. Washing of solids is NOT possible in one of the following centrifuges.

    A. non-perforated basket centrifuge B. Perforated basket centrifuge C. Semi-continuous centrifuge D. Super-centrifuge

SHORT QUESTION: -

1. Describe continuous centrifuges, giving their advantages.

2. Describe the construction and working of a Sharpies super centrifuge.

3. Describe the theory of centrifugation.


LONG QUESTION: -

1. Discuss construction and working of a discontinuous centrifuge for solid separation.

2. Describe the construction and working of a centrifuge used for the separation of slurry containing high percentage of solids.

3. Describe the construction and working of a centrifuge used for the separation of two liquid phases as in case of emulsions.

## *UNIT-V*


### *Syllabus*

• Materials of pharmaceutical plant construction, Corrosion and its prevention: Factors affecting during materials selected for Pharmaceutical plant construction, Theories of corrosion, types of corrosion and there prevention. Ferrous and nonferrous metals, inorganic and organic non metals, basic of material handling systems.


## MATERIALS OF PHARMACEUTICAL PLANT CONSTRUCTION

## INTRODUCTION

For manufacturing of pharmaceuticals, bulk drugs, antibiotics, biological products etc., number of equipment's are used. The equipment's are generally used for processing and packing of products. A wide variety of materials are used for manufacturing of theses equipment's. Some products are highly acidic while some are highly alkaline. Some products such as storage of biological products need to be handled carefully. Therefore, design of equipment, material selection and fabrication technique need to be considered carefully. These factors affect the success or failure of new chemical plant. If container will not compatible with material, then there are chances of contamination. So, the proper choice of material is very important both for construction of processing equipment's as well as containers and closers for storage of finished products. The choice based on expert advice, previous experience and laboratory tests.

## FACTORS AFFECTING DURING MATERIALS SELECTED FOR PHARMACEUTICALS PLANT CONSTRUCTION

The selection of a material for the construction of the equipment depends on the following properties:

### 1. Chemical factors

    a. Contamination of the products

    b. Corrosion of materials of construction

### 2. Physical factors

a.  Strength

b.  Mass

c.  Wear properties

d.  Thermal conductivity

e.  Thermal expansion

f.  Ease of fabrication

g.  Cleaning

h.  Sterilization

i.  Transparency

**3. Economic factors**

1. Chemical Factors

Each time a chemical is placed in a container or equipment, the chemical is exposed to the construction material of the container or equipment. Therefore, the material of construction may contaminate the product (contamination) or the product may destroy the material of construction (corrosion).

a) Product contamination: Iron contamination can change the colour of products (such as gelatine capsules), catalyse some reaction that can increase the decomposition rate of the products. The leaching of glass can make the aqueous product alkaline. This alkaline medium may catalyse the decomposition of the product. Heavy metals, such as lead, inactivate penicillin.

b) Corrosion of construction materials the products can be corrosive in nature. They can react with the material and can destroy it. This can decrease the life of the equipment. Extreme pH, strong acids, strong alkalis, powerful oxidizing agents, tannins etc., reacts with the materials, therefore, some alloys that having special chemical resistance are used.

2. Physicals Factors

a.  Strength: The material must have sufficient physical strength to withstand the pressure and stress required. Iron and steel can satisfy these properties. The tablet punching machine, the die and the upper and lower punches are made of stainless steel to withstand very high pressure. Glass, though has strength but fragile in nature. The aerosol container must withstand very high pressure, so tin containers covered with some polymers (lacquered) are used. The plastic materials are weak, so they are used in some packaging materials, such as blister packs.

b.  Mass: For transportation, lightweight packaging materials are used. Plastic, aluminum and paper packaging materials are used to package pharmaceutical products.

c.  Wear properties: When there is a possibility of friction between two surfaces, the softer surface disappears and these materials contaminate the products. For example, during milling and grinding, grinding surfaces can wear out and contaminate the powder. When pharmaceutical products of very high purity are required, grinding surfaces of ceramic and iron are not used.

d. Thermal conductivity: In evaporators, dryers, stills and heat exchangers, the materials used should have very good thermal conductivity. In this case, iron, copper or graphite tubes are used for effective heat transfer.

e. Thermal expansion: If the material has a very high coefficient of thermal expansion then as the temperature increases, the shape of the equipment changes. This produces unequal stresses and can cause fractures. Therefore, materials that are capable of maintaining the shape and dimension of the equipments at the working temperature should be used.

f. Ease of fabrication: During the manufacturing of equipment, the materials undergo various processes, such as casting, welding and forging. For example, glass and plastic can be easily moulded into containers of different shapes and sizes. The glass can be used as coating material for reaction vessels.

g. Cleaning: Smooth and polished surfaces facilitate ease in cleaning. After completing the operation, the equipment is thoroughly cleaned so that the previous product cannot contaminate the next product. The surfaces of glass and stainless steel can be smooth and polished.

h. Sterilization: In the production of parenteral, ophthalmic and bulk drugs, all equipment must be sterilized properly to avoid microbial contamination of the product. This is usually done by introducing high pressure stream. The material must withstand at high temperature (1210C) and pressure (15 pounds per square inch). If there are rubber materials, it must be vulcanized to withstand the light temperature.

i. Transparency: In the reactors and fermenters a visual port is provided to observe the progress of the process that takes place inside the chamber. In this case, borosilicate glass is often used. In the parenteral and ophthalmic containers, the particles, if any, are observed with polarized light. The walls of the containers must be transparent to see through it. The glass is used as perfect material.

3. Economic Factors

The initial cost of the equipment depends on the material used. Several materials may be suitable for construction from the physical and chemical point of view, but of all the materials only the cheapest material for the construction of the equipment is chosen. Materials that require a lower maintenance cost are used because in the long term it is economical. The material used for construction of plant is classified as metals (ferrous and non-ferrous) and non-metals (organic and inorganic).

**CORROSION**

It is defined as the reaction of a metallic material with its environment, which causes a measurable change to the material and can result in a functional failure of the metallic component or of a complete system. Exposure of surface to air, water and caustic chemicals are the measure causes of corrosion. The surface changes due to corrosion are carried through the equipment and destroy the performance and fabrication in due course. According to the environmental conditions corrosion can be of dry or wet type as follows:

1. Dry Corrosion: It involves the direct attack of gases and vapor on the metals through chemical reactions. As a result, an oxide layer is formed over the surface. This type of corrosion is not common.

2. Wet Corrosion: This corrosion involves purely electrochemical reaction that occurs when the metal is exposed to an aqueous solution of acid and alkali. The moisture and oxygen are also responsible. This type of corrosion is quite common.

$$\text{e.g. } Zn + 2HCl \rightarrow ZnCl_2 + H_2\uparrow$$

## THEORY OF CORROSION

1. Corrosion Reaction

on Single Metal A single piece of metal (e.g. Fe) when comes in contact with acid (e.g. HCl) small galvanic cells may be set up on the surface. Each galvanic cell consists of (i) anode regions and (ii) cathode regions.

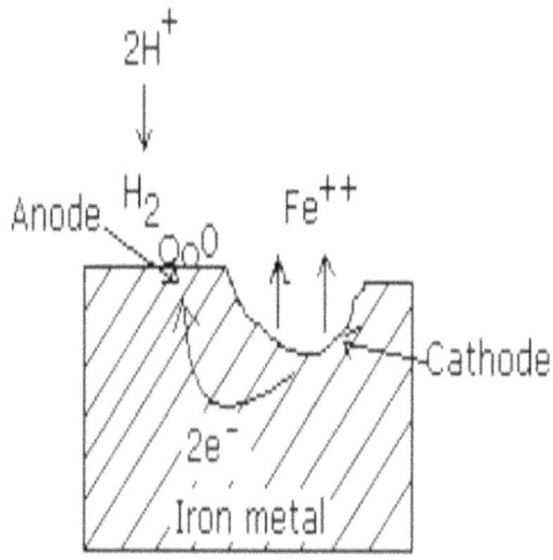


Electrochemical mechanism of corrosion

**Reaction at anode:**

Fe on the iron leaves two electrons to the metal and itself becomes Fe++ ion. Fe++ ion is soluble in water, so it is released in the medium. Thus, the iron surface is corroded.

**Reaction at cathode:**

The released electron is conducted through the metal piece into cathode region. Two electrons are supplied to two protons (H+) to form two atoms of H. Hydrogen atoms are unstable, hence two H atoms will combine to form a molecule of stable H2. In the absence of acid, water itself dissociates to generate H+ ion.

$2H+ + 2e- \rightarrow H_2\uparrow$, Hydrogen (H2) forms bubbles on the metal surface. If the rate of hydrogen formation is very slow then a film of H2 bubbles will be formed that will slow down the cathode reaction, hence the rate of corrosion will slow down. If the rate of hydrogen production is very high then hydrogen molecules cannot form the film on the surface. So the corrosion proceeds rapidly.

2. Corrosion Reactions between Metals

If two metals come in contact with a common aqueous medium then one metal will form anode and the other will form cathode. Now if both the metals are connected with a wire the reaction will proceed. Anode metal will be corroded and hydrogen will form at the cathode.

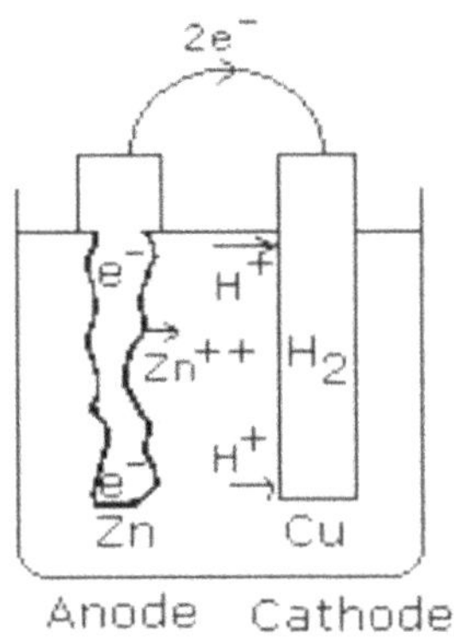


Galvanic mechanism of corrosion

For example, if a zinc and a copper plate is immersed in an acidic medium then zinc will form anode and will be corroded while hydrogen will be formed at copper plate.

Anode reaction: $Zn \rightarrow Zn^{++} + 2e-$.

Cathode reaction: $2H+ + 2e- \rightarrow H2\uparrow$

So, anode will be corroded and hydrogen will be evolved at cathode.

3. Corrosion Involving Oxygen The oxygen dissolved in the electrolyte can react with accumulated hydrogen to form water. Depletion (reduction) of hydrogen layer allows corrosion to proceed.

At cathode: $O2 + 2H2 \rightarrow 2H2O$

The above reaction takes place in acid medium. When the medium is alkaline or neutral oxygen is absorbed. The presence of moisture promotes corrosion.

## FACTORS INFLUENCING CORROSION

### 1. pH of the Solution

Iron dissolves rapidly in acidic pH. Aluminium and zinc dissolves both in acidic and alkaline pH. Noble metals are not affected by pH e.g. gold and platinum.

### 2. Oxidizing Agents

Oxidizing agents may accelerate the corrosion of one class of materials whereas retard another class.

> ➤ e.g. O2 reacts with H2 to form water. H2 is removed, corrosion is accelerated. Cu in NaCl solution follows this mechanism also.

> ➤ e.g. Oxidizing agents forms a surface oxide (like Aluminium oxide) and makes the surface more resistant to chemical attack.

### 3. Velocity

When corrosive medium moves at a high velocity along the metallic surface, the rate of corrosion increases because of:

> ➤ Corrosion products are formed rapidly and washed away rapidly to expose new surface for corrosion reaction.

➢ Accumulation of insoluble films on the surface is prevented.

➢ The corrosion is rapid in the bends of the pipes, propellers, agitators and pumps.

**4. Surface Films**

➢ Thin oxide films are formed on the surface of stainless (rusting). These films absorb moisture and increase the rate of corrosion.

➢ Zinc oxide forms porous films. Fluid medium can enter inside and thus corrosion continues. Nonporous films of chromium oxide or iron oxide prevent corrosion.

➢ Grease films protect the surface from direct contact with corrosive substances.

## TYPES OF CORROSION

1. Fluid Corrosion:

General When corrosion is generally confined to a metal surface as a whole, it is known as general corrosion. This corrosion occurs uniformly over the entire exposed surface area. e.g. swelling, cracking, softening etc. of plastic materials.

2. Fluid Corrosion: Localised

a. Inter-granular corrosion:

During heat treatment or welding, some components get precipitated at the grain boundary of the metal.

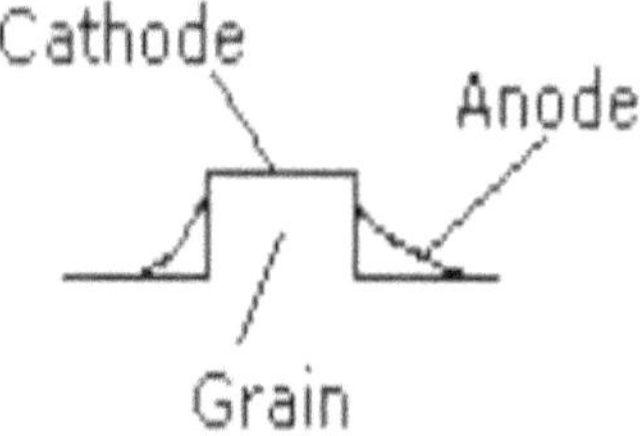


These boundaries act as anodes and grains as cathodes. So, corrosion of anode region occurs.

b. Pitting corrosion:

On metal surface small holes or pits are created due to local corrosion and these pits increase in size rapidly. In the pits the metals dissolve rapidly especially by chlorine and chloride ions.

c. Stress corrosion:

Certain area of metal may be subjected to thermal, mechanical or chemical stresses. The surface area becomes anode and acts as corrosion area.

d. Fretting corrosion:

Equipment showing high vibrations destroys the surface of metal (e.g. steels balls in ball-bearing) by mechanical hitting.

e. Corrosion fatigue:

Cyclic stress breaks the protective film, so corrosion increases.

3. Fluid Corrosion:

Biological Metabolic action of micro-organisms can either directly or indirectly cause deterioration of a metal by:

> Creating electrolyte concentration cells on the metal surface.

> Influencing the rate of anodic / cathodic reactions.

> Sulphates are converted in to hydrogen peroxide ($H_2S$) because of action of reducing bacteria on them. This reacts with iron to produce ferrous sulphide (FeS). Thus, the iron gets corroded.

## PREVENTION OF CORROSION

Following methods may be adopted for preventing or reducing corrosion:

1. Material Selection

> Pure materials have less tendency towards pitting, but they are expensive and soft. Therefore, only aluminium can be used in pure form.

> Improved corrosion resistance can be obtained by adding corrosion resistant elements. For example, inter-granular corrosion occurs in stainless steel. This tendency can be reduced by addition of small amount of titanium.

> Nickel, copper and their alloys are used in non-oxidizing environment, whereas chromium containing alloys are used in oxidizing environment.

> Materials those are close in electrochemical series should be used for fabrication.

> Corrosive materials are taken with suitable material of construction:

**List of materials of construction that can withstand the respective corrosive materials**

| Corrosive material | Suitable material |
| --- | --- |
| Nitric acid | Stainless steel |
| Hyfrofluoric acid | Monel metal |
| Distilled Water | Tin |
| Dilute sulphuric acid | Lead |
| Caustic | Nickel |

2. Proper Design of Equipment Corrosion can be minimized in the following conditions:

> Design for complete drainage of liquids.

> Design for ease of cleaning.

> Design for ease of inspection and maintenance.

> A direct contact between two metals should be avoided. They may be insulated from one another.

3. Coating and lining:

The metals are more prone to corrosion. To combat corrosion in metals, non-metals coating or lining should be used. Electroplating, cladding, organic coating can also be used. Galvanic corrosion can be controlled by applying barrier coatings or insulating both the anodes and cathodes to prevent the flow of electrons across the joint. Organic coatings are also used as lining of tanks, piping and shipping containers. Cladding is the bonding of dissimilar metals. It is achieved by rolling of two sheets of metal together. Cladding is also done for steel with an alloy is another approach to combat corrosion.

4. By changing the environment:

Corrosion can be prevented by removing air from boiler feed water which prevent steel from the corrosive effect of water. In case of nickel-based alloy the pumping of inert gas reduces air or oxygen content. The corrosive effect of acidic media on stainless steel alloys can be minimized by aeration. Corrosion can also be reduced by decreasing the temperature, by reducing the moisture and also by decreasing the exposure time.

5. Use of Corrosion Inhibitors:

Corrosion inhibitors are used to decrease corrosion of metals. The inhibitors are used in critical amount (less than 0.1% by weight). For example: Chromates, phosphates and silicates are used to protect iron and steel in aqueous solutions. Organic sulphides and amines are used to protect iron and steel in acidic medium. Copper sulphate is used to protect stainless steel from corrosion in hot diluted solution of sulphuric acid.

6. Cathodic and Anodic protection:

Cathodic protection is achieved by two methods as follows.

a. Sacrificial anode methods:

As the name indicates, anodes are kept in contact with protected metal (cathode), this cause scarification of anode. For example: zinc, aluminium, magnesium and their alloys are used as sacrificial anode for protection of iron and steel tanks.

b. Impressed emf methods:

In this method, external voltage is applied between tanks and electrodes. The anode is maintained always at positive. The natural galvanic effect is avoided. Thus, anode is non-consumed. So, any metal or non-corrodible alloys are used. For example: in case of sulphuric acid and deionised water, anodes are buried in ground while graphite and high silicone steel are compressed. The advantage of this method is: simple, most effective, inexpensive and used to store mild corrosive liquors.

In contrast to cathodic protection, anodic protection is one of the more recently developed methods for controlling corrosion. In anodic protection, predetermined potential is applied to metal. At initial stage, as current increases, metal dissolution or corrosion occur. At critical point passivation occurs. The potential develop at critical point is called passivating potential. Above the passivating potential, current flow decreases to minimum value. This is called passivating current. The main advantage of anodic protection is that it requires small current. This is used in transportation of concentrated sulphuric acid.


## CLASSIFICATION OF MATERIALS FOR PLANT CONSTRUCTION

The material used for construction of plant is classified as metals (ferrous and non ferrous) and non metals (organic and inorganic).

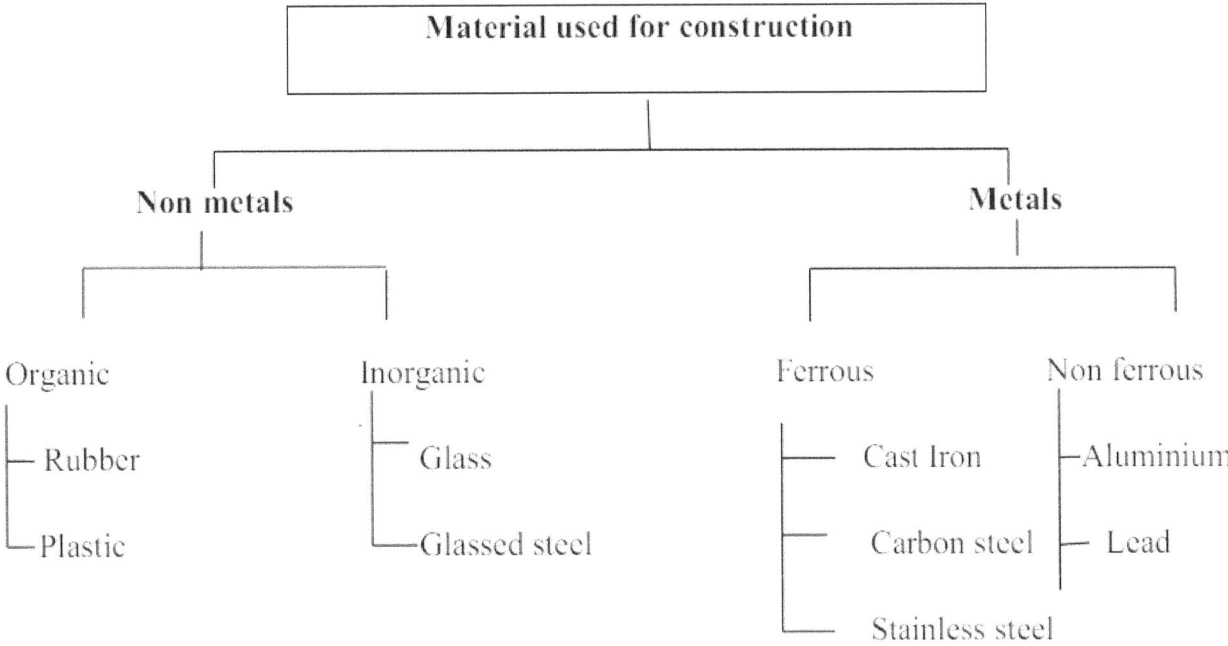



1. Non-Metals-Organic

a. Rubber It is used as a lining material

> Latex:

- Advantages: The latex is ready to use directly outside the container. Latex is economical, exhibits good abrasion resistance and is an elastic mouldable rubber. Latex moulds are also good for casting wax and gypsum. Disadvantages: Low-cost latex products generally shrink. Making moulds with latex rubber is slow and time consuming. Latex moulds are generally not suitable for melting resins.

> Polysulfide rubbers:

- Advantages: Polysulfide moulds are very soft, elastic and long lasting, even some have a useful life of 40 years. Disadvantages: It has an offensive smell. The polysulfides must be accurately mixed by weight otherwise they will not work. Polysulfide rubber costs more than latex.

> Silicone rubbers:

- Advantages: Silicone rubber has the best release properties of all mold rubbers. The combination of good release properties, chemical resistance and heat resistance makes silicone the best choice for the production of resin castings. Disadvantages: The silicones generally have a high cost.

> Polyurethane rubbers: Advantages: Polyurethanes are easy to use. They are less expensive than silicones and polysulphides. Disadvantages: As silicone rubber has the best release properties, urethane rubber has the worst release properties and adheres to almost anything. They have limited shelf life after opening.

b. Plastic

Plastic is commonly used material. It is light in weight. In plastic there are no chances of contamination as in metallic containers. They are available in variety of shapes. But plastic is not preferred in case of higher temperature. Generally, pipes and tubing are made of plastic material. They are used for storage of inorganic salt and weak acid. They can be easily cut as per requirement. Plastic do not corrode in air or water. It is also used as insulating material.

**Types:**

> Thermoplastic: They get softened with application of pressure and heat but regain their original shape on cooling.

| Thermoplastics | Uses |
| --- | --- |
| polyethylene | Cables, buckets, pipes |
| polypropylene | Milk, carsons, ropes |
| Teflon | Gaskets, coating |
| Polyvinyl chloride (PVC) | Manufacturing of gloves |

> Thermosetting: They are permanently shaped to rigid structure when pressure and heat is applied. e.g. Phenol-formaldehyde. They cannot withstand on severe abrasion.

2. Non-Metals-Inorganic

a. Glass

Glass container is widely used in daily life. It is composed of sand (pure silica), soda ash (sodium carbonate), limestone (calcium carbonate), and cullet (broken glass). Cullet acts as fusion agent for whole mixture. Glass is its solid state is considered as super cooled liquid.

Types: There are different varieties of glasses used such as

> Soft glass: They are made of sodium silicate and calcium silicate. It is used for making glass bulbs and window glasses.

> Hard glass: They are made of potassium silicate and calcium silicate. They are used for making glass apparatus.

> Flint glass: They are made of potassium silicate and lead silicate.

> Quartz glass: They are made of pure silica. They are used for making silica crucible.

> Pyrex glass and Jena glass: They are generally used for laboratory glassware's. The iron oxide is added to give amber coloured glass but iron oxide could leach into stored products. There are 4 types of glasses used in pharmaceutical industries according to I.P.

> Type1 (Borosilicate glass): It is highly resistance to alkali leaching. In this alkali and earth cations are replaced by boron. They are less brittle. Easy to clean and sterilize.

> Type II (Treated soda lime glass): In this type of glass, surface alkali is neutralized by sulphur dioxide vapours.

- ➤ Type III (Soda lime glass): It release 10 times more alkaline than type1 and type II. It offers moderate hydrolytic resistance. It is used for dry powder and oleaginous solutions.

- ➤ Type IV (General purpose soda lime glass): It is not used for parenteral. It is used as container for tablets, oral solutions, suspensions, ointment and liquid for external use. When glassware's are stored over a month in damp atmosphere having variation in temperature, it leads to Blooming or weathering. As a result, salt leach out of glass and appear as fine crystals. In this case salt is washed off with water and acid. Pharmaceutical glass containers should comply with official test for hydrolytic resistance.

**Advantages of glass container:**

**Physical aspect**

- ➤ They are quite strong and rigid.

- ➤ They are transparent which allows the visual inspection of the contents; especially in ampoules and vials.

- ➤ They are available in various shapes and sizes. Visually elegant containers attract the patients.

- ➤ Borosilicate (Type-I) and Neutral glasses are resistant to heat so they can be readily sterilized by heat.

- ➤ Glass containers can be easily cleaned without any damage to its surface e.g. scratching or bruising.

**Chemical aspect**

- ➤ Borosilicate type of glass is chemically inert. Treated soda lime glass has a chemically inert surface.

- ➤ As the composition of glass may be varied by changing the ratio of various glass constituents the proper container according to desired qualities can be produced.

- ➤ They do not deteriorate with age, if provided with proper closures.

- ➤ Photosensitive drugs may be saved from UV-rays by using amber colour glass. Economical aspect

- ➤ They are cheaper than other packaging materials.

**Disadvantages of glass container:**

**Physical aspect**

- ➤ They are brittle and break easily.

- ➤ They may crack when subject to sudden changes of temperatures.

- ➤ They are heavier in comparison to plastic containers.

- ➤ Transparent glasses give passage to UV-light which may damage the photosensitive drugs inside the container.

**Chemical aspect**

- Flaking: From simple soda-lime glass the alkali is extracted from the surface of the container and a silicate rich layer is formed which sometimes gets detached from the surface and can be seen in the contents in the form of shining plates – known as 'flakes' and in the form of needles – they are known as 'spicules. This is a serious problem, especially in parenteral preparations.

- Weathering: Sometimes moisture is condensed on the surface of glass container which can extract some weakly bound alkali leaving behind a white deposit of alkali carbonate to remain over there, further condensation of moisture will lead to the formation of an alkaline solution which will dissolve some silica resulting in loss of brilliance from the surface of glass – called weathering. To prevent weathering, the deposited white layer of alkali carbonates should be removed as early as possible by washing the containers with dilute solution of acid and then washing thoroughly with water.

## b. Glassed steel

It is an organic product of fusion. It is cooled to rigid condition without crystallizing. They are used in heavy vessels. It has excellent resistant to all acids. This is suitable in case of transparent pipes.

## 3. Metals-Ferrous

They are widely used as construction material because it is mechanically strong, easily available and economical.

## a. Cast iron

It is the combination of iron with carbon content greater than 2%. It is cheap and available easily so greater in demand. It is resistance to concentrated sulfuric acid, nitric acid and dilute alkalis. It has low thermal conductivity. The main disadvantages of cast iron are hard and brittle. Gray cast iron contains carbon, silicone, manganese and selenium. It is easy to mould into any shape. Gray cast iron prevents material from corrosion but it is not preventive against dilute acids. Malleable iron (white cast iron with carbon content 2.5%) is also available and it is also corrosion resistant. Nickel resistant cast iron has also superior toughness, easy to weld, corrosion and as well as heat resistant. A number of cast iron alloys like Duriron and Durichlor are available in market.

Uses:

- It is used to jacketed steam pans.

- It is used as lining material with plastic.

## b. Carbon steel

It is an iron alloy having low percentage of carbon content. It is cheapest and easy fabricate. It is most versatile metal used in industry. It is easily weldable and excellent ductility. But carbon steel has limited resistant to corrosion and it also react with caustic soda. Low alloy steel has high mechanical strength. It contains 0.4% Carbon, 0.7% Manganese, 1.85% Nickel, 0.8% Chromium and 0.25% Molybdenum. The properties of carbon steel can be altered by alloying with nickel, chromium and silicone. Carbon steel-Nickel alloy is tough and corrosion resistant. Carbon steel-chromium alloy increases hardness and more resistant to corrosion. At elevated temperature strength of carbon steel can be enhanced by preparing carbon steel-Molybdenum alloy.

Uses:

- It is used for construction of pipes and plates.

- It is used as supporting structure for plant vessels.

> It is used as fabricating material for large storage tanks for water, sulfuric acid and organic solvents.

## c. Stainless

steel It is an alloy of iron. It contains 12 to 30 % Chromium, 0 to 2% Nickel, low percentage of Carbon, Columbium, Copper, Molybdenum, Selenium, niobium, titanium. It is widely used in industries because it is heat resistant, corrosion resistant, easily fabricated, and has high tensile strength.

There are different types of stainless steel available

> Martensitic (type 410): It contains 12 to 20% chromium, 0.2 to 0.4% carbon and 2% nickel. It is mild resistant to corrosion and organic exposure. It is less ductile. It is used to prepare sinks, bench tops, storage tanks and mixing elements.

> Alpha-Ferritic (type 430): It contains 15 to 30% chromium and 0.1% carbon. It is better resistant to corrosion. It also resistant to oxidation and temperature. It is easy to machine. It is not good against reducing agents and hydrochloric acids. It is used in tower lining, baffles, beat exchangers, tubing, condensers, pump shafts and furnace parts.

> Austenitic: It contains 13 to 20% chromium, 0.1% is less than to 0.25% carbon and -22% nickel. It is highly corrosion resistant, east to weld, easily clean and sterilized. It can be easily weld. It is used in fomenters, evaporators, storage vessels, and extraction vessels.

> Others: Type 316, 316L and 317 with 2.5 to3.5% Molybdenum are most corrosion resistant.

## 4. Metals-Non-Ferrous

## a. Aluminium

It is available in large number of alloys. Aluminium is cheap and light in weight. It has adequate mechanical strength. Their maintenance and cleaning are easy. Thermal conductivity of aluminium is 60% of pure copper. Its tensile strength is 10000 lb/sq. in. It is resistant to corrosion. It can also use for concentrated nitric acid and acetic acid. It is used in wide variety of chemical equipment's. But mechanical strength of aluminium decreases greatly above 150 0C. For food and pharmaceutical uses super grade of aluminium is used. It is used as container for storage of meat. It is used in heat transfer applications. Aluminium alloy with improved mechanical properties and qualities are available which is also corrosion resistant. Aluminium clad alloy is used for greater mechanical strength. Hot dipped aluminized steel is preferred when sulphur is present. Aluminium is used in biosynthetic processes because it is non-toxic to microorganism. Uses: It is used for manufacturing of container (tank), rail tankers and barrels.

## b. Lead In pharmaceutical industry,

Lead is used in less percentage because in large amount it produces toxicity. It is cheap. It is generally used for non-food products. The addition of silver (Ag) and copper (Cu) makes lead corrosion resistant and fatigue resistant. Lead has poor structural quality due to low melting point. Therefore, antimony is added to harden the lead. Lead pipes are used for solution containing sulfuric acid. The main disadvantage of lead is high coefficient of expansion which may cause permanent deformation.

## c. Others

Copper and its alloy are also used in chemical processing because it has high temperature resistance properties. Nickel and its alloy are also used for handling alkalis and storing and shipping of high purity caustic soda and potash. It is also used to store chlorinated solvents and phenols. Titanium is also used as construction material due to strong, corrosion resistant, resistant to hot chloride solutions and nitric acid. But it is costly.

## BASICS OF MATERIAL HANDLING SYSTEMS

## INTRODUCTION

Material handling is the movement, protection, storage and control of materials products during manufacturing, storage, distribution, consumption and disposal. As a process, material handling incorporates a wide range of manual, semi-automated and automated equipment. Conveying is the process of transport of materials from one place to another. If there is delay in raw material movement as per production schedule, then manufacturing process will be slowed down. Conveyors are used in the production of tablets, capsule and liquid orals dosage form.

## OBJECTIVES OF CONVEYING

The objectives of conveying are

> - To decrease product cost.
> - To decrease manufacturing cycle time.
> - To decrease manufacturing capacity.
> - To decrease raw material cost.
> - To lower processing time.
> - To avoid contamination and dust formation.
> - High degree of uniformity and productivity at low manufacturing cost.
> - To provide better quality product without any damage.
> - To increase storage capacity.
> - To provide better working condition.

## APPLICATIONS OF CONVEYING

Conveyors have variety of applications

Ergonomics: Because they do the work of the movement of the load, the conveyors eliminate the possibility of the operator being injured by pushing or pulling.

Process flow: The conveyors can be used as part of an assembly or manufacturing process.

Safety: due to the fact that conveyers move loads along a fixed path, the conveyor belts eliminate the possibility of collisions associated with the movement of the forklift truck of the manual product.

Speed: The conveyor speed can be adjusted as per requirement.

Transportation: The conveyors facilitate the internal movement of containers or boxes with a minimum or no labour force.

**TYPES OF CONVEYORS**

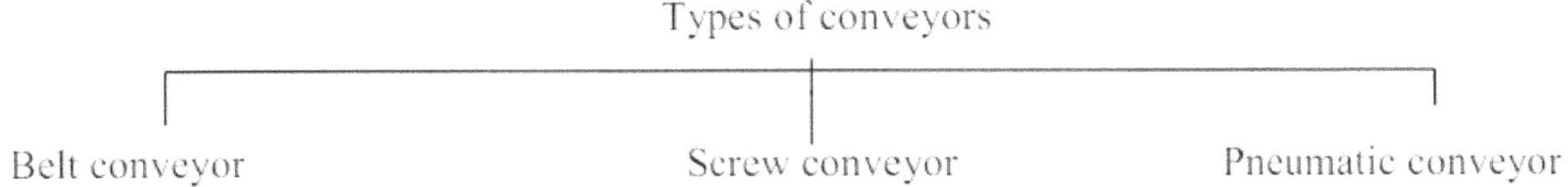


1. Belt Conveyors Principle: Belt conveyors are used to transport solid materials and bulk objects at high speed. The belt conveyors are based on the principle of material transport from the point of feeding to the point of discharge by rotating belt driven by motor in pulleys.

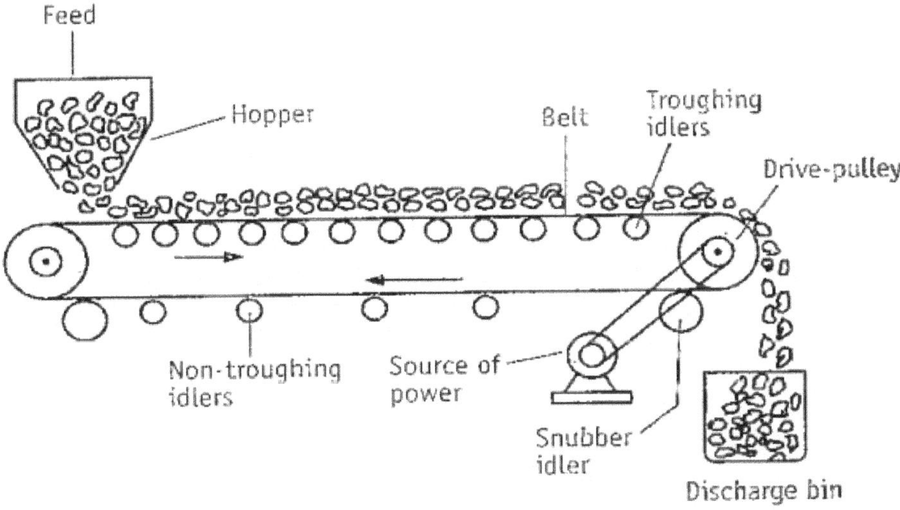


Construction:

The basic element of belt conveyors are belt and belt tightening system, belt drive and power supply, roller support, feeding arrangement and discharge arrangement. The belt consists of core of carcass of various plies of cotton duck in which each layer impregnated and bonded with rubber. The carcass is also coated with thin rubber layer that join plies with each other. The belt runs either in horizontal or inclined position. The belt runs continuously because both ends of belts are joined to each other.

To handle highly abrasive material, special grade of rubber belts are preferred. The belt of superior quality is made of neoprene and Teflon. Cord belts are also available. The belt should not be too thin or too thick because if belt is too thin for its width it will sag between idlers and if belt is too thick then it will not trough properly.

Due to temperature and humidity the length of belt is increased. Therefore tighteners are attached to maintain uniform stress on belt in all conditions. Belt drive is used to move the belt. The simplest device used to drive belt is bare steel pulley actuated with power source. The area of contact between belt and pulley can be enhanced by introducing snubber idlers below the pulley. Rollers which are arranged on shaft are used to support belt and these are called idlers. There are a significant number of idlers on conveyor. The selection of the correct type of idlers is very much important with respect to the optimum load carrying capacity of a conveyor and the environment in which the conveyor is to operate. The idlers are troughed to rise belt at edges and depress from centre.

Feed hopper is also attached at one end. Hopper is used to load feed at centre of the belt. To remove sticky material from belt, revolving brushes and rubber scrapper blades are used. The material at other side is collected in discharge bin.

Working:

When a rotor rotates, the conveyor belt will also rotate due to intense friction between the rotor wheel and the belt. This rotating movement of the rotor causes one side of the belt to move in one direction, while the other side moves in the opposite direction. There should be close contact between pulley and belt. Therefore, snubber idlers are used to maintain close contact between them. The material or feed with the help of the hopper is loaded from the one side to the centre of the belt as the belt moves continuously in the forward direction. This also allows the material to travel over the belt in same direction. The material is collected in the discharge bin from the end of the belt, either mechanically or manually. The selection of belt conveyor depends on speed of belt, width of belt, power required, mechanical and tensile strength of belt system, trough ability of belt and also on material size.

Applications:

> During production of dosage form (such as injections, liquid orals and ointments), belt conveyors are used to transport container for filling, capping, labelling etc.

> Stripes are conveyed through moving belt for strip and blister packing of tablet and capsule.

Advantages:

> Simple structure.

> Easy to maintain.

> Low energy consumption.

> Large load capacity. Belt conveyors run at speed of 1000 fpm and load 5000 tons per hr.
Disadvantages

> Costly equipment.

2. Screw Conveyors

Principle:

Screw conveyors are based on the principle of material transport from the point of feeding to point of discharge by rotation of helical screw driven by motor.

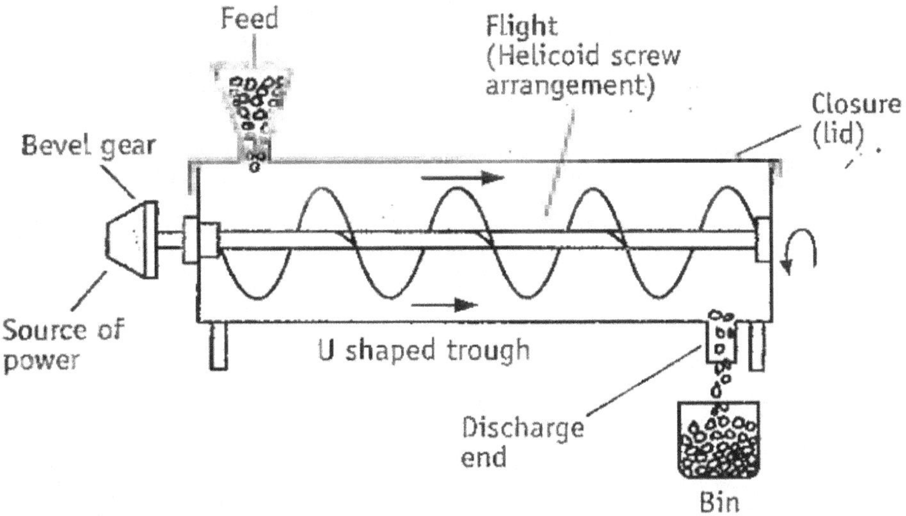



Construction:

The basic element of screw conveyors are trough system, feeding arrangement, flight and power supply and discharge arrangement. It consists of U-shaped trough which is made of steel. Spiral blade which act as screw element, also known as flight, is attached to the equipment. Power is transmitted through shaft to the flight or screw element.

The equipment is attached to helicoids screw arrangement which consist of one long ribbon twisted and wrapped into spiral shape. Flights are welded in to central shaft through hanger. Bevel gears are also installed at the drive end and used for maintaining speed and rotation for shaft. Hopper is used for feed arrangement. The drive end and discharge end are jointly called box ends. Various feed and discharge arrangements are available. Feeding arrangement such as plain spout, rotary van feeder and rack and pinion gates are available while different discharge arrangements are open end through, open bottom trough, flat bottomed rack and pinion gates, curved side gate, enclosed rack and pinion gates.

Working

Switch on the power system. Bevel gear maintains speed of rotation of shaft which rotates axially. The flight or spiral blade also rotates. Feed is introduced through hopper. Material gets trapped within the scrapper. Material move forward as a flight moves. The material is received in discharge bin using open end trough.

Applications:

> It is used to convey fine, pasty solids, abrasive and non-abrasive materials.

> It can transport material with capacity of 280 m3 /hr.

> Incorporated for in situ devices for mixing, heating, cooling etc.

Advantages:

> Operated at positive as well as negative pressure.

> It occupies less space.

> Material can be conveyed horizontally as well as vertically.

Disadvantages:

> High power consumption.

> High speed cause abrasive problem.

## 3. Pneumatic Conveyors

Principle:

In pneumatic conveyors, the transport of material from one place to another occurs due to the high velocity of the air stream that suspends individual particles in the air. This is known as fluidized bed system.

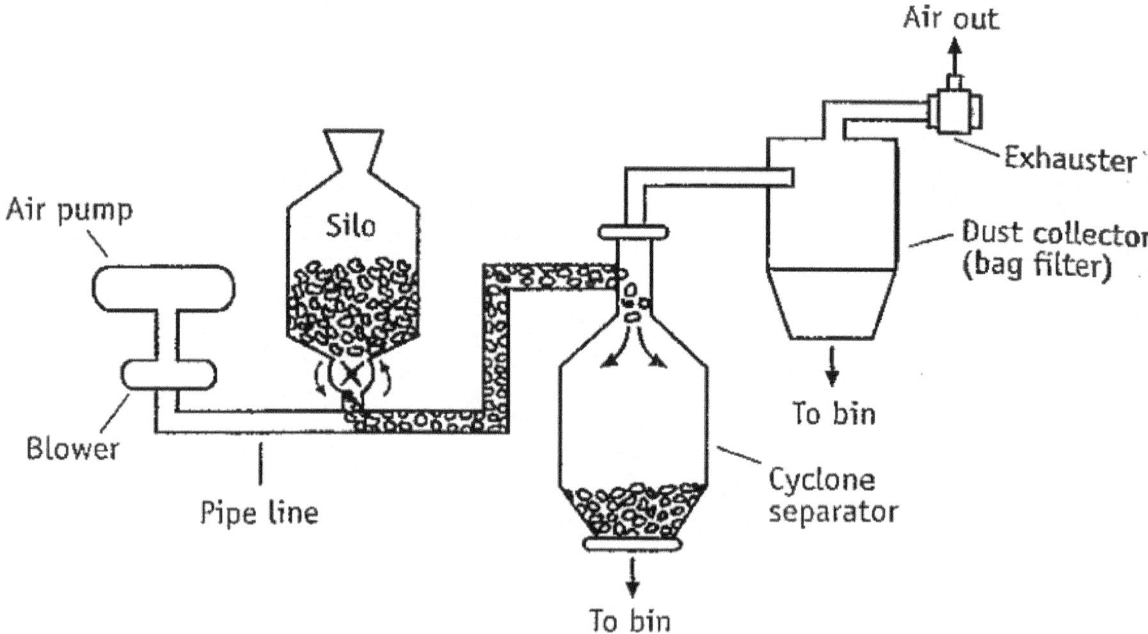



Construction: The equipment consists of Air supply system, Air slides, pipelines, feed arrangements, discharge arrangement etc. The system is attached to a pump. The conveying system consists of fans or cycloid blowers. The feed supply is connected to air slide through rotary feeder valve. The other end of pipeline is also attached to cyclone separator. The material is collected from other end of equipment and air is passed out.

Working: The air through cycloid blower generate at the pressure of 7 kilopascals. The cycloid blower produce air which pass through air slide. As a result rotary feed valve rotates and feed enters in to the pipeline. The solids are suspended in air stream. The suspension is then admitted to a cyclone separator where the separation of large and fine particles occurs. Large particle are collected in bin while fine particles removed in bag filters. The gas is recycled. Pneumatic conveyors are classified as pressure type, vacuum type, pressure vacuum type, fluidizing type and blow tank type.

Applications:

> It is used for transferring powders, granules, and other dry bulk materials through enclosed pipelines.

> It is used to move lightweight material quickly from one place to another without vessel. ¬ As it is a closed system, therefore also used to handle poisonous material.

> Fine powder having bulk density 1 to 200 lb/ft3 can be handled by pneumatic conveyors.

Advantages:

➢ The material travel from few meters to several hundred meters.

➢ It consists of simple, small diameter pipeline to transfer material.

➢ The system is totally enclosed and typically has few moving parts.

➢ Friction losses are small.

Disadvantages:

➢ A pneumatic conveying system requires more horsepower than other conveyor system.

➢ In case of large particle size and extremely sticky material there are chances of total pipeline blockage.

➢ Sometime attrition of solid occurs.

➢ Chances of erosion of internal surface.

**Question bank**

1. In belt conveyor, the main role of idlers is to:

   A. make tire belt under even-tension

   B. move the belt forward

   C. support the belt

   D. withstand the weight of materials

2. Idlers are generally troughed (depress the belt at the centre and rise at the edges), for:

   A. carrying more material without spillage

   B. giving the belt good shape

   C. reducing the risk of working

   D. sagging of tire belt

3. In belt conveyor, snubber idlers also help to maintain a close contact be¬ tween the following.

   A. Belt and hopper

   B. Belt and non-troughing idlers

   C. Idlers and belt

   D. Pulley and belt

4. In belt conveyor, the belt is NOT constructed with one of the following materials?

   A. Asbestos fibre

   B. Cotton

   C. Plastics

   D. Wood

5. Working efficiency of belt conveyor mainly depends on:

   A. load and speed of belt

   B. mechanical and tensile strengths of the belt

   C. power supplied and nature of idlers

   D. width and slope of the belt

6. In the construction of a screw conveyor, which is used for the movement of solid materials?

   A. Air pump

   B. Flight

   C. Idlers

   D. Pulley

7. The flight used in a screw conveyor is:

   A. round

   B. semicircle

   C. spiral

   D. square

8. In a belt conveyor, the carcass is usually impregnated and bonded with one of the following materials.

   A. Iron

   B. Plastic

   C. PVC

   D. Rubber

9. Pneumatic conveyor is used for the transportation of one of the following materials?

   A. Abrasive materials

   B. Highly density materials

   C. Pasty solids

   D. Toxic materials

**SHORT ANSWER QUESTION: -**

1. List advantages of screw conveyor and screw elevator. How do you com¬ pare these with pneumatic transport of solids?

2. Describe the construction and working of a screw conveyor.

3. Write the principle of belt conveyor with a neat diagram,

**LONG ANSWER QUESTION: -**

1. Describe the construction and working of belt conveyor system for solid transport.

2. Name the devices used for transportation of solids. Describe pneumatic conveyor.

3. Describe the factors influencing the selection of transportation equipment for solids.

<u>*About the authors:*</u>

**Ms. Prerana Sahu** is a young researcher and leading pharmacist, currently working as Assistant professor in Kalinga University, Raipur. She has more than 5 years of teaching experience. She has authored different books and book chapters by national and international publishers and also published 4 Indian patents. She also serves on the editorial board of various pharmaceutical journals. She has got published more than 55 research and review publications. She has received various awards like best faculty of the year, best employee of the quarter, best employee of the month, best paper presentation and best oral presentation awards. Her research interests include exploring different types of micro and nano delivery system.

**Mr. Divyansh Sahu** is a junior researcher of Rungta Institute of Pharmaceutical Sciences and Research, Bhilai. He has more than 15 research and review publications by national as well as international publishers/journals. He has published one Indian patent. He has received various awards such as best student award, best E poster presentation award and best oral presenter. His research concern shows representation of herbal drugs and includes Nano based delivery system.

**Dr. Gyanesh Kumar Sahu** is a young researcher and leading pharmacist currently working as Professor and Dean at Rungta Institute of Pharmaceutical Sciences. He has guided more than 50 post graduate students. He has authored different books published by national as well as international publisher and published 15 patents. He has published many research papers in high impact international journals. He also serves on the editorial board of various pharmaceutical journals and presented papers at various medical conferences and seminar. Dr. Sahu has received grants from various government funding agencies. His research interest includes exploring different types of micro & nano and herbal bioenhancer drug delivery system.

**Dr. Harish Sharma** is currently working as Professor and Dean at Rungta Institute of Pharmaceutical Sciences & Research. He has more than 18 years of teaching as well as research experience with specialization in Pharmaceutics. He has more than 100 publications in international and national journals of repute and published 15 Indian Patents. He also serves on the editorial board of various medical and pharmaceutical journals. He has received 12 grants from various government funding agencies. He has also received various awards like Chhattisgarh Gauravsamman, Utkrishtsamman, best paper presentation and winner in state level of different science exhibitions. His research extends from pharmaceutical nanoparticle and dermal drug delivery system.